AN INTRODUCTION TO THE FRANCISCAN LITERATURE OF THE MIDDLE AGES

An Introduction to the Franciscan Literature of the Middle Ages

by JOHN V. FLEMING

CHICAGO 1977
Franciscan Herald Press

Library of Congress Cataloging in Publication Data

Fleming, John V.
An introduction to the Franciscan literature of the Middle Ages.

Includes bibliographical references and index.
1. Literature, Medieval—History and criticism. 2. Franciscans in literature. I. Title.
PN682.F7F5 809.02 76-47531
ISBN 0-8199-0651-4

MADE IN THE UNITED STATES OF AMERICA

for my mother and father

JANET ELIZABETH FLEMING

and

MARVIN DALE FLEMING

TABLE OF CONTENTS

AN INTRODUCTION TO THE FRANCISCAN LITERATURE OF THE MIDDLE AGES

PREFACE AND BIBLIOGRAPHICAL FOREWORD

The modest and I hope virtuous ambition of this *Introduction to the Franciscan Literature of the Middle Ages,* explained more fully in the book's first chapter, is to encourage students of medieval literature to notice, appreciate, and investigate in their own research the importance of the Franciscan movement of the thirteenth and fourteenth centuries for the development of the European literatures. The field of study which it hopes to expose is large, rich, and underworked. Yet while it would be a difficult feat to miss altogether such a large target, it is no simple matter to hit the bull's-eye; and I have tried to follow the course which I hope will be most helpful to the general scholarly reader, a course which would eschew inappropriately detailed technical analysis on the one hand and merely superficial "literary history" on the other.

I must say a few words about the scholarly documentation of the footnotes, to which I have attempted to apply a strict principle of economy. The first purpose of the notes is to guide the interested reader to reliable primary sources, and in particular to good texts. I have also tried to offer specific bibliographical suggestions when appropriate, and to take into special account the convenience of an English-speaking audience. In an attempt to focus attention on primary texts of medieval Franciscan literature I have suppressed an elaborate apparatus of secondary reference. In general, I have made footnote citation of secondary studies only when they contain important bibliographical information or when they are in a quite strict and direct sense the immediate sources of statements and ideas.

I have proceeded in this fashion on the assumption that readers of this *Introduction* will have available some of the standard bibliographies of Franciscan studies. One of the most important of these is the *Bibliografia delle Bibliografie Francescane* of Ermenegildo Frascadore and Herwig Ooms, which first appeared in volumes 57 and 58 (1964-65) of the *Archivum Franciscanum Historicum* (Quaracchi) and which was then published in book form (Quaracchi, 1965). Of the periodical bibliographies, the most useful is that in the *Collectanea Franciscana* (Rome). These two journals (*CF* and *AFH*) are indispensable for the serious study of medieval Franciscanism. If there is a single indispensable book for English-speaking students, it is *St. Francis of Assisi, Writings and Early Biographies: English Omnibus of the Sources for the Life of St. Francis,* ed. Marion A. Habig (Chicago, Franciscan Herald Press, 1973). This *Omnibus,* as I cite it throughout my book, in addition to being true to the large claims of its title, contains an admirable and informed bibliography (pp. 1671-1760) which makes it in effect a vernacular encyclopedia of primitive Franciscanism. In this achievement it is a worthy contemporary heir of the scholarly tradition of Bartholomaeus Anglicus and Francesc Eiximinis.

What I have called economy others may feel disposed to call parsimony, or even downright meanness of spirit. There are many scholars whose work has shaped this *Introduction* but whose names appear only infrequently or not at all in my footnotes. They include Kajetan Esser, whose brilliant research has in a sense refounded the study of Franciscan origins, and Sophronius Clasen, who has redefined the "Franciscan question." M. Mollat and his students in Paris have greatly enriched our understanding of the theological and social meaning of medieval evangelical poverty. Of the many good surveys of Franciscan literature to which I have been able to turn, two in English deserve special mention. F. J. E. Raby has made as good an attempt to define a Franciscan poetic style as we have; and Bishop Moorman's recent *History of the Franciscan Order* contains a fine linear sketch of the major literary activities of medieval friars.

Of the dozens of other scholars whose debtor I am, I must mention four in particular. Giorgio Petrocchi's *Ascesi e mistica trecentesca* provides an elegant and economical introduction to the peculiar critical problems which attend popular religious literature in the vernacular period. Stephanus Axters' *Geschiedenis van de vroomheid in de Nederlanden* helped me understand the ways in which spiritual history and literary history are inseparable in the late Middle Ages. David Jeffrey, once my student and now my teacher, has recently published an important work, *Franciscan Spirituality and the Early English Lyric,* charged with suggestion for future lines of inquiry. Finally, I must pay homage to Kurt Ruh of Würzburg, the dean and pioneer of "Franciscan literary history" as I understand the term. The work of Ruh and his students on *Bonaventura deutsch* and on David of Augsburg, Berthold of Regensburg, and other master spirits of the German mission provides a model for the kind of scrupulous linguistic and critical examination of texts which will have so much to teach us about the Franciscan books of Italy, France, and England as well.

I marvel greatly that such a small book as this one has incurred for me such large debts of gratitude and friendship. Much of it was written three years ago, when, liberated from my wonted teaching and administrative duties by a semester's sabbatical leave from Princeton University, I was able to study at the Collegio San

Bonaventura in Grottaferrata (Rome). There I was welcomed by Fr. J. Guy Bougerol, the President of the International Bonaventure Commission, who generously helped me in many ways. To him, and to the entire scholarly community at Grottaferrata, I owe a pilgrim's thanks. I must make a particular acknowledgment of the kindness of two of the friars, Fr. Ignatius Brady and Fr. Romano Almagno, my compatriots in the earthly city and my spiritual colleagues in the study of Franciscan origins. Here at home, during the years I have worked on this book, I have enjoyed collegial conversation with three dear friends—Rosalie Green, Robert Hollander, and D. W. Robertson—each of whom has exerted an important influence on the way in which I have conceived of "Franciscan literature." As always, my greatest personal debt, and the one hardest to express, is to Joan Newman Fleming, my beloved wife. The long hours she has spent improving the manuscript—as the long years improving its author—may not yet have made a silk purse of a sow's ear, but they have saved the reader a good deal of verbiage and some nonsense. Finally, I want to thank Fr. Mark Hegener of the Franciscan Herald Press for encouragement and, I am afraid, patience.

Princeton, New Jersey
1976

1

What Is Franciscan Literature?

The "introduction" to the Franciscan literature of the Middle Ages which this book hopes succinctly to effect is of three kinds. It seems desirable in the first place to supply students and scholars whose primary interests are the literary or cultural history of medieval Europe with a general book which places before them in a reasonably comprehensive fashion the major contours of the literary achievement of the Franciscan movement during the first two centuries of its history. There is at the same time a real sense in which it is appropriate, and I hope not pretentious, to encourage the smaller but on the whole better-equipped army of Franciscanists to make a general review of an important topic clearly within their domain which, for reasons I shall come to in a moment, they have too often passed over. Finally, the book is an introduction in the sense that its intention is to stimulate serious and sustained research into various topics in Franciscan literary history, and especially on subjects involving the important relationships between the international Franciscan movement and the major vernacular currents of late medieval literature.

It is the expected attitude, and perhaps the stylistic duty, of a scholarly author to claim, against the silent incredulity of his unseen readers, that his topic has in the past been strangely neglected. It is in fact the case that the Franciscan literature of the Middle Ages has been neglected, strangely so I would have to add; but in the face of the remarkably vigorous pace of Franciscan studies in general in the last several decades, and the particular attentions which have been lavished on such writers as Bonaventure and such books as the *Fioretti,* in essays and studies so numerous that their very citations fill hefty octavo bibliographies, such a claim would require a more lengthy justification than this book could appropriately sustain. My aims will perhaps be better served by a brief explanation of how the book understands the phrase "Franciscan literature," and how this understanding may differ from that of traditional Franciscan studies. I mean by the term Franciscan literature primarily those works of poetry, fiction, song, and the historical and visual imaginations which are related, stylistically and ideologically, to the great Franciscan spiritual movement of thirteenth- and fourteenth-century Europe. Franciscan literature thus conceived of course does not include all books written by medieval Franciscans, nor is it limited to works written by them only. The phrase inevitably lacks absolute precision, but its compensating convenience is that it can remove the examination of certain important medieval texts from their wonted context of discussion—the history of the Franciscan Order—and relocate them at some slight distance away within the context of medieval literary history. The aim is by no means to expropriate one of the technical tasks of "Franciscan Studies," but to draw the relevance of that task to the attention of a larger audience of medievalists and other students of European literature in the pre-modern period.

What has usually been meant by Franciscan literature is quite simply literature written by Franciscans. Such is the fundamental premise of Franciscan bibliography, supported by a long-standing tradition and useful scholarly convention. Not the least enduring of the scholarly monuments of the seventeenth and eighteenth centuries —the heyday of the religious antiquaries within the Franciscan Order as elsewhere—were the vast compilations of bibliography, biography, hagiography, and monumental sources devoted to the history of the various orders. I have in mind such works as Mabillon's *Acta Sanctorum Ordinis Sancti Benedicti* and his *Annales,* the *Speculum Carmelitanum* of Daniel of the Virgin Mary, and Quétif and Echard's *Scriptores Ordinis Praedicatorum.* There were, naturally, major Franciscan contributions in the same genre—the *Annales* of Friar Luke Wadding (1588-1657), for example, or the *Firmamentum Trium Ordinum.* Such works have proved to be of permanent scholarly value, but the assumptions on which they are based have not been without their unfortunate results for modern research in the field of medieval religious history.

For the tradition which such works established, or rather handed on from the Middle Ages themselves with impressive scholarly skill and the advantages of movable type, is always potentially narrow and can easily become myopically chauvinistic. The idea that Franciscan (or Dominican or Carmelite) literature is the same thing as a list of books by authors in gray (or black or white) cowls is implied by the very impulse from which these great catalogues were born. They focus on famous men, *illustri,* giants of the Order, major figures of the "high culture" of medieval Europe. One important body of primitive Franciscan literature, however, is popular and derivative in nature and anonymous in its artistic claims. We have no idea who, precisely, wrote the Cortona *laude* or the *Sacrum Commercium,* and no sure idea about the *Meditationes vitae Christi* or the *Fasciculus Morum.* These books are "Franciscan" not merely or even chiefly because of the supposed religion of their authors, but because of their style, their themes, their peculiar way of giving expression to cherished Christian values. For the student of medieval European literature, of Dante or Chaucer or Jean de Meun, the stylistic characteristics of Franciscan literature and the relationships between Franciscan texts or "influence" and the larger literary mainstreams of the emerging vernaculars are matters of intense interest which are hardly hinted at in the pages of Wadding and Sbaralea.

Literary history itself has a history, and a clear view of the larger shape of medieval Franciscan literature has been obscured by the scholarly emphasis, in itself entirely admirable, on the history of scholastic thought. Insofar as there has been a conscious Franciscan "literary" history, it has been the history of the Franciscan school and its great luminaries, such as Alexander of Hales, Duns Scotus, William of Ockham, and above all St. Bonaventure. An event of the greatest possible significance in the history of Franciscan studies was the establishment, late in the nineteenth century, of the Collegio S. Bonaventura at Quaracchi, Florence. The "college" was in fact a research institute, staffed by a diverse group of talented textual scholars commissioned with the great edition of the *Opera Omnia* of Bonaventure. This edition, the final volume of which appeared with the new century, remains a standard monumental source. It at once established a new criterion of excellence in the editing of medieval theological literature and also set the pattern for the future work of the college and for that of several other scholarly institutions of which it is the spiritual parent. It has been continuously active since its foundation in editing medieval Franciscan texts—particularly notable are the editions of Alexander of Hales and St. Bernardino of Siena—and since 1907 in the quarterly publication of the *Archivum Franciscanum Historicum,* the most prestigious and influential of the many scholarly journals devoted to the study of the Franciscan heritage.

No student of Franciscan literature can take a step without relying on the pioneering work of the Quaracchi Fathers, but their general approach to the question of medieval Franciscan writings has left two questions of vital importance to European literary history largely unexplored. It is in the first place necessary to underscore the fact that, in primitive Franciscanism, there is a marked strain of anti-academicism more or less formally hostile to the learning of the university and to its academic methodologies. In Francis' own writings, in his attitude toward books and learning reported in the early biographies, and in his self-description as an *idiota* (an unlearned person), there is at the very least a rich ambiguity about the appropriateness of magisterial scholarship in the vision of his Order which has proved to be almost endlessly controversial.

Indeed the ghost of the "scholarship question," like that of the "poverty question" to which it is bloodless kin, makes occasional appearances in the Franciscan journals even today. During certain episodes of medieval Franciscan history there was a fairly clearly demarked conflict between those who did and those who did not think that an academic career was consistent with the "poverty" of Franciscan vocation. This attitude was a distinguishing characteristic of the so-called "Spirituals," but it was by no means theirs alone. Furthermore, it was an attitude held by a number of very important literary figures, and its classical expression will not be found in an arid polemical tract but in the spirited poem of Jacopone da Todi, "Oh Paris, you have destroyed Assisi!" We may well call this tradition anti-intellectual if we wish, but it was a tradition with a substantial literary heritage. If Alexander of Hales or William of Ockham had never written a page, we would at most have to rewrite one or two footnotes to our history of medieval poetry. If the obscure penitential confraternities of the March of Ancona and Provence had not written their simple hymns, a great deal would have to be rewritten.

A second imbalance of Franciscan literary history is logically related to the first. Franciscan scholarship has for the most part lavished its interests and energies on texts written in Latin and has avoided profound engagement with vernacular traditions. This, of course, is in one sense not surprising. Medieval vernacular traditions are by their nature parochial and, so far as Franciscan texts are concerned, vernacular books are usually dependent upon a Latin "source." Furthermore, the problem is complicated by the fact that many presumably vernacular texts (especially, of course, sermons) have been recorded only in Latin versions. Yet the resultant situation is somewhat paradoxical. We have a fine Quaracchi edition of the *Stimulus Amoris,* but no authoritative history of that work's very substantial vernacular impact on European spiritual literature in many countries. We can read the lovely but hermetic *Meditatio Pauperis in Solitudine* in a critical edition in the "Bibliotheca franciscana ascetica medii aevi," but we shall not find there an edition of the *Laude* of Jacopone da Todi. James

Ryman, O.F.M., who left behind him the largest assignable body of medieval English lyric poetry we have, has so far as I know never been mentioned once in nearly seventy volumes of the *Archivum Franciscanum Historicum.* It is in this sense that Franciscan literature has been a neglected topic.

It is likewise in some ways unfortunate that "vernacular" Franciscanism has been conceived of primarily if not exclusively as a chapter in the cultural history of Italy. The temptation to do so is very great. Francis was an Italian and, like Dante and Mazzoni, he has become a major cultural industry in his native land. His earliest followers, including many who were to be important in the Order's history, were likewise Italians: Brother Leo, Brother Thomas of Celano, the "three companions," indeed the whole impressive list of authorities who make up the classical repertory of primitive Franciscan history and hagiography. Furthermore, a number of the earliest texts of the Franciscan movement are of considerable importance in the history of Italian letters of the *duecento* and *trecento.* One need only mention by way of example the *Cantico di frate sole* itself, surely among the most carefully studied of European vernacular texts, or the *Fioretti,* the crown jewel in the treasury of Tuscan prose, the *Laude* of Jacopone, the most important unified collection of lyrics which we shall find in the vernacular Middle Ages. Yet this cisalpine splendor is by no means the whole picture. Franciscan literature, like the Franciscan Order itself, was profoundly international in motive and achievement. With few exceptions, its major productions found international audiences through a process of *vulgarisation* which as often as not involved imitation, adaptation, and imaginative improvisations more than simple translation. On the basis of presently published materials it is impossible to make an accurate measurement of the vernacular disbursement of Franciscan literary materials through the nations of Europe in the thirteenth and fourteenth centuries, but the extraordinary work of Kurt Ruh and his students at Würzburg, dealing with the vast German language areas, gives some exciting suggestions. Without dealing with France and England, where very large numbers of medieval Franciscan texts have survived, one can find whole local literatures—such as that of Catalonia, for example, or of Flanders—in which the compositions and "translations" of friars play not merely an important but a decisive role.

There is a further bold feature of the primitive Franciscan ideal which had profound implications for the Order's history from its very inception, and which helps to distinguish Franciscanism from the other religious movements within its own immediate spiritual climate, movements with which it otherwise shares so much in common. It is, furthermore, a feature decisive in the Order's literary history and crucial to consider when attempting to explain the almost astonishing range of early Franciscan writings. I refer to what might be called the "double movement" of the Franciscan conception of the religious life.

In the life and writings of Francis himself we find yoked together, always dramatically and sometimes paradoxically, the centrifugal spiritual aspirations of ascetic withdrawal and plenary, vigorous Christian service in the world. Among Francis' legislative writings is a brief but fascinating rule for the ordering of hermitages, dating from an early time in which the more prominent features of institutional Franciscanism were not yet defined. Its first paragraph reads as follows: "Those brothers who wish to live as religious in hermitages should be three in number or at the most four. Two of them should be 'mothers,' and should have two 'children,' or at least one. The former will lead the life of Martha, and the other two the life of Mary." The scriptural images are obvious, for in medieval exegetical tradition Mary and Martha from the New Testament, like Rachel and Leah from the Old, represent the *vita contemplativa* and the *vita activa*. These concepts, of active and contemplative life, will be familiar ones to almost any reader of medieval poetry. They find beautiful expression in Dante's *Purgatorio,* for example, and are an important subject of discussion in *Piers Plowman.* Francis presents the twin ideals with typical simplicity, and without the elaborate discussions of hierarchical gradation or theology of perfection which typically accompany medieval discussions of the "two lives." He is content to state that the two, like Mary and Martha, should live beneath a common roof.

There is nothing at all remarkable in the statement itself, and the major originality of the document is to be found elsewhere. For our purposes, however, it is a very useful and poetic statement of the "double movement" of the Franciscan life as it poured its energies on to the written page. For although Francis is here specifically addressing himself to the fraternal life of the desert, the twin ideal which he enunciates is apt for the entire Order as we find it developing in the first two centuries of its history. It is an Order made of "mothers" and "children," of Maries and Marthas, an Order of great masters of the interior life and of great apostles to the world. One need only consider any of the diverse yet representative giants of early Franciscan history—Pecham, Bonaventure, Angelo Clareno, St. John of Capestrano—to see how fully and dynamically the twin ideals could be fused in a single life. The author of the *Soliloquium de quatuor mentalibus exercitiis* and the *Lignum vitae* was also the administrative genius who skillfully guided the burgeoning order through some of its most difficult years. The revered master of one of the major schools of medieval mysticism made repeated missionary journeys to Africa before finally gaining his long-desired martyrdom at the hands of "Saracens." Such examples are by no means unique to the Franciscan Order or to the religious life of the later Middle Ages, but they are conspicuously representative of a major Franciscan ideal.

It is this "double movement" of Franciscanism which accounts for the extraordinary breadth and range of Franciscan literature. We find on the one hand a literature of the "Maries," a profundity of mystical and ascetical expression which demands its place among the library of the desert fathers or the great Cistercian spiritual writers of the twelfth century. On the other, there is a vast literature of the "Marthas," a very substantial part of which might be called the evangelical press of the thirteenth and fourteenth centuries. If the writings of the "Maries" have been more carefully edited and more closely studied than those of the "Marthas," it is nonetheless the latter which enjoy the most intimate and catalytic relationships with the literature of the secular world, and which have most clearly left their impress on the shape of the literary history of medieval Europe.

Thus it is that any introduction to medieval Franciscan literature which hopes to be even reasonably comprehensive must address, or at least bring to mind, a range of texts which are very considerable in number and which constitute a major anthology of the kinds and styles of late medieval European literature. I have set aside works of a purely scholastic character, the works that have been the very heart of traditional Franciscan studies. I must say in passing that the loss to my subject has not been inconsiderable. The *Collyrium adversus haereseos* of the legist Alvaro Pelayo is "purely" theological in its intention and scholastic in its method; yet it is buttressed throughout with the authority of exemplary "literary materials." Even making this draconian exclusion, the scholar is still faced with creating a context for the consideration of such texts as the *Testament* of St. Francis, the *Sacrum Commercium,* Bonaventure's *Apologia pauperum, Vitis mystica,* and *Legenda major,* the fiction of Ramon Lull, the *Examples by ABC,* the sermons of Anthony of Padua, the "love-rune" of Thomas of Hales, and the penitential *summa* of Friar Jean Rigaud. None of these works is simply accidentally Franciscan, by virtue of the votive affiliation of its author; each is radically Franciscan—that is, each reveals at its most intimate sources some important aspect of the "double movement" of Franciscanism.

If there are dangers in defining Franciscan literature quite narrowly as literature written by Franciscans, there are difficulties as well in defining it simply in terms of a style or "spirit." Medieval Franciscanism was a diverse and very broadly based spiritual movement which reached into all the far-flung dioceses of the Latin Church and beyond to the mission fields of Africa and the crusading kingdoms. Though it exhibited certain distinctive features of emphasis, it was in one sense merely the most important and vital institutional expression of the European evangelical revival which witnessed the growth of all kinds of groups dedicated to a *vita apostolica,* to the reforms of the Lateran Council of 1215, to the flourishing of the other mendicant orders, and to the general spiritual fervor which characterized European religious life in the second half of the thirteenth century. There is inevitably much in medieval Franciscan literature which is in no way unique or even markedly distinctive. Poverty, though it is the Franciscan theme *par excellence,* is not monopolized by the Franciscans. Penance, a theological and pastoral preoccupation of the Franciscan missionaries, was even more the literary specialty of the Dominicans. The greatest "Franciscan" masterpieces of penitential literature are probably those of Dominicans, such as the Frenchman Peyrault and the Italian Passavanti. Most of the books which this study will "introduce" are indeed the work of Franciscan writers, but this is to some extent a contrived accident of economy.

We must address, or at least make a feint at, the question of the way or ways in which the Franciscan vision of evangelical life leads to literary implications rather different from those of other medieval religious groups. It is after all a valid axiom of medieval literary history that the formal organization of the religious life—or, to put it another way, the peculiar characteristics and aspirations of the religious orders—exercised a crucial influence on literary developments during all periods of medieval history. The *religious* (in the technical sense of that word) control of medieval literary culture has so far been most generally acknowledged, and most carefully studied, with regard to the great Benedictine establishment which dominates the intellectual and scholarly life of the period from the time of Gregory the Great to that of St. Bernard. Perhaps because monastic culture was, for at least six centuries, the heart and conscience of Western learning in ways too numerous and too obvious to need rehearsal, its importance for literary historians has most often been expressed in terms which are general and sweeping, and not infrequently hackneyed. The vague "monk in his cell," the "monkish interpolator," the "monastic scribe"—all are well-known players in the *dramatis personae* of our conventional literary history. Sometimes they are villains, responsible for a superstitious preoccupation with miracles, for "pious fables," for bad Latin, and for an annoying infatuation with allegory; but they can be heroes, too, the loving and on the whole careful middlemen to whom we owe practically everything we know about the classical heritage of Roman letters. What is needed now, perhaps, is a discriminating investigation, sensitive to local nuance and historical change, of the "literary" visions of the religious movements before and beyond Benedictinism.

We may wish to consider, for example, the eremitic institutions of late Antiquity and the early Middle Ages. It is a remarkable fact that, of contemporary literary genres of the period, none enjoyed a wider success, apparently among all classes of literate society, than the *vitae* of the great saints of the desert. Particularly notable in this respect was the *Vita Antonii,* written in Greek by Athanasius, translated into Latin by Evagrius, read (it would appear) by the entire world of the early Middle Ages. These lives, which present as a *social* ideal concepts of eremitic asceticism nearly incredible in their severity, are filled with epic encounters with beasts and demons, lurid tableaux of viscid temptations heroically resisted, and haunting images of surrealistic landscape, abandoned tombs, caves, quarries, foetid pools, and sulphurous fires. They are, in short, excellent reading, and their general influence on other kinds of literature, both historical and fictional, was enormous and long lived. Neither such a religious work as the *Heliand* nor such a secular one as *Beowulf* could have taken their precise shapes without what might be called the "desert tradition" behind them. Another example, which could be developed at length, is the literary impact of the canonic reform of the eleventh and twelfth centuries, out of which grew on the one hand the theological and spiritual literature of the school of St.-Victor and its cultural levellers, and, on the other, a rich literature of a popular and pastoral nature quite unlike that of the Benedictine period.

Hence it is in no way surprising, given the fact that the mendicant movement was beyond question the most important spiritual development of the later Middle Ages, that the friars exercised an important and distinctive influence on the shape of their world's literature. We should have expected as much from the general pattern of medieval literary history, even granting that the friars arrived in a world in which literacy was by no means the near monopoly of religion, as it may have been in the eighth century or the tenth, and in which the religious cadres themselves were considerably more diverse in their literary impulses. There are, however, two particular circumstances which can help explain the quite extraordinary influence of the mendicant religious institutions on the literature of the larger secular world about them. The first is the simple fact that mendicant religion appeared and then flourished in Europe at precisely the time that the major European vernaculars were claiming the prerogatives of versatile literary languages. One cannot call this an accident of history, because the two phenomena to some extent share common social causes, but it is a crucial fact of mendicant literature, and of Franciscan literature in particular.

There are, to be sure, major vernacular *works* before the thirteenth century, but it is difficult to identify convincing vernacular *literatures*. Anglo-Saxon England seems to provide an exception, but its vernacular tradition, always fragile, was effectively and violently erased in the eleventh century, to make an impressive revival only some three hundred years later. So far as the Continent is concerned, it is the thirteenth century which was decisive in the formation of the modern literary vernaculars. Literary historians sometimes give the impression that French as an elegant literary language was created by Chrétien de Troyes, or Italian by Dante Alighieri. This impression is at best only half-true, or perhaps better, only half-false. What is beyond question is the fact that the period during which the mendicant movement was making its most revolutionary impact on Europe was also the period of the crucial triumph of the European vernaculars.

The second circumstance which explains the particular literary importance of the mendicant movement, and of the Franciscans in particular, is its social dimension. The friars' image of themselves was not one of monkish scribes, let alone flagpole hermits, but of plenipotentiary practitioners of the "apostolic life": evangelists, missionaries, doctors of the spirit. Their arena was to be that very world which Christ had come to save and into which He had sent His Apostles, whose successors in fact they were. Their language would be the language of the world. This is clear, for example, in the discussions attendant upon the foundation of the Order of Preachers. The Dominicans were to be *preachers,* and would do little good to harangue the Cathars in Latin, however orthodox. The same impulse is evidenced by the capitular legislation of the Augustinian Hermits and the Carmelites. But above all it is evidenced by the Franciscan Order, which was, so to speak, the vernacular order *par excellence.* For from its very inception, which is to say from the heart and mind of Francis of Assisi himself, the Friars Minor were consciously to exploit not merely the language of the people among whom they practised their apostolate but also their customs, songs, and fables. The early friars consciously thought of themselves as missionaries in their own native lands, and their evangelical techniques, as we shall see in greater detail in a later chapter, explicitly addressed the vernacular cultures among which they lived.

Since literary works are the artifacts of the human imagination, literary history must inevitably be as complex and mysterious as the hidden faculties of human intellection. When we speak of literary developments, literary sources, literary forms, taste, and style, we often speak of little more than the evanescent crests of bright foam on the whitecaps of an ever-changing sea. In writing of "Franciscan mystical literature" I cannot hope to honor the complexity, but I must at least acknowledge the mystery. I shall several times in this book have occasion to suggest that the peculiar qualities and importance of Franciscan literature, of mendicant literature generally, are intimately related to the broadened social sense of the religious life which more friars shared. A number of the specific features which defined the newness of this increased vision have been identified by Heribert Roggen in a provocative study which analyzes primitive Franciscanism in terms of its double challenge to the values of traditional feudalism on the one hand and those of an emerging bourgeois culture of the Italian commercial towns on the other.[1] He finds this challenge formulated not in the terms of self-conscious social criti-

[1] Heribert Roggen, *Die Lebensform des heiligen Franziskus von Assisi in ihrem Verhältnis zur feudalen und bürgerlichen Gesellschaft Italiens* (Mechelen, 1965).

cism but as a response to the gospel, a gospel viewed as a vibrant manual of Christian living rather than as a remote theological authority.

Roggen traces four major "Franciscan" trends, common in different measure to other religious movements of the twelfth and thirteenth centuries, but crucial and defining for the friars and the folk who heard their message. In the first place, Franciscan religion recast the rhetoric and the spiritual psychology of the religious life from that of a rigorous militarism of sharp relationships between superiors and inferiors to a profound and practical conception of religious *fraternitas.* Secondly, it honored the shared ideal of a common *minoritas,* but one founded in penitential perception removed from social distinction. The edifice of Franciscan spirituality was built upon the foundation of an evangelical *paupertas,* so that the very institution of Franciscan religion implied a confrontation with emerging bourgeois values. Finally, the Order fostered an extraordinary and in some ways paradoxical *libertas* founded in fraternity which remarked and valued the individuality of each brother—and each sister.

The implicit Franciscan "challenge," thus perceived, was fundamental, and included social, political, psychological, and stylistic aspects. The internal conception of mendicant evangelism implied powerful external manifestations. At its best, Franciscan evangelism took cloistered aspirations into the busy world or highway and market fair, actively seeking out the publicans and sinners of thirteenth-century life as well as the centurions and pharisees. Late medieval spiritual movements had a broad social base, and we can see in the confraternities (rural as well as urban phenomena), in the trade guilds, in the *béguinages,* and in other small social groupings a renewed religious sociology within a society different in kind rather than in degree from that of the feudal centuries. These spiritual families, most of which either had formal connections with the fraternal orders or had been significantly influenced by them, provided an arena in which serious religious aspiration could become, really for the first time in the Middle Ages, *popular* and accessible to peasants, married men and women, and others who fell outside the elitist vision of medieval monasticism.

The new dynamic of Franciscan religious life facilitated significant stylistic changes in ascetic expression and social organization. Among them, Roggen identifies several which are of considerable importance for a study such as this one. Franciscan religion moved from a cult of God the *Dominus* to focus upon the Incarnate God—visible, accessible, suffering, welcoming in his human nature. The millennial awe of the Byzantine Pantocrator and the Romanesque *Judex* is not entirely absent from the Franciscan Christ, but it is tempered and qualified by the engaging familiarity of the *Bambino* and the pathos of the Man of Sorrows. The knowledge of God—that is, the immediate, personal, and individual experience of Christ—became a general social ideal; the gospel life, a practical social possibility.

Roggen raises the "woman question." In the hierarchical organization of medieval feudal and ecclesiastical life women found limited opportunities for the exercise of authority in either Church or State. Medieval social convention did not encourage the participation of women in public intellectual life. They could not be members of the clergy and did not attend the schools and later universities whose formal purposes were defined by programs of clerical education; nor did they, with rare exceptions, occupy important ancillary positions in chancery life. "I do not suffer a woman to teach," said St. Paul; and medieval women "teachers" and "preachers," like Chaucer's Wife of Bath, are usually risible emblems of social disorder. Under these circumstances, the influence of women on literary developments was limited but by no means negligible, and in Gothic Europe there were at least two major arenas in which they exercised considerable literary "power." In the first, the influence was passive and oblique, in the second, active and direct; both were important to the Franciscans.

One major shaping force of Franciscan literature is audience. Whatever the situation may be with regard to other literary periods, it is surely a mistaken notion to seek medieval "women's literature" exclusively or even primarily in works written by women or in works which, though written by men, deal with "women's themes." In the world of secular letters there are to be sure a few remarkable women authors, such as Marie de France in England; but the paradoxical truth may be that women exercised a far greater "influence" over the development of medieval romance as "readers" than as writers. A courtly audience, largely female in its composition, was the self-conscious arbiter of taste in important literary centers throughout Europe. Women were likewise the defining audience for much late medieval religious literature. If we have a good deal to learn about the social world of Wolfram von Eschenbach from his implied readers, we have no less to learn about the strategies of the mystery plays and the affective energies of the passion lyrics from *their* audiences. It is in no sense a mere literary accident that Francis sang his *Cantico di frate sole* for the sisters of San Damiano, or that John of Caulibus addressed the *Meditationes vitae Christi* to a Poor

Clare, or that Friar Thomas of Hales dedicated his "love-rune" to "a certain young woman."

It is often said that the exercise of more positive intellectual leadership was "limited" to the cloister. I think it is more accurate to say that such leadership was actually enabled and strengthened by the changing institutions of medieval religious life. Certainly the most important literary contributions made by women come from the convents and hermitages, within whose closed and largely self-sustaining worlds women religious could write, for small but significant audiences, in a wide spectrum of literary genres. We have precious evidence from the ages of antique and Benedictine monachism in such masterpieces as the pilgrimage diary of Etheria, the witty Terencian plays of Hrotsvita of Gandersheim, and the polymath erudition of St. Hildegard of Rupertsburg. Yet the kinds of literature most notably associated with medieval women writers are, as we would expect, the genres of spiritual letters which grow out of and nourish the interior life, "mystical" works. Late medieval spiritual literature, if not quite dominated by women writers, is certainly greatly enriched by them: in Germany, Gertrude and Mechtild; in Scandinavia, Bridgit; in Italy, Catherine of Siena; in England, Julian of Norwich. Even a partial list is impressive.

The Franciscan contribution to this spiritual literature, though important, is modest when compared with that of the Dominican nuns. Yet we shall find throughout the broad social spectrum of the Franciscan movement, from the royal paupers of the aristocratic congregations in France to the humble members of the confraternities, evidence of literary possibility. The letters of St. Clare herself, written to the noble sister Agnes of Bohemia, are by no means without literary ambition and achievement; but a more dramatic, even revolutionary, example is that of blessed Angela of Foligno. She was born in the hamlet which gave her her name, a few kilometers south of Assisi, around the middle of the thirteenth century. She led a secular life for some forty years, marrying and bringing a family into the world, before her profound but obscure conversion around 1290. She became a Franciscan tertiary, and a member of the group expounding the most radical doctrine of Franciscan poverty. Quite apart from her remarkable "writings" she would claim a place in the history of the Order as the person who converted Ubertino da Casale to the strict observance. She died in the new year of 1308, leaving behind her the local reputation of a saint and the book for which she is still remembered today.

In fact the *Book of Blessed Angela of Foligno,* as it is usually called, is not so much a "book" as it is a dossier of miscellaneous documents.[2] These include some thirty-five pieces in all, letters, prayers, brief meditations, and various spiritual "position papers," but the most important of them is the lengthy memoir, compiled in Latin by a certain Brother Adam of Assisi, Angela's confessor, and later reviewed by Angela herself. This memoir is a remarkable work of exemplary autobiography. Though it has some clear generic kinship with a number of well-known books from the middle of the thirteenth century, it is in many respects highly original, pointing much more in the direction of the mystics of the medieval twilight—Rolle, Julian of Norwich, the Rhineland visionaries—than back to the elegant cadences of Thomas of Celano or the almost shrill lyricism of John Pecham. In her "book" we find the authentic voice of a new and

[2] *Le livre de la Bienheureuse Angèle de Foligno,* ed. P. Doncoeur (Paris, 1926); see Doncoeur's article "Angèle de Foligno," in *DS,* I, 570-571.

"bourgeois" spirituality which had redefined the traditional categories of medieval ascetic experience for a religious society greatly expanded in its numbers and in its social breadth.

Another important attitude which helps to characterize Franciscan literature is an attitude toward language. The language of Franciscan books—language understood in a broad sense to include not merely a vocabulary but also a spiritual syntax and a range of characteristic idiom —is the language of the Scriptures. For Francis, however, the very *words* of the Scriptures have a sacramental character, for they are not merely written by God but are true archeological vestiges of the Incarnation. This is made clear in the remarkable letter addressed by Francis to all the priests of the Church, exhorting them to be reverent and meticulous when handling the consecrated elements of the Eucharist. The title under which the tract is published in the Quaracchi *Opuscula*—"De reverentia corporis Domini et de munditia altaris"—can give only a partial indication of the work's content, and Francis is concerned not only with the sacramental elements of the altar, but with the sacramental words of Holy Scripture as well. He writes thus: "Indeed, in this world there is nothing of the Most High himself that we can possess and contemplate with our eyes, except his Body and Blood, his name and his words, by which we were created and by which we have been brought back from death to life."[3] Nor is the relationship between God's "body and blood" and His "names and words" merely a metaphoric one. Francis frequently writes of the Sacrament, always stressing a distinction between the elements visible to the "animal man" (I Cor. 2:14) and

[3] *Opuscula Sancti Patris Francisci Assisiensis* (Quaracchi, 1949), p. 22; *Omnibus,* p. 101.

the invisible but necessary spiritual reality mysteriously alive within them. In his first *Admonitio,* "De corpore Christi," he draws the explicit analogy between Christ's visceral and His sacramental bodies, both of which hide mysteries.

Francis argues that the Son of God must be seen as spirit. "That is why all those were condemned who saw our Lord Jesus Christ in his humanity but did not see or believe in spirit in his divinity, that he was the true Son of God. In the same way all those are damned who see the sacrament of the Body of Christ which is consecrated on the altar in the form of bread and wine by the words of our Lord in the hands of the priest, and do not see or believe in spirit and in God that this is really the most holy Body and Blood of our Lord Jesus Christ. . . ."[4] All the more remarkable, then, is Francis' reverence for the words of Scripture, regarded as it were as physical objects, precious elements of ink and parchment sacramentally consecrated by the articulation of their divine author. For he insists on the point that it is not merely the outward and visible signs of the sacrament which should be treated with reverence and decency but also the *words*—"In the same way, God's name and his written words should be picked up, if they are found lying in the dirt, and put in a suitable place."[5] As usual, one could wish that Francis had written more, but even the riddling statements we do have are exciting with suggestion for the student of the "critical theory" which lies behind the Christian poetry of the Middle Ages. Francis' attitude is one best understood by a poet. Dante understood perfectly.

[4] *Opuscula,* p. 4; *Omnibus,* p. 78.
[5] *Opuscula,* p. 23; *Omnibus,* p. 101.

A reverent and expectant waiting upon the names and words of God, a "primitive" fascination with the authority and integrity of the written word—such attitudes help explain the remarkable purity of the textual tradition of Francis' own brief writings. Francis de Beer has drawn attention to a number of arresting texts in Francis' own writings which seem to reveal a deference to the written word almost "magical" in its character.[6] He constantly urges his readers to follow his words *ad finem,* to understand them in their clarity and their simplicity, in their sufficient and definitive exposition, without recourse to gloss or extrinsic explication.

The most famous such injunction comes at the end of the *Testament,* where he says that the friars should have it always with them *juxta regulam.* "And in every chapter meeting it should be done thus: when they read the rule, they read also these words." But constantly in his letters as well, he ends with injunctions that they should be studied *ad finem,* memorized by the illiterate, not tampered with. This insistence on the inviolability of the received text—especially as regards the provisions of the rule and the *Testament*—was to become the marching orders for the Spirituals, but there is evidence that it was widely subscribed to in the early foundation. The saint's letters, for example, have been preserved in a careful textual transmission which has scrupulously maintained what one squeamish philologist has termed the "gross Italianisms" in the Latin words which came from Francis' own lips or pen.

One further implication must be drawn from the biblicism of Francis' mental habits and literary imagination, and that is that literature is powerful, practical, af-

[6] Francis de Beer, *La Conversion de Saint François selon Thomas de Celano* (Paris, 1963), p. 154*n*.

fective, consequential. The *Cantico di frate sole* was not merely sung, but *used*—to bring peace to Assisi, to comfort the Poor Clares of San Damiano. The imperative power of the sacred text as a goad to immediate and radical action was unquestioned, and Francis, together with Christians as far removed in time and place as Augustine and John Wesley, practiced *sortes,* divination through random consultation of a scriptural passage. One of the narrative clichés of hagiography is that the reading or hearing of a text—a scriptural text, above all—should have an immediate, powerful, indeed definitive effect upon its readers or hearers. An excellent case in point is the literary history of Francis' own "conversion experience," effected by the chance audition of the lectionary passage from Matthew 19, "If thou wilt be perfect, go, sell all thou hast, and give it to the poor . . ." This is a spiritual quotation of the moment in the *Vita Antonii* which, in a slightly different way, controls the history of Augustine's conversion in the eighth book of the *Confessions.*

Early Franciscan texts typically aspire to a borrowed biblical authority to make things be and happen. Francis wrote for his brethren, or rather compiled for them from the Scriptures, a document which was not merely a "monastic rule" but a "life." The word is striking, especially in the abrupt prologue to the *Regula non bullata* of 1221. "In the name of the Father and of the Son and of the Holy Spirit. Amen. This is the *life* Brother Francis asked to be permitted him and approved by the lord Pope Innocent." The larger phrase of the first paragraph, which became the keystone of the ratified document of 1223, is "the rule and life of the friars." *Vita et regula.* Beneath the surface of this plain yet perplexing phrase we can find one of the most constant indices of Franciscan thought and temper, a profound vision of the vivifying energies of the Incarnation. The fraternal rule is not a *vita* because it prescribes a way of life, though it does do that in the two precepts of the New Law. Rather it *is* life, because it is of Christ, the way, the truth, and the life. It is life because its words are those of the Word made Flesh.

The claim that the rule embodied the unmediated will of Christ, shocking and even scandalous to many within the Order as well as without, is explicitly advanced in the prologue to the *Speculum Perfectionis.* Brother Elias, fearful of the rumored severity of the *regula bullata,* then in the process of being drawn up by Francis, murmured against it. "At this blessed Francis raised his face to heaven and spoke to Christ, saying, 'Lord, was I not right when I said that they would not believe me?' And all present heard the voice of Christ answer from heaven, 'Francis, nothing in this Rule is yours; for all is Mine. I wish the Rule to be obeyed to the letter, to the letter, without a gloss, without a gloss.' "[7]

In the context of the *Speculum Perfectionis* the idea is clouded and perhaps compromised by its polemical intentions, but we shall find it implied and acted upon everywhere in the most noble documents of the Order. Life, grounded in Christ, is likewise grounded in Scripture. Its words are not an opaque medium between perceived historical life and an ancient Incarnation; they are the very words of life itself. Of all the medieval poets who shared with Francis of Assisi the excitement of a living connection between words and *the* Word, none is more happy in its expression than Dante Alighie-

[7] *Speculum Perfectionis,* I; Omnibus, pp. 1125-26.

ri. In his celebrated survey of Franciscan history in the twelfth canto of the *Paradiso,* Dante puts into the mouth of St. Bonaventure, or rather the *vita di Bonaventura,* his soul and living presence, a brilliant metaphor in which the Franciscan rule, Franciscan life, and the Franciscan Christ all merge in a daring irresolution:

> Ben dico, chi cercasse a foglio a foglio
> nostro volume, ancor troveria carta
> u' leggerebbe 'I' mi son quel ch'i' soglio . . .'

(Nevertheless, I say, he who should search our volume leaf by leaf might still find a page where he would read, 'I am as I always was . . .')[8]

A close reading of the passage will reveal that the *volume,* the "book," is at once the Bible, the rule, and the human architecture of the Order, whose "pages" are individual friars. Dante's own insistent pretense that his book, the *Commedia,* is in a sense scriptural, is a "Franciscan" attitude.

All of medieval Christian literature is "influenced" by the Bible and by the spiritual attitudes and exegetical expectations which its Christian readers brought to it; but to attempt to do justice to the radically scriptural nature of Franciscan literature in such general terms would be to say that the gull is "influenced" by the air through which it glides, or the potter by the clay he shapes.

Gregory the Great had remarked, in connection with his account of the signs and wonders wrought by the saints of Italy, that his readers should not be surprised to see repeated and relived in the lives of contemporary holy men those identical miracles which are the authenticating marks of God's special grace working through the

[8] *Paradiso,* XII, 121-123; ed. and trans. by C. S. Singleton (Princeton, 1975), pp. 136-137.

prophets of the Old Testament and the One to whom they pointed in the New. For him the familiarity of the pattern of sacred history was a comforting and confirming reassurance, not a source of doubt or a clue to "lateral contamination." The authenticity of the holy works wrought by Benedict is guaranteed by the fact that we have seen them before in Elijah and Elisha. Indeed, we shall see them again, until the end of time, wherever we find the special saints of God.

A similar attitude dominates the Franciscan historical imagination, convinced as it was of the unique significance of Francis and of the founding of his Order. It is not merely the language of the Bible which infiltrates practically all imaginative Franciscan literature. It is as well its poetic strategies and narrative rhythms, its whole sense of the appropriate way in which words can express religious ideas. Though we shall find few traces in medieval Franciscan texts of learned or "humanistic" allegory in the mode of Prudentius and the Chartrians, we shall indeed find a kind of pervasive and generalized luminescence of quasi-scriptural allegory, especially in the treatment of the actual events of the life and works of Francis.

There is a vivid not to say baroque example of this kind of allegorical infiltration of the early narrative and biographical texts at the beginning of the third of the *Considerazioni sulle Stimmate,* a late fourteenth-century work. Brother Leo, disobeying Francis, secretly observes by moonlight one of the master's moments of tansfixed rapture. In ecstatic discourse Francis repeats time and again, "Who are you, my dearest God? And what am I, your vilest little worm and useless little servant?" Brother Leo "marveled greatly at this," and raising his eyes to heaven, he saw a great flame descending to Francis' head. From the flame came a voice, speaking words incomprehensible to Brother Leo. At this he quietly drew a little further away but continued to watch as Francis reached out his hand three times toward the flame. Later, Leo confessed his act of disobedience to Francis, but he begged not merely pardon but an explanation of the extraordinary vision of which he had been a pious *voyeur.* Francis, "seeing that God had revealed to him or allowed the humble Brother to see some things," gave the following explanation: "God was in that flame which you saw, and He spoke to me under the form of that flame, as He had formerly spoken to Moses. And among other things which He said to me then, He asked me to give Him three gifts. And I replied: 'My Lord, I am entirely Yours. You know that I have nothing but a habit and cord and breeches, and those three things are likewise Yours. So what can I offer or give to Your majesty?' . . . Then God said to me: 'Put your hand in your bosom and offer me whatever you find there.' I searched and I found there a coin of gold . . . and then I offered it to God. . . . And I did this three times. And after making the third offering, I knelt down and blessed and thanked God, who had given me something to offer."[9]

In the exegesis which follows Francis explains that he was given to understand that the three gold coins represented the religious vows—*la santa obbedienza, l'altissima povertà, e la splendidissima castità.* The episode is thick with scriptural suggestion and scriptural language; one thinks of Joseph's dreams and Ezekiel's vision. Its central idea is purely religious and in a sense

[9] *I Fioretti di san Francesco,* ed Guido Bonino (Turin, 1972), pp. 178-179; *Omnibus,* pp. 1444-47.

entirely commonplace, but it finds its expression in a "historical" event of scriptural pretensions.

The stylistic ramifications of this literary biblicism are very far-reaching, and some of them must occupy our attention in succeeding chapters. Francis' own modes of expression habitually involve a harmonic construction in which the literal "text" plays against an implied or subsumed scriptural image. Some of the complexities of what might be called Francis' "literary imagination" are revealed by an analysis of the saint's *Testament,* probably the most carefully studied of his Latin works outside the *regulae* themselves, and one which exercised an enormous authority on a large part of the Order in the thirteenth and fourteenth centuries. It is a document which presents few obvious textual problems. Indeed, there is good reason to believe that it is the textually purest of Francis' *opuscula*—a brief document, overtly "plain and simple" in its form and content, dictated by a dying man to scribes as solicitous of his every word as they would have been of those of the Scriptures themselves. Yet in fact we cannot get beyond the title before encountering serious problems of literary analysis. Though generally known as the *Testament* from an early period in the Order's history, it is not clear whether the title ever had Francis' own sanction. He himself says that it is not a *rule,* but instead his "*recordatio, admonitio* and *exhortatio,* and [his] *testamentum.*"

In it he does in fact "remember" the exemplary moments of his life, how God gave him the grace "to begin to do penance," how when he still was "in his sins" the sight of lepers was painful to him, how the Lord gave him brothers. Likewise he admonishes and exhorts his brothers—to be obedient Catholics, to remain true to the rule of poverty, to "read these words" whenever gathered together in chapter. But in what sense is the work a *testamentum*? The richness of the word is by no means exhausted by the meaning of "will" or deathbed legacy, though such a meaning is appropriate to the circumstances. The primary meaning of the *testamentum* is precisely that of the two "testaments" of the Scriptures: promise, alliance, contract, bond. A Dutch Franciscan scholar, A. van Corstanje, has written a beautiful little book which elegantly demonstrates how the subliminal image of the Exodus infiltrates Francis' thinking in the *Testament,* and directs the work's ideographic structure.[10] The bond, the article of alliance as it were between Jehovah and his chosen people, is, for Francis, holy poverty. The idea itself is an arresting one; but what is perhaps more relevant to our introduction to medieval Franciscan literature is the manner in which it lies submerged beneath the text of the *Testament,* like a shell of mother-of-pearl brightly but indistinctly visible beneath the rippling waters of a clear stream.

[10] Auspicius van Corstanje, *Het verbond van Gods armen* (1964); translations in German, French, and (by G. Ready and S. A. Yonick) English, *The Covenant with God's Poor: An Essay on the Biblical Interpretation of the Testament of St. Francis of Assisi* (Chicago, 1966).

2

Some Medieval Biographies of Francis

Scholarly discussion of Franciscan literature has usually meant the examination of the "Franciscan question," the riddle of the small and by now classical repertory of thirteenth- and fourteenth-century texts which deal directly with the life of the founder. Though the aims of this book include an exhortation to look beyond these lavishly studied books, it is not possible to look around them. In the Middle Ages the quest for a definitive and "authentic" Francis, and for a single "true" account of his vision of fraternal life, tragically rent his Order; in our own day it has often made the study of Franciscan origins partisan and polemical. No one can answer the "Franciscan question," but there is no way, either, that an introduction to medieval Franciscan literature can avoid asking it.[1]

One can only wish that the "Franciscan question" were as simple in its roots and ramifications as the famous

[1] The primary texts are collected in the *Legendae S. Francisci Assisiensi saeculis XIII et XIV conscriptae* (Quaracchi, 1926-41); except as noted, they are available in translation with rich commentary in *Saint François d'Assise: Documents*, edd. T. Desbonnets and D. Vorreux (Paris, 1968) and in the *English Omnibus of the Sources for the Life of St. Francis*, ed. Marion A. Habig (Chicago, 1973). For a recent, thorough bibliography of the "Franciscan question" see Sophronius Clasen, *Legendae Antiquae S. Francisci* (Leiden, 1967).

upas tree; but it is a complicated tangle of philological problems, textual mysteries, and editorial guesses. The most difficult, and often unstated part of the question has been this: which among the wide variety of the early biographical materials give the most authentic picture of the life of the founder and of the early Order? One's attitude toward this part of the question influences other lines of inquiry. Can the "official" lives of Thomas of Celano and Bonaventure be given full authority, or must they be screened for establishmentarian bias? What documents were lost as a result of the action of the General Chapter in 1260? Who compiled the *Speculum Perfectionis,* and when? Have any of the undoubted works of Friar Leo survived? The search for an authentic Francis, and for a single "true picture" of the early Order, has been as much a controlling motive of modern Franciscan scholarship as it was an occasion for medieval polemic within the Order. It is, however, a search unlikely to be satisfied by the evidence of colophons and textual variants; indeed, it it unlikely to be satisfied at all, for the truth about the man will hardly be less nuanced and many-sided than those documents which tried to enshrine him in parchment and ink. The pages which follow make no pretense of dealing with the "Franciscan question." They have a different aim, and that is to give some suggestion of the range and nature of early Franciscan biography and to show how its themes, techniques, and historical assumptions have literary implications which were to reach far beyond these hagiographic texts themselves.

Though I abjure the intention of answering the "Franciscan question," it is probably just as well to attempt some description of its scope. One special problem is the problem of Brother Leo. Brother Leo was one of the closest of Francis' friends, his scribe, and his confessor. We have it on the authority of several thirteenth- and fourteenth-century writers that Brother Leo was among the saint's biographers. The "Spiritual triumvirate"—John Peter Olivi, Ubertino da Casale, and Angelo Clareno—all testify to the existence of some *rotuli,* or manuscript scrolls, written in Leo's very hand. Ubertino actually goes so far as to cite one of the works in question and, in another place, to lament the report of their probable loss. It has proved possible, by working carefully with citations, allusions, and some manuscript fragments which came to light around the turn of the century, to publish two of Leo's opuscules, the *Intentio Regulae* and the *Verba Francisci.*[2] It seems at least likely that both of these are merely surviving portions of longer, more ambitious works. In addition, it has been argued that two extended biographical compositions—the so-called *Legend of Perugia* and the *Speculum Perfectionis*—are in fact the work of Brother Leo. John Moorman, the English Franciscanist, would add the *Legend of the Three Companions.* Taken as a group, these writings are often called the "Leo sources" or the "Leo documents," though in fact only the slightest and the most fragmentary of them have any probable claim to be Leo's own work. The "Leo sources" reflect an essentially Spiritual view of Francis and the Order's early history, a rigorist position on the poverty question, and an insistence on the absolute authority of the literal *Rule.*

Discussions of the authenticity of these works, and their relationships with the biographies officially endorsed by the Order in Chapter, have been a prominent feature of the "Franciscan question." A crucial issue

[2] These two texts are edited by K. Lemmens in *Documenta antiqua Franciscana,* I (1901), pp. 83-106.

is that of the adjudication of dates. Here we have a few fixed beacons in a veritable ocean of speculation. The *Vita prima* of Thomas of Celano, the first "official" biography, dates from 1228, the *Vita secunda* from 1248. Bonaventure's *Legenda major* was commissioned in 1260, completed in 1263, and pronounced the sole authorized biography by capitular action in 1266. The questions which then arise are several. What documents, if any, survived the censorship of 1260? Most conspicuously, of course, the two lives of Thomas of Celano survived. They must have been recognized as the major sources of Bonaventure's biography and therefore enjoyed a kind of special immunity. But there must have been many texts which were in fact destroyed and lost to history. Celano's *Vita secunda,* as is well known, was written in response to the open invitation of the Minister General Crescentius of Jesi, issued at the Chapter of Genoa in 1244, to send in materials concerning the life and miracles of the founder. The *Legend of the Three Companions* is apparently another such response to the request. Whether the two lives of Thomas of Celano depended on written as opposed to oral sources has been a hotly debated issue. What a hundred years of careful investigation has not been able to call in doubt is that Thomas of Celano wrote the first formal biography of Saint Francis.

Thomas was born in the Abruzzi, probably in the 1180's.[3] In one of the very rare instances in which the biographer draws attention to himself, he lets drop that he was among a group of "noble and learned" men who presented themselves to be received into the Order by Francis himself. That would have been in 1215, so

[3] See Silvana Spirito, *Il francescanesimo di fra Tommaso da Celano* (Assisi, 1963).

that Thomas, though not among the select group of Umbrians who were with Francis since before the Order's foundation, was an early recruit. He spent the early 1220's in the great mission in Germany and returned to Italy, probably in time to see Francis die. He was at the Portiuncula in 1228 and witnessed with his own eyes the fantastic scene which took place at the church of St. George outside the walls of Assisi on July 16, 1228, when the *poverello* was formally enrolled among the saints of the Church.

Thomas of Celano was no doubt chosen for the role of official biographer because of his literary accomplishments. He exemplified the Franciscan "literary" ideal exactly as Francis himself had, for he was both a poet and a notable preacher. There now seems no reason to doubt his authorship of the *Dies irae,* one of the most famous Latin hymns of the Middle Ages, and while his sermons have not apparently survived, there is unequivocal contemporary testimony to their high quality.[4] Yet his biographical works present serious problems for the modern reader, even as they demand his attention. In all, he wrote four different works concerning the life of Francis: two formal biographies (known simply as the *Vita prima* and the *Vita secunda*), a *Tractatus de miraculis,* and a brief liturgical legendary. Though they differ considerably in motive and historical importance, they all bear the distinctive mark of Thomas' literary style. The two *vitae* and the collection of miracles are particularly important.

The reader who wishes to avoid disappointment in sampling the works of Celano must approach them in a spirit of active cooperation and bring to them, insofar

[4] Aniceto Chiappini, "La sequenza 'Dies Irae, Dies Illa' di fra Tommaso da Celano," *CF,* XXXII (1926), pp. 116-21.

as is possible, medieval rather than modern expectations. Medieval biography in general, of which hagiography is of course by far the largest part, is exemplary in nature. It has little if any interest in placing its subject in a complex and defining historical context, or in the detailed delineation of the subject's family history, his "early years," his education, his personality, or indeed, most of the other features which characterize the biographical mode as it has developed in recent centuries. The aims of the medieval hagiographer are quite different. He seeks to demonstrate the sanctity of life of his subject, and to do so in such a fashion as to give intelligible and whenever possible practical example to his readers. The readers' expectations are likewise important: they are assumed to be a practical edification which can lead to an amendment of life, a desire not so much to know the intimate and pedestrian details of the saint's life as to be able effectively to imitate his spiritual actions.

Furthermore, few medieval saints' lives make any sustained effort at originality of narrative conception; and they reveal not merely a profound conventionality of form but, to a remarkable extent, a conventionality of content as well. One reads a medieval *vita* with a continuing sense of *déjà vu*. Borrowed miracles and dialogue, recurrent narrative clichés, are mixed in a seemingly random fashion with historical and local details of an altogether more "authentic" stamp. The "parent text" is often quite obvious; it is usually the Bible, or one of the standard classics of early Christian exemplary literature such as the *Confessions* of St. Augustine or the *Vita Antonii*. In the *Dialogues* of Gregory the Great the acts of St. Benedict repeat the miracles of the Old Testament prophets, with a fruitful confusion of Monte Cassino and Mount Carmel.

In the *vitae* written by Thomas of Celano this conventionality appears in a variety of forms.[5] There is in the first place little by way of a chronological narrative of Francis' life. The first book of the *Vita prima,* though it advertises itself as a "chronological" history, in fact spends less than three chapters dealing with Francis' early life. The *Vita secunda* moves with even greater haste into its exemplary purposes. In it there is but one brief chapter concerning the saint's life before the time of his capture by the Perugians as a young man, and most of that deals with the significance of the name "Francis" and with prophetic aspects of his childhood. Furthermore, the focus is not on specific empirical history, but on generalized spiritual history. Thomas of Celano writes with the Bible on his writing desk, and St. Augustine at his shoulder, with a handy reference library of grave authorities on his study shelf. The first sentence of the first chapter is a manipulation of the first sentence of the book of Job, and in the first two paragraphs of the work there are at least twenty scriptural borrowings, two overt allusions to the *Confessions* of St. Augustine, and a formal citation of the *Moral Epistles* of Seneca. The reader is further isolated from any immediate and vital sense of Francis' presence by an elevated and artificial rhetorical style.

Nonetheless, the two lives of Thomas of Celano do provide the specific biographical details by which the world has seemed to know Francis best: his heroic poverty, his stupefying humility, his eccentricities of behavior which inspired embarrassment, shock, outrage, and, above all, awe, wherever he went. Francis, a legend

[5] For evidence of Thomas' literary culture—evidence rather curiously interpreted, it must be added—see Nino Tamassia, *S. Francesco d'Assisi e la sua leggenda* (Padua, 1906); English trans. (London, 1910).

in his own lifetime, lived on in the legend of Thomas of Celano. Some scholars have accused him of attempting to reduce the complexity and controversiality of his subject to the proportions which would be acceptable to the "Church" or the "Order." The *Vita prima* was commissioned directly by Pope Gregory IX, who had been Francis' friend, who had (as the revered Cardinal Hugolino of Franciscan historiography) been the Order's first appointed protector, and who had presided at the rites of canonization. Gregory can be expected to have wanted a *vita* which would be useful to the Church, just as he wanted to use the spiritual energies of the new Order in the Church's service. Certainly the extent to which subliminal controversial motives directed Thomas' pen is a discussable question, even if we cannot accuse him of rewriting the life of Francis of Assisi as that of Francis of Rome. A significant attempt to define with some precision the differences in motive and vision between the *Vita prima* and the *Vita secunda* has recently been made in a stimulating but eventually inconclusive book by the French scholar Francis de Beer.[6]

Thomas left two other works concerning the life of Francis. As an "official" biographer, he had to be concerned not merely with biography but with the establishment of the saint's cult as well. He had in his possession for some time the saint's relics, and Jordan of Giano records that Thomas gave them to him in 1230. About the same time he edited from the *Vita prima* a liturgical legendary, generally called the *Legenda ad usum chori*. It is brief and elegant, and has some special importance for the few biographical details which it adds to the *Vita prima*, such as that the seraph of the stigma-

[6] Francis de Beer, *La Conversion de Saint François* (Paris, 1963).

tization spoke secret words to Francis. Its interest to literary historians, however, is limited.

Such is not at all the case with the *Tractatus de miraculis,* which Thomas compiled around 1252/1253, and which was destined to be an extremely important source of iconographic detail in the visual arts and in popular literature. In it, Thomas attempts to provide a *catalogue raisonné* of nearly two hundred miracles, distributed into chapters according to subject matter. Though it finally loses its coherence in a kind of fabulous *materia medica* (with chapters devoted to childbirth miracles, ruptures, blindness and deafness, leprosy, insanity, and fractures), the structure of the *Tractatus de miraculis* displays the same editorial abilities which characterize the two *vitae* and which would by themselves be enough to justify his commission as the Order's official hagiographer.

Thomas begins the *Tractatus* with a particularly bold and felicitous stroke. "At the beginning of this narration which we undertake concerning the miracles of our most holy father Francis," he writes, "let us first of all describe that most solemn marvel which was for the world a warning, a stimulation, a thunderclap: I mean that religious foundation, that *fecundity of a sterile woman,* that descending into innumerable branches."[7] The "fecundity of a sterile woman" is an allusion, at the literal level, to the birth of the prophet Samuel, but it is here charged with a heavy weight of allegorical meaning which Thomas does not long leave dark. The sterility is the ineffectuality of a corrupt and maimed Church in a world of sin. The first miracle of Francis is the foundation of the Franciscan Order.

[7] *Tractatus de miraculis,* I, 1; *Legendae S.F.A.,* p. 272. The *Omnibus* includes only selections from this text.

That is not, however, the Franciscan miracle *par excellence*. The miracle *par excellence* was the reception of the stigmata. In the mystery of the stigmata, indeed, Thomas finds the definitive, unprecedented, and absolutely extraordinary sign which, for him as for many in the early Order, could alone be the decorous seal of a human life likewise unprecedented and extraordinary. He insists not merely on the authenticity of the stigmata, but on the absolute necessity that the miracle be actively believed and its mystery venerated, with what might be described as a defensive aggressiveness. The second long chapter of the *Tractatus,* the first which deals with miracles properly speaking, is an attempt to create a historical context in which the granting of the stigmata is a logical if not an inexorable event. This context is the history of Francis' often miraculous commerce with the cross. Brother Sylvester saw a golden cross come from his mouth, the arms of which encircled the entire globe; Brother Monaldo saw him crucified in the flesh as he listened to a sermon of St. Anthony about the cross. Francis honored the sign of the cross with a special devotion; he marked all the habitations of the brothers with its image and signed his letters in no other way that with the mysterious Tau. "Thus, there is nothing astonishing, neither to the eyes of reason or to those of faith, that the cross, the object of such a great love, should in return heap such honors upon Francis. For this reason nothing is more normal that what is reported to us concerning the stigmata."[8]

Thomas had been among the hundreds, perhaps thousands, who had seen Francis' corpse, and he is eloquent in his own testimony to the mysterious marks of the Passion branded into the flesh: "What we tell you about

[8] *Tractatus de miraculis,* II, 3; *Legendae S.F.A.*, p. 273.

this, we ourselves have seen; we have touched with our own hands what our hands here describe. . . . All this history tends to the glory of Christ. What sane man would dare deny it? There have, however, been those who have not believed. Let us recount their punishment, in order to convince skeptics and to encourage believers in their devotion." The exemplary stories used to that end are remarkable if crude. A canon in Potenza, ill for a long time, goes into a church to pray for a return of good health. He sees there a painting of Francis stigmatized, kneels before it in devotion, and begins to pray fervently; but the enormity of the miracle preys on his mind. "Can this be true? . . . No, it must be an invention, perhaps even a conscious fraud made up by the friars. It goes too far beyond the bounds of human understanding. It is too squarely at odds with common sense."[9] God punishes him with a sudden and horrible wound. His gloved left hand is pierced through with an arrow wound which leaves no mark on the glove. In another story the stigmata, left out of a picture of Francis through the negligence of the artist, miraculously appear there in response to the pious concern of a believing woman.

In 1244 the General Chapter had been more than happy to see new biographies of the founder. As we have seen, the Minister General issued a broad invitation asking for biographical materials from anyone who might have them, rather in the fashion of scholars who make appeal in the small print of the *Times Literary Supplement.* Such was the genesis of the *Vita secunda,* the *Legenda Trium Sociorum,* and, no doubt, other works as well. In 1260, things had changed dramatically.

[9] *Tractatus de miraculis,* II, 6; *Legendae S.F.A.,* p. 275.

In its General Chapter of that year the Order took steps to see that all these materials, as well as any which antedated them, be destroyed. From the ashes of the bonfire would rise a new, authoritative, indeed definitive *vita,* to be written by Bonaventure of Bagnoreggio. The reversal of policy and the drastic censorship which it involved are puzzling in the extreme. Though many commentators have attempted to explain the episode, none has so far done so in an entirely satisfying fashion.

The easy answer, certainly the one most frequently adduced by medieval historians, is that the capitular action of 1260 reflected in an obvious if not a blatant form an ideological struggle within the Order. The heirs of the Franciscan revolution, like other second-generation revolutionaries both before and after their time, were profoundly aware of the necessity of controlling their own history, of being its masters rather than its slaves. The tensions between the two broad tendencies within the Order (the Community and the Spirituals, as they would come to be called), though they had not reached the critical point at which they arrived in the final decades of the century, were already clearly articulated; and the whole question of the Order's mission within the Church, around which the tensions developed, had been brought permanently to the fore by the attacks of the secular masters at the University of Paris in the 1250's upon the mendicant orders and the whole theology of mendicancy. Bonaventure, an honest moderate, universally admired as the great spokesman for Franciscanism within the Church, would be commissioned with the composition of a *vita* at once unimpeachable in its authority and sensible in its general conception of what the Order was about. It would be a document at which none could cavil, and its exclusive patent of publication might put an end to the troublesome proliferation of books of the genre of the Leo sources, with their explicit contradictions of official policies of the Order.

Easy answers are not always wrong, and there is probably a good deal of substance in this one. But there are surely other factors to be considered. The year 1260 was not an innocuous one in Europe, especially in Franciscan Europe. The forty-two stations of the Exodus, the forty-two generations from the birth of Christ were fulfilled in that year, and Joachimite expectations were riding high. This sort of thing had already once in the recent past embarrassed the Order and occasioned the attacks on mendicancy which Bonaventure's *Apologia Pauperum* had sought to silence. For Salimbene of Adam, as no doubt for others in the Order, the uneventful passage of the "apocalyptic" year discredited a kind of dangerous Joachimism which linked melodramatic historical expectations with an extravagant ecclesiological view of Franciscanism. A new life of Francis was needed for a new age. And Bonaventure, while no Joachimist, certainly held a poetic and, indeed, a prophetic vision of Francis of Assisi, "the angel of the sixth seal."

It can credibly be argued that St. Bonaventure is the greatest Franciscan writer who ever lived. Certainly he claims a place among a very select group of the most profound and influential spiritual geniuses of the Middle Ages. So varied are his contributions to Franciscan literature that he must find a place in every chapter of this book, though major consideration of his achievement will be postponed until we examine his mystical works, in the fifth chapter. Hagiography was merely a sideline for Bonaventure, and he undertook the composition of the *Legenda major* only in humble obedience to the will of the Order.

The *Legenda major* (so called in retrospect to distinguish it from a second and shorter *vita* written by Bonaventure) was designed, above all, to provide an authoritative and uniform portrait of the founder to all members of the Franciscan Order. If it had no other merits its importance to Franciscan literature would remain enormous by simple virtue of its extraordinarily wide publication and influence. It must surely be one of the most widely disseminated texts of the later Middle Ages. The General Chapter held at Paris in 1266, which confirmed the work, decreed as well that every convent in the Order should be supplied with a copy of it. In Dante's time there were well over a thousand Franciscan houses in Europe, and in Chaucer's there were nearly two thousand, counting those of the Second Order. It was thus the required reading for a spiritual army, numbering at the very least in the hundreds of thousands, which included among its ranks some of the most important cultural arbiters of a century of European history. Its influence in the popularization of Franciscan legend in poetry, painting, and cult is unquestioned. Several Franciscan texts regarded as of considerable importance have survived in only a few copies. One or two—such as the Perugia *Legenda* and Bonaventure's sermon on the *Rule*—exist in a single medieval manuscript. There are over four hundred surviving manuscripts of the *Legenda major.*

The *Legenda major* relies to a marked degree on the two lives of Thomas of Celano. Bonaventure has edited, shuffled, and polished the earlier materials, but the general effect is that of a Thomas of Celano *redivivus* so far as the narrative content of the *Legenda* is concerned. This is of course puzzling. Why is the "new" life merely an old life rewritten? Bonaventure did not, in my view, bring to his task an original conception of the content of Francis' life. What he did, instead, was to place the verbal iconography of Franciscan legend within a rigorous speculative structure. The *Legenda* is a distinctly "theological" biography, and its structure reveals a tautness of theological schema which the casual reader may hardly notice. Bonaventure distributes his materials among fifteen chapters, not counting the prologue. The numbering is not haphazard—it seldom is in sophisticated medieval works—for the *Legenda* is structured around certain numerological conventions which, though formally extrinsic to Bonaventure's material, add legitimate significance to its articulation. The "biographical" chapters are six in number. Four at the beginning deal with the youth and conversion, the two at the end deal with the final illness and death. The ratio is the harmonic 2:1, beloved of St. Augustine. The center of the work is taken up with a trinity of "threes," in which Thomas of Celano's biographical anecdotes are exposed according to the tripartite "ways" made famous in his mystical system: the purative, the illuminative, and the unitive. The great "unitive" mystery of Francis' life, the stigmata, thus maintains the same high importance it did for Thomas of Celano.

The sense of melodrama, vaguely present throughout the *Vita prima* of Celano, is at times almost oppressive in the *Legenda major*. The two biographers share a vision of Francis as an exalted "restorer of the Church," and Bonaventure clearly sees the foundation of the Order in apocalyptic terms. Like Thomas, he begins his work with an extraordinary prologue; to call it "poetic" is to do it an injustice. It is a *poem,* its cadences those of the Vulgate major prophets. In its carefully composed mosaic of highly charged scriptural themes and images Francis is the morning star, the rainbow, the messenger of true peace. He is an "angel"; like Michael, he has conquered devils; he has brought the light of faith to unbelievers, as Raphael did to Tobias; and he has announced the good news to all mankind, as Gabriel did to the Virgin Mary. But finally, and in a sense definitively, Francis is the apocalyptic angel of the sixth seal: "There is every reason to believe that it is he who is referred to under the image of an Angel coming up from the east, with the seal of the living God, in the prophecy made by another friend of Christ the Bridegroom, St. John the Apostle and Evangelist. When the sixth seal was broken, St. John tells us in the Apocalypse, 'I saw a second Angel coming up from the east, with the seal of the living God' (Ap 7:12)."[10] Thus does one of the treasured and audacious themes of Franciscan literature find its classical expression.

Like Thomas of Celano before him, Bonaventure composed a brief liturgical legendary from the resources of his larger biography. This is usually called, out of habit, the *Legenda minor*. The work is a remarkable *tour de force* which does full credit to two of Bonaventure's most conspicuous literary talents. The first of these is an ability to say much in brief compass, and the second is a genius for Gothic organization which can reduce even the most disparate narrative materials and dense theological commentary to a dazzling formal arrangement. The *Legenda minor,* medieval hagiography's most graceful surrender to the demands of the lectionary, redistributes without noticeable mutilation the disparate materials of a major biography into seven brief chapters of nine paragraphs each.

[10] *Legenda major,* preface, 1; *Omnibus,* p. 632.

To certain *aficionados* of the "Franciscan question," the *Legenda major* has seemed a document too compromised by its official sanction and the monopoly of authority which it was allowed to enjoy for it to merit credence as an "authentic" treatment of its subject. It seems quite unjust, however, to go so far as to say that (as some have said) it is a tendentious document which systematically edits away the Francis of the Spirituals, leaving only a plaster saint acceptable to the Community of friars and useful to Rome. Numerous textual passages strongly suggest what the historical context alone could not fail to suggest, that Bonaventure picked his way carefully through the biographical episodes most charged with controversy in the poverty debate, and his conscious attempt was to stress Francis' remarkable role as a mediator of reconciliation and peace. Tact is not the same thing as insincerity, however, and the *Legenda major* (when compared with the *Speculum Perfectionis,* for example) is conspicuous for the discreet submergence of its compiler's own motives.

This of course does not mean that Bonaventure had no point of view on the issues which were splitting the Order, or that his point of view is totally concealed behind a strategy of reconciliation. It is quite true that his very appointment as the official biographer was hostile to the rigorists in the Order, for the position which he had already taken in the *Apologia Pauperum,* his magisterial defense of mendicancy which he wrote at Paris during the 1250's, involved a conception of the Order's place in the Church inevitably at odds with that which would more and more come to characterize Spiritual thought. The point of view which subtly pervades Bonaventure's biographical thought, if we may call it that, can be seen in the emphasis given to the episode which he takes as the confirmation of Francis' complete conversion: the saint's resolution to repair the church of St. Damian. The story is not to be found at all in the *Vita prima* of Celano, and in the rhetorical structure of the *Vita secunda,* from which Bonaventure adapts it, its force is rather different from his own. One day Francis retreated to the countryside to meditate and happened by the church of St. Damian, a building in a sad state of neglect and disrepair. Impelled by the spirit, Francis entered the church and prostrated himself before the crucifix to pray. "All of a sudden, he heard a voice coming from the cross and telling him three times, 'Francis, go and repair my house. You see it is all falling down.' "[11] Francis followed the command literally, and only later did he come to understand that the voice spoke not of mortar and stone but of "that Church which Christ has purchased with his blood" (Acts 20:28). A second episode (*Legenda major,* 3:10), also quarried from the *Vita secunda,* takes the idea one step further. Among the portents which convinced Innocent III of the worthiness of the proposal for the foundation of a new order brought before him by Francis was an oracular dream. In it the pontiff saw his church of the Lateran about to crumble and fall, but it was supported by a poor and humble man of unremarkable appearance, who held it up with his shoulder. "There indeed," thought the Pope, "is he who by his action and his teaching will support the Church of Christ."

Perhaps the most remarkable fact about the official and drastic censorship of Franciscan biography in the middle of the thirteenth century is that so many texts either survived it or were put together in the face of it. It is to the most important of them that we must now

[11] *Legenda major,* I, ii, 1; *Omnibus,* p. 640.

turn our attention—the "Leo sources" of the period of the poverty debate and the mystical biographies of the fourteenth century. Of the former, one of the most attractive and unassuming is the *Legend of the Three Companions (Legenda Trium Sociorum).* Despite its charm, the *Three Companions* is problematical. It remains one of the very few major documents of early Franciscan history which has yet to be published in a critical edition, and it is by no means easy to penetrate the thick fog of controversy which surrounds it.

On the face of it, the *Three Companions* is a book of rather casual memoirs of three of Francis' earliest friends —Brother Rufino, Brother Angelo, and Brother Leo, "who once were, in spite of their unworthiness, the companions of the blessed Francis." This information is gleaned from the work's most controversial part, an epistle dedicatory addressed to the Minister General, Crescentius of Jesi, and dated from the convent of Greccio in August, 1246.[12] The letter goes on to say that the work was compiled in response to the general request of the Chapter of 1244, and to define its purpose in a way which seems at least implicitly critical of Thomas of Celano. "We do not limit ourselves to a recitation of his miracles," write the Companions. "Miracles do not make sanctity; they merely manifest it. We wish, above all, to show his characteristic habits of behavior and the ideal of his holy will. . . . Our modest contribution should be able to find a place among the histories already written, if you should choose to see it so. We are in fact convinced that if the venerable biographers had been aware of our testimony they would not have passed over it in silence but that they would, at least in part, have deco-

[12] *Omnibus,* pp. 887-888.

rated it with their elegant literary style and thus given it to the memory of posterity."

This last remark would seem to have some connection with Thomas of Celano's statement at the beginning of the *Vita secunda* to the effect that his new biography contained some materials which had previously not come to his attention. But what connection? There is only one brief chapter of the *Vita secunda,* in which are grouped a number of miracles concerning Francis' power over creatures and inanimate objects, which has any concentrated correspondence with the *Three Companions.* Looking at the same stick from its other end, there is only one section of the *Three Companions* which has materials not to be found in one or both *vitae* of Celano. This concerns the primitive history of the General Chapter.

It must be said that the dedicatory epistle is problematical in the extreme. Its authenticity has been questioned by some scholars, and others, though accepting the document itself as an authentic record of the "three companions," have debated whether or not it describes the text of the *Three Companions* which it accompanies and whether it has been edited out of a totally different text of which we have no surviving trace. The *Three Companions* certainly does bear several marks of a work somewhat casually put together by "divers hands," and its persistent air of informality is one of its greatest charms. There is no attempt at a rigorous thematic organization, and anecdotes whose relationship one with another is by no means always clear are frequently linked together through a process of conversational association. On balance, however, the *Three Companions* perhaps comes closer than any of the other thirteenth- and fourteenth-century biographical materials to satisfying our normal expectations of a biography. Its ordering is chronological, and its focus seldom moves from its subject, Francis, observed for the most part in concrete and revealing human situations. It offers little in the way either of biographical or exemplary material which is unique among the documents of the "Franciscan question," but it does have a quite distinctive and pleasing flavor of lived experience. The *Three Companions* is sprinkled with anecdotes and narrative details which, even when they have clear analogues in other texts, seem to bear the stamp of authenticating first-hand experience fondly remembered after many years. We find in it, as we find in few other documents, a sense of what it must have been like to have been one of the first friars.

We can see the random citizenry of some dusty Italian village listening with mixed emotions of respect, fear, and amusement, while Francis preaches to them not a proper sermon but repeated exhortations to penance. Brother Giles wanders through the crowd, encouraging them to listen: "Listen, Brother Francis is giving you good advice!" Women and girls hide in fear when they see friars approaching their town. Friars walking along a country road are suddenly and without further explanation stoned by a madman.

However, the work is by no means uniform in tone or texture. It does not in fact limit itself to the personal memoirs of the three companions but attempts a full, if at times sketchy, life. The early chapters, dealing with Francis' youth and the stages of his conversion, are pallid and conventional. One misses in them Thomas of Celano's theological reflectiveness and Bonaventure's sense of prophetic mission. It is the central chapters, dealing with the first few years of the Order's history, which are the richest and most satisfying; in them personal recollection becomes authoritative. Even here there is a puzzle, however, for the work effectively comes to an abrupt end with an account of events which took place in 1221, five years before Francis' death. The treatment of his remarkable death and of the canonization, both subjects of rhetorical and theological emphasis in the official lives, are treated almost as afterthoughts.

Which of the three companions actually took pen in hand to record these lovely memoirs? There is no clearer answer to this question than to any of the dozen others which the work raises. The *Three Companions* is one of the few early Franciscan documents whose claim to a rusticity of style is actually honored on the page. Yet it is not the prose of Brother Leo, whose work is characterized by a number of endearing eccentricities not to be found in this text. Since one of the ancient references to the "four evangelists" of the Order ascribes a biography to Brother Angelo, we may perhaps ascribe the *Three Companions* to him, at least for the purposes of poetry.

A compilation closely related to the *Legend of the Three Companions* is the *Legend* of Perugia, so called because it was discovered in a fourteenth-century manuscript now in the library of that city. The materials in the *Legend* of Perugia seem to have been used by Thomas of Celano in putting together his *Vita secunda.* Like the *Three Companions,* it is an anthology of vivid first-hand anecdotes which present a striking and most attractive sketch of Francis' life. The unknown compiler of the work makes only the slightest nod to the conventions of stylish hagiography, and is much more interested in presenting forceful biographical *exempla* than in making a balanced *vita.* Though it shares the honest rusticity of style of the Leo documents, the vivacity of its narration is impressive, and at times exciting. Some sense of its dynamic qualities is conveyed by its opening paragraph: "In the early days of the Order, that is to say, at the time when Francis began to group a few brothers around him, he lived with them at Rivo Torto. One night, around midnight, when all were sleeping on their poor straw mattresses, one of the brothers began to cry out: 'I am dying! I am dying!' "[13] Working on the theory that both the *Three Companions* and the *Legend* of Perugia represent different parts of a single lost collection, one Franciscan scholar has recently put together an interesting but speculative "reconstruction" which he has called the *Flowers of the Three Companions.*

Of the several texts which pretend to give a picture of Francis as his earliest and closest followers knew him, however, it is the *Speculum Perfectionis* which is the most controversial. It may be true that the *Speculum Perfectionis* is a work more written about than read, for it has been its not altogether fortunate fate to be the crucial document of the "Franciscan question." It was discovered and published, late in the last century, by the great French Franciscanist Paul Sabatier. Sabatier was convinced that it reflected an "authentic" Francis, historical, without the cosmetic and establishmentarian touches of the official biographies of Thomas of Celano and Bonaventure. He published it with the very provocative subtitle "the most ancient life of Francis" and "the memoirs of Brother Leo." This was skating on thin ice; for the first part of the description is certainly wrong, and the second part can be true only in a general sense. Several Franciscan Franciscanists—some of whom at least gave the unpleasant impression of being unable to forgive a Protestant for having made the most vital and original contributions to Franciscan studies in more

[13] *Omnibus,* p. 977.

than a century—spent the next several decades demolishing in neo-scholastic Latin Sabatier's elegant but errant acceptance of the early date (1227) found in several of the manuscripts. Sabatier himself took up a rather unproductively defensive stance and died, with a critical edition of the *Speculum* nearly ready for the press, still convinced of the document's antiquity.

Sabatier's scholarly judgment has proved to have been wrong in the light of the most probable arguments of textual analysis, but his literary response to the work was dead right; he took the *Speculum Perfectionis* to be exactly what its editor wanted it to be taken as. The work does not date from the early decades of the thirteenth century at all, but from the early decades of the fourteenth, probably from the year 1318. It was composed during one of the most bitter periods of the poverty debate and it is an oblique but thorough argument for the strict observance, presented as the immediate and unmediated eyewitness account of Francis' most intimate brethren.

The anecdote which is set apart as a prologue to the work is an extraordinary one which gives the clearest possible indication of the point of view from which the *Speculum Perfectionis* is written. It concerns the composition of the *Rule* of 1221, the so-called *regula non bullata.* After the loss of the primitive rule (referred to in the text mistakenly as the "second" rule), Francis climbed a mountain in the company of Brother Leo and Brother Bonizo of Bologna to write another. This he did "under the guidance of Christ." When they heard what Francis was doing, a number of the provincial ministers came to Brother Elias to express their fears that the new rule would be severe beyond their endurance and to ask him to intercede with Francis. "Let him make it for himself, and not for us." Brother Elias accordingly approached Francis and explained the scandalous problem, whereupon the saint turned his face to heaven and spoke directly to Christ, "Lord, was I not right when I said that they would not believe me?" Christ, in a voice clearly audible to all, answered thus: "Francis, nothing in this Rule is yours; for all is Mine. I wish the Rule to be obeyed to the letter, to the letter, without a gloss, without a gloss. . . . So let those who are not willing to obey the Rule leave the Order."[14]

If the *Speculum Perfectionis* were merely a cleverly designed piece of "Spiritual" propaganda in the guise of an anecdotal biography, it would still claim a place in this book on the basis of its literary importance, but that place would be in the next chapter, along with the formal and informal documents of the poverty debate with which it shares a common motive. It is, however, much more than that, and its real originality is editorial rather than inventive. There are, in fact, absolutely no unique anecdotes in the work, and few significant variants. Even the extravagant prologue can be found, in almost identical form, in the Perugia *Legend.* The point of view of the work is revealed not through the devices of fictive invention, but through those of editorial selection and arrangement. The *Speculum Perfectionis* is indeed what the manuscripts claim it is, "a work compiled in the form of a legend following those things which the companions of Francis once wrote or had written"; but both the chosen anecdotes and their ordering within the book reflect a profoundly partisan purpose.

The *Speculum Perfectionis* is, *par excellence,* the "friar's biography" of the founder, seen from a controversial point of view to be sure, but nonetheless focused

[14] *Omnibus,* pp. 1125-1126. Cf. p. 26 above.

on the Order in a way which none of the other major biographical materials are. Thomas of Celano and, after him, Bonaventure wrote as Franciscans too; but central to their common purpose was the delineation of a concept of sanctity which went far beyond the Order and which had more or less formally declared designs upon the Church and world. For Thomas of Celano, Francis was a mirror to all mankind. "Every person, of no matter what age or sex, will find in him not merely shining truths which they need to know, but also splendid examples of what they ought to do to become saints." The *Speculum Perfectionis* is a much more closed work, and it is doubtful in the extreme that its compiler thought of an audience outside the Franciscan Order. Francis' life is here considered as the "mirror of perfection of the state of a Friar Minor." In its pages, the world outside the Order hardly exists, save as an arena for the performance of Franciscan virtue. It has been said of Salimbene that one could read his *Chronicle* without any significant awareness that its author was a Franciscan. There is no such danger with the *Speculum Perfectionis,* which one could easily read with no serious awareness that Francis' life might have social significance for those outside Franciscan houses.

The *Speculum* has 124 "chapters," most of them no more than a few hundred words long, casually distributed among twelve books or "parts," organized around important hagiographical themes. There is, however, little that is casual about the book's strategy, which is to develop an inexorable and cumulative anecdotal argument from narrative. The work's setting is a primal, and mythic, golden age of the Franciscan Order, and the work itself at once a bill of indictment and an exhortation to the citizenry of an iron age but dimly sentient of its glorious heritage. It deals, more or less schematically, with the following subjects: Franciscan poverty, Francis' charity and love of neighbor, his humility and obedience, the general zeal within the early Order for the observance, Francis' zeal for the perfection of the brothers, his love of Christ and his devotion to the Passion, his example in prayer and in reading the office, his temptations, his prophetic gift, the fashion in which Providence provided for the needs of the early Order, Francis' love of God's creatures and theirs of him, and finally his death.

One of the most important sections is of course the "poverty chapter," placed in an initial and emphatic position. Its anecdotes touch, one by one, upon each of the specific recurrent points of the poverty debate: whether friars could own books; the quality of cloth of which the habit should be made; the materials appropriate for the construction of Franciscan churches. The little stories have been gathered with care and edited with skill, mainly from the sources of the Perugia *Legend* but also from Celano and Bonaventure. Many of them are vivid, witty and "literary." For example, Francis expresses his displeasure with friars who seek to have books (even a simple psalter) with a reference to Charlemagne and Oliver. Moderns attempt to gain the glory of the heroes of the *chansons de geste* or of the martyrs of the early Church merely by writing about them, as though the literary act were worthy of the same praise and admiration as the deeds described.[15]

The nostalgia for a vanished Franciscan "golden age," conscious attempts to resolve the complicated problems of the Order's governance through the appeal to supposedly unambiguous literary authority, and the widely felt need for a single, unified, and uncomplicated pic-

[15] *Legenda Perugina,* 72; *Omnibus,* pp. 1048-1049.

ture of the founder were among the most important factors controlling the energies of Franciscan biography during the second half of the thirteenth century. By the fourteenth century, these same impulses had given birth to a rich and often bizarre Franciscan myth system which both in its general historical presuppositions and its specific literary manifestations has a good deal to teach us about the broader sweep of Gothic allegory between the time of Jean de Meun and that of Geoffrey Chaucer. In a number of the more influential histories of the Order, the fourteenth century has been treated as a "period of decline," an embarrassment first of strife and heresy and then of laxity and the corruption of good morals—an unfortunate desert lying between the oases of the "Franciscan springtime" of the thirteenth century and the vigorous renewal of the Order in the age of St. John of Capestrano. The generalization, like most generalizations, has left a good deal to quarrel with. So far as the literary history of the Order is concerned, the fourteenth century saw the production of a number of the most precious texts in the whole Franciscan repertory, including two of the most fascinating and imaginative attempts to place the life of Saint Francis in an adequate mythic framework.

The first of these works is the *Fioretti,* the *Little Flowers of Saint Francis,* which surely must be the best-known document, in a popular sense, in the *dossier* of the "Franciscan question." Its modern popular success has been enormous. It has been translated into many languages, illustrated by famous artists, lavishly printed by prestige presses. Alone of the texts touched upon in this chapter, it usually makes its way into general literary histories of the *trecento* and books about the medieval "achievement"—in several of the latter, it must be admitted, under the curious misapprehension that it is a book written by rather than about Saint Francis. It has been, in short, the Franciscan text *par excellence* for the general reader.

The "little flowers," lovingly collected from the large spring field of Franciscan legend, are anecdotes, usually of an extravagant character, concerning Saint Francis and numerous other friars contemporary with him. Not in the most casual sense do they constitute a recognizable biography, and the reader leaves them not so much with a coherent picture of one saint's life in the world as with a vivid sense, communicated through disparate images and impressions, as of an enormous, diffuse, and constantly surprising power which emanates from that life. The *Fioretti,* of course, is the title given to the vernacular (Tuscan) collection put together in the second half of the fourteenth century. The actual contents of the work is more clearly indicated in the title of the Latin collection which is their narrative source, the *Actus Beati Francisci et sociorum ejus.* About this collection a certain amount can be deduced from internal evidence. It was put together, sometime between 1328 and 1343, by a certain Brother Hugolino of Monte Giorgio, working with an anonymous collaborator.

Though the Tuscan *Fioretti* is clearly posterior in its date of composition, it is not a mistake, in this case, to pay more attention to the "translation" than to the "original." No medieval writers ever believed more firmly that, if the letter kills, the spirit gives life, than did medieval translators. In general, they took a much less restricted view of their task than do their modern counterparts, and they often felt free to make a liberal exercise of their creative as well as their linguistic prowess. Hence it is that medieval "translations" often look very different indeed from their parent work. The translator may edit, add explanatory comments, or, in some cases, completely restructure the work being "translated." There are examples of medieval translation in which the "original" is merely the drab occasion for the *tour de force* of genius. In this case the relationship is not so much one of simple derivation as it is that of the artist and his raw materials, the relationship of Shakespeare to the *novelle* which gave him the plot line of *Romeo and Juliet* or *The Taming of the Shrew.*

The "translator" of the *Fioretti* did, as a matter of fact, follow his Latin original reasonably closely, yet at the same time he added, rearranged, emphasized, or excised to an extent which makes the work his own. He was, clearly, a writer of considerable narrative skills. The peculiar charm of the *Fioretti* lies in the fact that it is a text captured in the midst of an exciting change from literary hagiography to unapologetic exemplary fiction. Its materials are those of the former, its most distinctive narrative conceptions those of the latter. Of course most of the texts which make up the "Franciscan question" reveal a point of view about questions current in the Order at the time of the composition, and several, as we have seen, combine biographical and propagandistic motives with differing degrees of success. But the *Fioretti* moves far beyond the mere presentation of a "point of view," while it is at the same time free of obvious partisan bias with regard to the questions which had split the Spirituals and the Community. One is tempted to say that the *Fioretti* removes the problem of Francis from the context in which it had been discussed for a century to a new setting, which is that of a fully developed myth. In the *Fioretti,* for the first time in a major text, the most daring and extravagant attitudes and presuppositions of

Franciscan historiography are given free reign. Francis is prophet, wizard, king, and martyr—as well as *poverello.* He shares, in all but the most unthinkable aspects, the full mystery of Christ.

Thus, several of the anecdotes in the *Fioretti* are prophetic in nature, describing miraculous visions in which is revealed the course of future history, particularly the history of the Order. In some of these not merely the modest verisimilitude of hagiography but simple theological coherence is abandoned for other literary ends. In one such episode, for example, Francis was granted a vision of the apostasy and eventual damnation of Brother Elias, after which he could hardly bear even to see him. Elias eventually forced Francis to explain his sudden coolness, and, when he learned of the vision, begged Francis to pray that it might not come to pass. Through Francis' prayers, God revoked the sentence of damnation on Elias, who, though he died outside the Order, rejoined on his deathbed the company of the elect. The most elaborate of the prophetic visions is also the most chaotic from a literary point of view. In it Brother Jacopo of Massa sees a "tree" of Franciscan history, a tree which, for all its roots of gold and other exotic features, is clearly enough a crude adaptation of Bonaventure's *lignum vitae.* The tree represents in its foliage, fruit, limbs, and twigs a kind of arboreal biography of all friars past and present, with the Minister General John of Parma occupying a prominent and, as it were, trunk position. If the reader does not find enough difficulty with the tree itself, he soon has the opportunity to tax his wits on a purple allegory of the transfer of power from John of Parma to Saint Bonaventure.

The stories in the *Fioretti* make of Francis' life a kind of running Pentecost. In one of them, St. Clare very much wants to eat one meal with Francis. Though she repeatedly sought the favor, he would never grant it until taken to task by some of his companions. "Father, it seems to us that this strictness is not according to divine charity." They remind him that it was in response to his preaching that Clare left the world and that "if she were to ask an even greater favor of you, you should grant it to your little spiritual plant." Francis, persuaded, decides that if it is worth doing, it is worth doing well. Accordingly, he invites her to come from St. Damian to St. Mary of the Angels to make, *all'italiana,* something of an outing of it as well. The appointed day arrives, and Clare realizes her great desire when she sits down at the table with her spiritual master. Francis—"at the first course," as the text puts it— began to speak of heavenly things, and a fiery rapture fell upon the whole table. The entire citizenry of Assisi as well as the inhabitants of another nearby village, Bettona, seeing the flames, think that the monastery and indeed the whole woods around it are ablaze and come running to help fight the fire.[16]

Fire, indeed, is a recurrent theme of the *Fioretti,* which is also the source of the lurid account of Francis' sexual temptation which made such an impression on Bartholomew of Pisa. During his missionary journey in the land of the Saracens, Francis met a woman, "very beautiful in face and body but very foul in mind and soul," who invited him to fornication. "If you wish me to do what you want, you must also do what I want," he is reported to have said. Stripping naked, he threw himself on the fire in the hearth, and invited the woman to take her clothes off and lie down with him "on this splendid, flowery, and wonderful bed." When she saw that he

[16] *Fioretti,* I, 15; *Omnibus,* pp. 1332-1334.

stayed there a long time without being burned or singed, the Saracen woman not merely repented but became a convert to Christianity.[17]

Francis, like Christ, is in the *Fioretti* a source of power which shines incandescently through the lives of others. A most charming and "Franciscan" miracle is reported of St. Anthony when he preached against the heretics of Rimini. The heretics would not listen in spite of his wisdom and his eloquence, so he went down below the town to the strand where the river joins the sea. There he preached to the fishes, who lined up in massive but orderly numbers to attend his homily. He encouraged them to praise (as best they could with their small, voiceless mouths) the God who in his bounty had given them the choice of fresh or salt water to live in, exempted them alone of all unreasonable life from the terrors of the Flood, equipped them with fins, and granted them the boon of being Christ's nourishment "before His Resurrection and in a mysterious way afterwards." The fish mouthed back their watery praises, and Anthony blessed God that unreasonable fish had more piety than insolent heretics—at which, of course, the heretics themselves were converted.[18]

To the Tuscan editor of the *Fioretti* we can also ascribe with reasonable certainty a very strange work called *Le considerazioni sulle stimmate.* The two works, which are found together in all the most ancient manuscripts, share a substantial number of formal and stylistic characteristics, as well as a general air of the extravagant and the fantastic. The *Considerazioni,* unique among the early biographical documents, are known only in an Italian text, and there is a rather remote possibility that they

[17] *Fioretti,* I, 24; *Omnibus,* pp. 1354-1355.
[18] *Fioretti,* I, 40; *Omnibus,* pp. 1391-1393.

are a vernacular composition. Though no close Latin original has yet been found, the work's general and more remote sources are clear and unsurprising; they are the official biographies of Celano and Bonaventure, and the traditions associated with the name of Brother Leo, whose testimony concerning the central miracle is regarded as crucial. What is by no means clear is the work's unstated rationale, and it cannot be said with confidence whether the little book is purely "historical" and devotional in intent or whether it is a conscious reply to critics in defense of the authenticity of the stigmata. There is a good deal in it which makes the latter hypothesis an attractive one; Thomas of Celano, in his day, had already realized that the miracle of the stigmata was to be the *pons asinorum* of the Franciscan legend, at once the "Franciscan" miracle *par excellence* and the "occasion of scandal" of the gospels.

The five "considerations" around which the work is structured attempt to give a precise and ordered account of the exact circumstances under which Francis received the stigmata. To this extent, the work submits itself more readily to the normal demands of history than do any of the other biographies. The five "considerations," chronologically delineated, are these: the circumstances under which Francis went to Mount Alverna; the life of the friars in their retreat there; the apparition of the seraphim; Francis' return to Saint Mary of the Angels; and miraculous affirmations of the stigmata granted to various brothers after the death of Francis. But when one moves from form to tone, one leaves the unexcitability of history for the same fabulous *mise-en-scene* against which the action of the *Fioretti* takes place, a kind of Tuscany in technicolor. Like the *Fioretti* as well, the *Considerazioni* are characterized by a vivid and novelesque sense of narrative detail and the patterns of dialogue. It is a work which deserves to be better known.

All the surviving hagiographic documents of the thirteenth and fourteenth centuries make more or less extraordinary claims, often enough explicit ones, about the "newness" of Francis. Francis is not merely a great saint or even, perhaps, the greatest saint. He is a saint different in kind. There is also external literary evidence—in the episode of the *Everlasting Gospel,* in the writings of Archbishop Fitzralph, in Geoffrey Chaucer's "Summoner's Tale"—that Franciscan speculation about the uniqueness of the founder could be considered dangerous, troublesome, offensive, arrogant, or simply ridiculous. When Thomas of Celano wrote of the stigmata, and Bonaventure of the angel of the sixth seal, they were walking a razor's edge. Many others tumbled, headlong, into the heady and, as it was to prove, unacceptable extravagances of Franciscan Joachimism.

The "newness" of Francis was his total conformity to the life of Christ. The idea is stated with classic simplicity in the very first sentence of the *Fioretti:* "We must consider first how Saint Francis, in all the acts of his life, conformed to the blessed Christ." The statement is in itself in no way remarkable. Christ, who stands at the center of the medieval Christian vision of history, is likewise the tropological referee or exemplar of the Christian life, and ascetic masters from the pre-Benedictine era on write about the religious life as a "following" or an "imitation" of Christ, often within a metaphoric framework which makes close reference to the specific details of his life and, especially, his Passion. The most widely diffused ascetic manual of the end of the Middle Ages is appropriately entitled *The Imitation of Christ.*

What *was* remarkable about the Franciscan idea of the conformity was its exhaustively schematic character. If Christ had twelve disciples, so had Francis. If one of them betrayed Christ, so another betrayed Francis. If Christ was crucified, so was Francis. From the literary point of view, one of the most interesting sidelights of the process was the idea of Francis' "four evangelists." "Saint Francis had four successors who wrote his life with great accuracy, just as Christ has the four evangelists," wrote the author of a little work called *De cognatione Sancti Francisci* in 1355. Each Franciscan evangelist shared the symbolic beast of his earlier counterpart: Thomas of Celano, the angel; Brother Leo, a lion (*Leo, leo!*); Julian of Spire, an ox; the mystical Bonaventure, a bird, no doubt the soaring eagle of the Fourth Gospel. Refracted through the prism of prophecy, the life of Francis became no mere ascetic imitation of that of Christ, however remarkable for its perfection, but rather a true, unique, and supernatural type of Christ's life. That is why some Franciscans could write of the founder, audaciously but without conscious blasphemy, that he was a "second Christ."[19]

In the *Fioretti,* an apocryphal rather than a canonical gospel, the theme of the "conformity" is already an old one, which, indeed, is already present, faintly sketched, in what must be the earliest surviving "biographical" document which came from the Order. That is the general epistle in which Brother Elias announced Francis' death. Elias' lament is written in a contrived and literary prose which probably would have made Doctor Johnson doubt whether it left room for honest grief, but the very literary conceits are most revealing of the historical vi-

[19] See Stanislao da Compagnola, *L'angelo del sesto sigillo e l' "Alter Christus"* (Rome, 1971).

sion which Elias brings to Francis' life. Early in the letter are echoes of the Creed ("light of light") and of major prophecies of the Advent ("those who dwelt in darkness") which appropriate to Francis a privileged language traditionally reserved for Christ. Then comes the explicit statement that the seal of Francis' life is the new miracle of the stigmata: "Et his dictis, annuncio vobis gaudium magnum et miraculi novitatem. A saecula non est auditum tale signum, praeterquam in Filio Dei, qui est Christus Deus."[20]

The theme of the "conformities" had significant literary development in the thirteenth century. Salimbene, in the *Cronica,* speaks of having written on the subject "elsewhere," and the idea finds important poetic expression in the late thirteenth-century *Meditatio Pauperis in deserto.*[21] But its culmination is the remarkable and little studied work written in the twilight of the fourteenth century by Bartholomew of Pisa, the work called the *De Conformitate vita beati Francisci ad vitam Domini Jesu.*[22] The *Book of Conformities,* encyclopedic in its ambitions and audacious in its design, is an attempt to demonstrate, by sheer massive weight of detailed evidence a supernatural congruence at levels literal and figural between the life of Christ and that of Francis. Bartholomew was a learned man, and he brought to bear on his book an impressive command of the Scriptures, the works of the fathers of the Church, and the major theologians of the later Middle Ages. His researches into the Franciscan legend were exhaustive, and scholars turning over the "Franciscan question" have been able to learn a great

[20] *Acta Sanctorum, Octobris,* II, p. 669.

[21] *Meditatio pauperis in solitudine,* ed. F. Delorme (Quaracchi, 1929).

[22] *De Conformitate vita beati Francisci ad vitam Domini Jesu,* 2 vols. (Quaracchi, 1906-1912).

deal about what hagiographic texts were known and credited at the end of the fourteenth century by making a careful collation of his pages. Perhaps embarrassed by its bizarre contents and its vulnerability to Reformation ridicule, most Franciscanists have been content to treat it as though it were a kind of textual charnel house, unsavory but of considerable archeological importance. In fact, the *Book of Conformities* is among the Franciscan texts of greatest potential interest to general literary scholars.

The *Book of Conformities* is one of the three great Franciscan "tree" books, finding its structural inspiration in the *Arbor vitae crucifixae* of Ubertino and directly in Ubertino's magisterial source, the *Lignum vitae* of Bonaventure. Its matter is divided into forty sections or "fruits," distributed among three books. There are twelve "fruits" each in the first and third books, sixteen in the second. The number of books, the number of "fruits," and the proportions by which they are arranged all have numerological significances and owe a good deal to Bonaventure. Though no very thorough study has been made of the orchestration of Bartholomew of Pisa's figural *schema,* it surely must rival that of Dante in its ambition, complexity, and *garbo.*

Bartholomew of Pisa carefully avoids the dangerous theological line of Franciscan Joachimism taken up by the disgraced Gerard of Borgo San Donnino and reflected in another way in the schismatic tendencies of the Ancona "Spirituals" and the *fraticelli.* Nonetheless, the *Liber Conformitatum* is radically and fundamentally "Joachimist." This fact is not so clearly demonstrated in the work's occasional but overt applications of specific prophecies of Joachism to Francis and the Franciscan Order—this was, after all, commonplace among Franciscan writers—but in its central belief that Francis' whole life was a prophetic fulfillment of the life of Christ. Francis is an *alter Christus* not because he issues in a new dispensation of grace above and beyond that promised in the Old Testament and accomplished in the New, but because his life is a unique and undeniable reaffirmation of the fulfillment of scriptural promise. There is no renovating "age of the Holy Ghost" in the pages of the *Liber Conformitatum;* instead, the Incarnation remains the central event in history, but an event prophetically pointed at, as it were, both by the past and by the future.

In this respect it is most significant that the first "fruit" of the *Conformities* is that of *prophecy.* Bartholomew collates seventy-three prophetic passages from the Old Testament which point to Christ with seventy-four texts from the Franciscan "scriptures" of the legendaries. It is shown in each case how the biblical foreshadowing, fulfilled in Christ, has a valid parallel prophecy which points to Francis. Many of these are rather vague in character and have to do with general moral qualities shared by Francis and Christ, but there is also a number of examples which deal with specific biographical details of Francis' life. For example, the third fulfilled prophecy of Francis' life was his imprisonment by the Perugians, which had been foreshadowed in the Old Testament by the incarceration of Joseph (Genesis 39:20). Francis' control over animals, attested to in a wide spectrum of early documents and among the most charming aspects of his popular cult, is a realization of the power of Adam, to whom dominion over the lower orders was granted by God (Gen. 1:26).

Even the few examples given here can show that, for Bartholomew, scriptural types have a prophetic validity not merely for the life of Christ, as in the classical tradition of medieval scriptural exegesis, but for the life of Francis of Assisi as well. This extraordinary claim is made explicit in the second half of the first fruit, which is given over to ten Old Testament figures which, after applying to Christ, apply peculiarly to Saint Francis. These ten prophetic images are particularly revealing in the diversity of range and focus. Francis is, in the first place, the man "made after the image of God"; the literal reference is to Adam, but the prophetic reference is to the stigmatized *poverello.* Francis is, furthermore, the dove sent forth from the ark (Gen. 8:8) and Jacob, whose seed was as "the dust of the earth" (Gen. 28:4).

A particularly startling image is that of Pharaoh's giving of his ring from his own hand to Joseph (Gen. 41:42). This, too, is a type of the stigmata, for "to no other saint did Christ give the ring of his own image, namely the *stigmata,* except to blessed Francis." Jacob's blessing of his two sons (Gen. 48:15) is a type of Francis' blessing on Brother Bernard and Brother Elias (*Speculum Perfectionis,* 107).

There are three important ecclesiological types. The first is the triple vine (Ps. 79), which foreshadows the three Minorite Orders. Secondly, Francis is signified by the young Joshua, who served Moses (Numbers 11:28). But the most important of all the prophecies relating to the Church comes from the well-known story of Nebuchadnezzer and the children in the fiery furnace (Dan. 3:24-25). "Did not we cast three men bound into the midst of the fire? . . . Lo, I see four men loose, walking in the midst of the fire, and they have no hurt; and the form of the fourth is like the Son of God." According to Bartholomew, the four men typify the four great religious founders of the Middle Ages—Basil, Augustine,

Benedict, and Francis. Francis, of course, is the fourth visage, the one "like the Son of God."

Not all of the forty fruits are as heady as the fruit of prophecy, but the total effect of the work in its unflinching willingness to pursue the myth of the *alter Christus* wherever it may lead is, in truth, staggering. A century and a half after its formal presentation to the General Chapter, it was published in a vernacular version by a noted Protestant scholar. He called it the *Alkoran of the Barefoot Friars,* and it had a successful run in a coffee-table edition as a kind of early *History of Maria Monk.*

3

The Poetry of Poverty

Of all the titles of respect, veneration, or of simple heartfelt affection which have been afforded to Francis of Assisi for seven hundred years there is one which more than any other has come closest to capturing the essence of his life and ministry. Francis is, and forever will be, the *poverello,* God's poor man. This is as it should be, for the historical center of primitive Franciscanism is a radical articulation of the meaning of Christian poverty which daringly collated the highest aspirations of Western ascetic tradition with the more active and evangelical impulses of the "apostolic life." The will to be poor was a defining imperative of Francis' life. In his death, it became the crucible in which his followers would be tested.

The medieval history of the poverty debate, written in blood as well as ink, has been and must continue to be an important subject on the agenda of intellectual and social historians, for what was at stake were the most basic concerns of medieval spiritual and, indeed, social life.[1] The contest within the Franciscan Order itself, be-

[1] The most recent general treatment of the subject is M. D. Lambert, *Franciscan Poverty: The Doctrine of the Absolute Poverty of Christ and the Apostles in the Franciscan Order 1210-1323* (London, 1961); still useful is K. Balthasar, *Geschichte des Armutsstreites im Franziskanerorden bis zum Konzil von Vienne* (Münster, 1911). There is a very good bibliographical article by Octavius a Rieden, "De quibusdam commentariis circa paupertatem Franciscanam nuper in lucem editis," *CF,* xxxii (1962), 445-460. For an illuminating theological account of Francis' conception of poverty, see K. Esser, "Mysterium paupertatis: Die Armutsauffassung des hl. Franziskus von Assisi," *Wissenschaft und Weisheit,* xiv (1951), 177-189.

fore it became hopelessly blurred by the rhetoric of theological polemic and consistory courts, was in one sense simple enough, a clash of conceptions, of poetic images, as to what the Order must be. Was it the Order of Francis of the backroads, eremitic, studiedly anti-intellectual? Or of Francis of the Pope's dream, "restorer of the Church"? Here the simplicity ends, and Franciscan scholars have increasingly demonstrated, over the last few decades, the rich complexity of issues involved. Franciscan poverty can never have been easy; but what was possible for one great saint and a few of his followers was perhaps simply not possible for a substantial and organized religious order. Within a few decades in the middle of the thirteenth century the Order of Friars Minor was transformed from what appears in the pages of the *Speculum perfectionis* as a small band of backwoods pilgrims into an international religious movement numbering in the thousands, divided into well-organized battalions directed by an efficient and vigorous general headquarters. The "first generation" Franciscans were Peters and Johns, "simple men," not a few of them illiterate. Their heirs were Pauls and Augustines, the doctors of the Church and its princes.

The student of medieval literature will profit from some knowledge of the poverty debate, which in ways both overt and subtle infiltrates a number of the most important and admired secular texts of the thirteenth and fourteenth centuries. For the student of Franciscan literature, the topic must be considered in all its breadth, for the debate controlled much of the literary energy of major and minor writers for more than a century. We have already seen the deep impress which a particular vision of Franciscan poverty made on Francis' own *Testament* and on early hagiographic texts at a time when the debate was more anticipated than joined. The action taken by the General Chapter of 1260 to suppress unauthorized lives of the founder is the most vivid possible evidence of the extent to which the literary image of poverty was being vividly contested within the Order by mid-century. Once the issue was formally joined, the ink flowed, first in rivulets, then in cataracts. The literature more or less formally connected with the debate over Franciscan poverty, displaying an extraordinary range both of style and achievement, includes lyric, dramatic, and narrative poetry, prose both fictional and historical, sermons, academic *questiones,* commentaries on the *Rule,* and formal treatises on mendicant poverty which range from rank polemics to enduring masterpieces of controversial theology.

For many thinkers in the later Middle Ages, poverty was what the Franciscan Order was *about,* so that from a certain point of view, frequently reflected in the literature, the ups and downs of the poverty contest are not so much an episode in the Order's history from the time of the death of Francis to the promulgation of *Cum inter nonullos* (1323)—the view taken by many later commentators—as the very essence of that history. Angelo Clareno, who came closer than any other contemporary writer to formulating a history of Franciscan poverty, would be able to trace those backsliding tendencies which from his point of view became triumphant under John XXII back to the very days of Francis' life. He divided his matter into seven "tribulations," which began with the "subtlety of philosophy" and cupidity hidden within the heart of Brother Elias and ended with the martyrs of Narbonne. For purposes of gaining access to the literature it is probably more convenient, if just as arbitrary, to think of three general *loci* or movements of controversy. The first of these is the growing division between the "Community" and the "Spirituals" within the Order; the second, the debate between secular and regular masters at the University of Paris in the 1250's; and the third, the pontificate of John XXII and the heresy of the *fraticelli.*

It is of course slovenly to talk of the poverty "question" at all, for there was not a single question, but many. Those raised by the emerging parties of the rigorists and the Community centered on the *Rule,* its specific provisions, and the source of authority for its interpretation. At Paris, the issues were, suitably enough, more academic: the essence of Christian perfection and the nature of the Christian ministry. At Avignon the question also seemed academic: whether Christ and the Apostles, either as individuals or in concert, owned property. But it became in fact a contest of spiritual authority between the Pope and the unmediated words of Francis, dead for a century but alive in his *Rule.* A rich repertory of arguments, technical terms, and above all scriptural images developed around the controversies, a repertory which would be taken up and exploited in such major works of the European Middle Ages as the *Roman de la Rose,* the *Divine Comedy,* and *Piers Plowman.* The continuing dialogue within the Order subjected to close examination that set of prohibitions which came directly through the *Rule* from the scriptural accounts of Christ's commission to the first "friars." What did it mean that they were to have neither scrips nor staves nor food for the journey? Could a friar handle money if he wore gloves? Such arcane questions were argued not merely by a few Franciscan academics, but by the thinking community of Europe. Crowned heads debated whether a friar might wear shoes. Then there was the question of perfection. How was it "perfect" to "have no purse," when Christ Himself used one? Finally, how could Christ be said to "own nothing"? He ate food, and even invited Zacchaeus to dine with Him. He had sandals (which John the Baptist was unworthy to unlatch), a seamless robe, and once again the troublesome purse. We would be mistaken to regard the specific points at issue as trivial, though they may strike us as bizarre, and they are particularly important for Franciscan literature because they provide the basis of a privileged language of poetic imagery. Likewise important is the language of the solutions offered to problems raised. Throughout the thirteenth-century discussions there is an important distinction, for example, between ownership (the exercise of *dominium*) and simple use *(usus)*. To "own" property was to possess it in a dimension both legal and personal—as to own a house, which one could sell for profit or loss, or one's "own" copy of a book. *Use* on the other hand is the contingent and insecure relationship with the necessities of life, such as food and clothing and sufficient shelter from the elements, enjoyed not by continuing legal right but as charity and Providence might each day provide. The friars were *mendicants* precisely because they owned nothing, living from day to day only by the "poor man's use" *(usus pauperis)*. The effect of the early papal interventions into Franciscan polity in the pontificate of Gregory IX was to rationalize the apparent paradox of the increasing real wealth of the mendicants by investing the Pope with the technical ownership of Franciscan properties, leaving the friars with their *usus pauperis*.

The technical language of the debate increasingly permeates the literary documents concerned with the Franciscan ideal as they become more consciously expository and polemical during the course of the thirteenth century, and there are few in which controversial intent is subordinated to narrative or historical design with such satisfying results as in the *vitae* considered in the last chapter. Among these few is the so-called *Sacrum Commercium,* perhaps the single most brilliant example of the simple but lapidary allegory which was to become a major mode of spiritual writing in the later Middle Ages.[2] The *Sacrum Commercium* has been ascribed, with varying degrees of plausibility, to at least five different famous Franciscans, including three Ministers General, St. Anthony of Padua, and Archbishop Pecham. Several of the candidates seem distinctly unlikely, especially in the light of stylistic analysis, and none is compelling. We shall probably be wise to respect the anonymity of its authorship, following Ubertino of Casale, who attributes it simply but so rightly to a "certain holy doctor, a professor and staunch defender of this holy Poverty." The matter of the work's date of composition is rather different. On paleographical evidence it can be no later than mid-thirteenth century, and several of the manuscripts claim that it was written in July of 1227, less than a year, that is, after the death of Francis. Given the general polemical context of the poverty debate, we must be wary, but there is no very good reason to reject such an early date out of hand. Kajetan Esser, the most profound of the work's modern students, judiciously weights what evidence there is, only to conclude that no positive answer is possible. It does seem clear that even if the work does not antedate *I Celano,* as its colophon pretends, it does belong to the earliest phase of the poverty debate and deserves to be studied in that context.

[2] *Sacrum Commercium S. Francisci cum Domina Paupertate,* edd. Quaracchi Fathers (Quaracchi, 1929).

Its spirituality, and its poetry, are never far from the Portiuncula.

The audacious argument of the *Sacrum Commercium,* an argument for which poetry was perhaps the only appropriate dialectic, advances evangelical poverty as the defining characteristic of theological perfection since the creation of the world through the sapiential Christ. The heart of the work, taking up thirty-three of its sixty-nine numbered paragraphs in the Quaracchi edition, is Poverty's eloquent autobiography and her searching critique of the religious life through history. "I am no upstart *(rudis),* as many think," she says, "but old enough and full of days, knowing the ordering of things, the varieties of the created order, the transiencies of ages." The resplendent image of Poverty seems clearly enough to fit into a literary tradition, of which the author elsewhere demonstrates awareness, which begins with the scriptural personification of Wisdom, finds its classical medieval embodiment in the Lady Philosophy of Boethius, and embraces Dante's Beatrice.

Poverty was, she says, in Paradise with the nude Adam, an eyewitness to his expulsion, a homeless wanderer through the age of the Patriarchs, whose promise was not the promise of poverty, but that of a land flowing with milk and honey. She then speaks of the coming of Christ, whose testimony she cites in a kind of dramatic anthology of scriptural statements on poverty. Then follows a brief description of her life among the Apostles (no. 32) and among their first followers (no. 33). But the story then becomes one, alas, of Poverty's persecution. The decadence of the religious life of the Church, already a time-honored literary topic in the thirteenth century, finds vivid and original statement in her dramatic portrayal of Avarice, her archenemy. Avarice assumes false names, like "Discretion" and "Human Providence"; sometimes she works alone, and sometimes she joins Accidia, as Pilate joined Herod. The "historical survey" of the vicissitudes of religious poverty is followed by a general exhortation, conflated from the Old Testament and the Epistle to the Hebrews, and a special invitation to Francis and his friars. Poverty dines with the brothers, probing the depth of their paupers' commitment. The piece ends extravagantly but brilliantly with Poverty's oracular description of the joys of the Heavenly Jerusalem at the conversion of the friars: "In conversione vestra, carissimi, caeli vices magna celebrarunt gaudia et coram aeterno Rege nova cantica cantaverunt." The friars' festival hymn is nothing less than the new song, the martial music of God's poor ones.

Though in fact the *Sacrum Commercium* is, in form, a prose narrative, its flesh is pure poetry and its bones pure drama. The dramatic element, indeed, is particularly remarkable. Certain cardinal moments in the piece —the scene in Paradise, for example, or the Franciscan "feast"—bear so clearly the stamp of dramaturgy that the student of medieval literature may suspect the existence of a cognate *ordo,* or play, which shares its major metaphoric patterns and perhaps established the iconography of Francis' "mystical marriage" in the visual arts. This "marriage" does present a problem at the literary level, as a scholar has recently pointed out, for although commentators since the time of the Middle Ages have spoken of it, there is no marriage in the literal text. The "marriage" is, rather, a visualized implication of the dramatic (as opposed to the narrated) action, and of the major pattern of scriptural language. Much of the simple narrative action on the other hand (for example, the brothers "look here and there for a towel" but find none) reads like the narrative stage directions in the *Jeu d'Adam.*

The *Sacrum Commercium* has been strangely neglected even by Franciscan scholars, and it has never been examined closely in terms of its literary techniques. Like much else in the Franciscan anthology, its often-praised "simplicity" can be deceptive. Certainly the full elegance of its spiritual argument and its real theological sophistication depend in large measure on a skillful manipulation of scriptural language which is by no means apparent on a casual reading. While it is hardly possible to communicate the work's subtle complexities in brief compass, some idea may be gained by the following example. Near the end of the *Sacrum Commercium,* in an emphatic dramatic position, is a paradoxically ascetic feast *(convivium)* which is the friars' final, and triumphant, testing. The friars bring Poverty down from the Mountain: "Et descendentes de monte, duxerunt dominam Paupertatem ad locum in quo manebat; *hora* enim *erat* quasi sexta." The scriptural detail about the time of day (John 4:6), a small matter, may go almost unnoticed. It is "about the sixth hour," the noontime, the time for the midday repast. The friars will now eat. Yet to collate the context in the gospel from which the detail comes with the context of its use in the *Sacrum Commercium* is to demonstrate how deeply the former text infiltrates the latter and, as it were, takes command of its literary energies. The scriptural episode is that of the meeting of Christ and the Samaritan woman at Jacob's well. Jesus, "tired from his journey" *(fatigatus ex itinere),* sits on the wellhead to rest as the Samaritan woman comes to draw water. What follows is a haunting, riddling conversation about true and false refreshment, about the water which can slake the thirst for an hour and that "living water" which refreshes through eternity. In the *Sacrum Commercium* it is the friars who are tired from the long journey *(ex longe itinere fatigati)*; and it is they who entertain their noble guest, Lady Poverty, to a paradoxical feast, punctuated by her dramatically feigned surprise, which consists of a few crusts and a single vessel of cold water. The highest aspirations of the poverty of the Christ-life, boldly linked with the most generous promises of Christian grace, lie veiled behind a narrative detail which on its surface is at best drab: *hora enim erat quasi sexta.*

The *Sacrum Commercium* is a poetic attempt to define through fiction the concept of radical poverty of an already mythic Franciscan Golden Age. In it we can see the faint outlines of that impractical nostalgia which increasingly becomes the hallmark of the Spiritual cause, and it is not surprising that the work found an enthusiastic audience in men like Olivi and Angelo Clareno. Yet it is a work totally free from those grosser intrusions of polemic which characterize most of the literature of poverty for the rest of the century and beyond, especially those steaming documents associated with the dispute between the teaching friars and the secular masters at the University of Paris in the 1250's. This dispute was fundamentally different from the one which is the unstated context of the *Sacrum Commercium,* for it was no family argument but a powerful and popularly supported attack on the validity of the concept of the "apostolic life" held by the friars, Franciscans and Dominicans alike, from the outside. Its literary documents compose the standard dossier of the "poverty question" in the thirteenth century.

Before recalling this tragi-comic episode, so well known to ecclesiastical and intellectual historians, it is well to remember the extraordinarily rich historical context in which it took place.[3] The University of Paris in 1250 was just entering what, in retrospect, was to be the headiest period in medieval intellectual history. Among the strong spiritual movements of the time was a strain of popular apocalypticism, which we may rather loosely call Joachimism. Furthermore, the Order of Friars Minor was going through a period of dynamic growth and evolution which had brought it, together with the Dominican Order, to a position of visible intellectual leadership within the Church. What happened when the friars came to the university was perhaps not inevitable, but it was entirely explicable.

The preachers and teachers of the new orders made a major impact at Paris, as they had elsewhere. By 1252 the university legislation shows that many of the secular masters had begun an organized campaign to limit the friars' participation in the life of the university. The issues involved—academic rights and privileges, the number of teaching chairs to be allowed to religious, and so forth—were local in nature. But the discussion took on immediately broader implications in the polemical literature which they occasioned. Several secular masters attacked the very legitimacy of mendicant life, and although the poverty question was not always at the center of their objections, it was one of their major concerns.

The most famous of the opponents of the friars' academic privileges, and of their claims to authentic "apostolic life," was William of Saint-Amour, who published in 1254 his notorious *De periculis novissimorum temporum (On the Dangers of the Last Times).* Taking his text from the third chapter of 2 Timothy, William identified the friars in his vitriolic attack with the evil men who

[3] The best general account of the quarrel will be found in P. Glorieux, "Le conflit de 1252-1257 à la lumière du Mémoire de Guillaume de Saint-Amour," *RTAM,* xxiv (1957), 364-372.

will infest the earth in the "last times" of the world. The friars, in William's pages, become the apocalyptic types of the Pharisees; their chief characteristics are self-love and hypocrisy. As a group, they represent a diabolical force to be associated with the Antichrist. William was scandalized by what he considered to be the hypocrisy of practice of the Franciscans on the matter of poverty, and tries to quote their own rule against them in the fashion of a Spiritual polemicist. But much more fundamental to his argument is an implacable hostility toward the concept of Christian perfection as mendicancy, and to the validity of the mendicant ministry, particularly a mendicant ministry of penance, which the friars practiced with a dramatic effectiveness.

William's work fell under the papal censure, and he himself was banished from the university. Yet his importance to the literary history of the later Middle Ages was considerable, for the judgment of popes is not always the judgment of poets. The *De Periculis* and another of his works, *De Antichristo,* provided a scriptural basis for antifraternal satire, and his images of friars as "pseudoapostles" and "creepers into houses," indeed an elaborate caricature language of bad friars, live on in the poems of Rutebeuf and Chaucer and Langland. His contribution to the literary history of the Franciscan Order was that which the irritant grain of sand makes to the oyster.

Were he not remarkable on his own merits, William of Saint-Amour would earn a page in Western intellectual history as the man who was attacked at length by the two most famous theologians of the thirteenth century, Thomas Aquinas and Bonaventure. Bonaventure's writings on evangelical poverty are numerous and, though less well known than his mystical and exegetical works, make up an important chapter in the history of the literature of poverty.[4] The most important of them is his refutation of William, the *Apologia pauperum*. Its structure is both ingenious and exasperating. Though Bonaventure suggests in various places that he distributes his material in conformity with the "attacks" of his "adversary," the end result owes as much to Bonaventure's profound and life-long fascination with the mysteries of number and metaphor as it does to anything in William's own pages. The attack to which he replies is, he says in the prologue, "aimed first at toppling the pinnacle of evangelical perfection; second, at demolishing its defenses; third, at subverting its very foundation; fourth, at defaming with false accusations the sincerity of those who are poor for Christ, in order to make them seem loathsome to the world. Against such a fourfold assault, a fourfold reply must be constructed as four lines of defense; and each line must have three sides, as the subject matter demands, so that the soldiers of the Gospel, surrounded by these triangular fortifications, may remain invulnerable and protected against the sharp points of flaming darts." The result is a veritable epic in twelve books, covering with encyclopedic exhaustiveness the whole range of arguments, actual and potential, against the Franciscan doctrines of perfect poverty.

No other single book connected with the Parisian episode of the poverty debate—or indeed with Franciscan poverty in general—had more influence within the mainstream of the Order than did the *Apologia*, yet its very

[4] For bibliographical information concerning St. Bonaventure, see note 3 on p. 194. The *Apologia pauperum* will be found in the *Opera Omnia*, vol. VIII, along with many other writings on the poverty question not discussed here. Citations are from the translation by José de Vinck, *The Works of Bonaventure* vol. 4, *Defense of the Mendicants* (Patterson, 1966). A useful commentary to the *Apologia* is provided by S. Clasen, *Der hl. Bonaventura und das Mendikantentum* (Werl, 1940).

inclusiveness and the individuality of its author's approach to his subject make it all but impossible to summarize. The third and fourth "lines of defense" (chapters 7 through 12) are probably the most important parts of the work in terms of the doctrinal history of poverty, for in them Bonaventure deals directly and at length with the respective questions of the relation of poverty to Christian perfection, and the validity of the polity and ministry of the friars within the life of the larger Church. The entire work, however, is an elaborate edifice of Gothic argument with a stunning ornamental facade, surprising carved bosses, and misericords delightfully tucked out of sight behind the supporting columns of the "fourfold defense." The full force of the argument is serial and cumulative, but it is a work which can also be browsed through with pleasure.

One of the criticisms made of the friars by William of Saint-Amour and his numerous and distinguished allies was directed at the prevailing style of scholastic discourse in which, according to one critic, "all true theology is given over to sophistry, and Paul to Aristotle." William at one point refused to have further "sophistical" debate on the friar question, but challenged all comers to a "Catholic collation of the Scriptures" on the issues involved. Bonaventure's *Apologia* takes up this challenge. It is not at all a demonstration through scholastic disputation, but a massive argument from the authority of the Bible and patristic tradition. Indeed its freedom from the formalistic academic prose of the university is one of its signal virtues, which becomes all the more apparent when one compares it with other poverty tracts of the immediate period, such as the *Manus quae* of the English Franciscan Thomas of York. Bonaventure stalks his opponents on their own native grounds.

All of Bonaventure's works display the seal of a brilliant original mind, but none, aside from the *Soliloquy* and certain of the exegetical writings, displays a more complete command of the Bible and of the repertory of the Christian classics. He exhibits, lightly, a particularly profound study of the four doctors of the Church—Ambrose, Augustine, Gregory, and Jerome—and of the great Greek father John Chrysostom; but his inkwell is also full of apt citations from the early monastic writers, from the Victorines, from St. Bernard. The *Apologia* becomes a kind of vast ecumenical council of the weightiest names from a thousand years of Church history, all solemnly assembled to testify on behalf of mendicancy.

In terms of the history of the poverty debate, Bonaventure's *Apologia* has a special importance which is twofold. In the first place, his answers to specific *questiones disputatae* proved so satisfying that they in effect became the standard "position" of the Order. A good example is his treatment of the endlessly controversial "little purses" *(loculos)* carried by Judas, a subject which he deals with in passing in the tenth chapter, entitled "The First Point of the Fourth Answer, in which the Religious Life of Those Who Have No Purse is Defended against Error, and the True Right of Ecclesiastic Possession is Explained." William had argued that the friars mistakenly seek perfection in their poverty, since their master, Christ, had dominion over a purse, and "no disciple is above his teacher" (Mat. 10:24). Bonaventure tries to demonstrate that, on the contrary, Christ's use of the purse was a condescension to the weakness and needs of others, that is, the charitable condescension of the perfect to the imperfect. His commission to His apostles, on the other hand, contains injunctions to perfection which are sufficiently explicit. The commandments to go barefoot without scrips and staves, and to take nothing for the journey, are attested to in Catholic tradition by "Ambrose, Augustine, Jerome, Chrysostom, Bede, Rabanus, and Bernard, all of whom affirm that the teaching of Christ to the apostles on the advisability of not carrying money is to be understood literally." The *use* of the purse thus foreshadows the just exercise of ecclesiastical possession in a Church made up of perfect and imperfect alike, just as the specific abdication of the use of the purse, vowed by the Friars Minor, reflects the will to accede to a counsel of perfection.

A second important point about the *Apologia* might be described as its general position with regard to the function of the Franciscan Order within the Church. Bonaventure defends a "hard line" with regard to poverty, and certainly argues (in the eleventh chapter) what was to be the position of the discredited Spirituals under John XXII. He is likewise sympathetic, however, to the interventions of Gregory IX to rationalize the increasingly complex affairs of the Order. The friars, he writes, "never profess that no one is to provide for them, or to make alms personally or through an interposed person, since this would be impossible and foolish for a community of mendicant poor: they merely profess that, in the manner handed down through the Gospel by evangelical men, they possess no money whatsoever." The word "community" is important, and in terms of the clash of images which was dividing the Order over the poverty question, there is no doubt where Bonaventure eventually stood—side by side with Francis at the wall of San Giovanni in Laterano. For Bonaventure, the Franciscan Order was a therapeutic community within a ravaged Church, an army of the disciplined poor whose sacred duty was a fully apostolic ministry within a protecting Church, "lifted like another Esther up among nations as the mother of all churches, as their queen and teacher to propose and defend the truths of both morals and faith." The final chapter of the *Apologia,* as emphatic in its rhetoric as in its positioning, is given over not to a discussion of questions of abstract perfection, but to a defense of the evangelical ministry of the mendicants within the Church, considered under "the sevenfold scriptural metaphor" of the builder, the gardener, the shepherd, the bailiff, the physician, the watchman, and the leader.

Both because of its intrinsic merits and because of its authority within the Franciscan Order, Bonaventure's *Apologia pauperum* is the most important of the academic defenses of poverty, but it is by no means the only one which deserves the attention of the literary historian. Among the many others are those of the English friar John Pecham, who became Archbishop of Canterbury in 1279, and who was among the most vigorous and versatile apologists of mendicancy in the thirteenth century.[5] Pecham was a poet of very considerable abilities—the *Philomena,* his famous sequence on the Passion, is one of the most brilliant poems of his age—and even when he must perforce work within the sometimes brutal conventions of contemporary polemic his tracts on the poverty question reveal a witty poetic intelligence, a sure sense of literary form, and, above all, a powerfully intimidating impression of authority. Pecham took on all comers. In the *Tractatus pauperis,* the most conventional of his poverty pamphlets, he answers the attacks of the Parisian seculars, particularly William of Saint-Amour and Gerard of Abbeville. Another essay sets out to refute arguments

[5] On Pecham, see the article by A. Teetaert in the *DTC,* XII, i, cols. 100-140 (s.v. "Pecham, Jean"). For a full biography, see Decima Douie, *Archbishop Pecham* (Oxford, 1952).

against Franciscan practice brought forward by the English Dominican Robert Kilwardby. In yet another genre, his lucid commentary on the *Rule* argues strenuously along the lines traced by St. Bonaventure, for the strict observance of the mid-century settlement. At his best moments, Pecham has the rare grace to be able to move beyond opaque polemic and, like the author of the *Sacrum Commercium,* write about poverty with both lyric grace and considerable theological sophistication.[6]

Such moments are rare in the *Tractatus pauperis,* which, like the *Contra Kilwardby,* is an academic piece clearly intended for a limited university audience. Both in its general conception and its specific lines of argument it is characterized by a rhetoric always on the simmer and often enough at full boil, and by a good deal of Bernardine overstatement. Pecham attacks a certain anthology of anti-mendicant tracts ("Three books bound up in one volume"—which, precisely, it is impossible to tell) which he compares to the inelegant croaking of so many frogs. Like Bonaventure's *Apologia,* on which of course it leans heavily, the *Tractatus* is an elaborate and incremental argument from authority, depending for its effectiveness on the sheer weight of scriptural, patristic, and canonic *exempla.* If the resulting document is more heated and hurried than the *Apologia,* it is nonetheless impressive. Pecham's discussions of the recurrent *questiones disputatae* of the controversy—the significance of the "little purses," the propriety of wearing sandals, and so on—

[6] Of the texts discussed here, the *Tractatus contra fratrum Robertum Kilwardby,* the *Defensio Fratrum Mendicantium,* and parts of the *Tractatus pauperis* (sometimes also called the *De evangelica perfectione*) are edited in *Fratris Johannis Pecham quondam archiepiscopi Cantuariensis Tractatus tres de paupertate* edd. C. L. Kingsford, A. G. Little, and F. Tocco (Aberdeen, 1910). The *Canticum pauperis pro dilecto* was published by the Quaracchi Fathers together with the *Stimulus amoris* of Jacob of Milan in the third volume of the "Bibliotheca ascetica franciscana medii aevi" (Quaracchi, 1905).

will be of real interest to students of the verbal and visual arts in the thirteenth century, but on the whole the *Tractatus* is of less literary significance than two other of Pecham's works that are less clearly defined by the context of academic polemic.

The first of these is the *Canticum pauperis pro dilecto,* a strange and uneven work which is difficult to categorize. Though in fact a prose tract, the work merits its conventional title of the *Canticum pauperis,* for it is, at its best moments, an eloquent and lyrical celebration and defense of the aspirations of the *Rule.* Its form is that of a dialogue between a narrator and a certain very wise elder, or *senior.* The narrator is a stock figure of medieval didactic allegory in the Boethian tradition, a confused and disturbed *ignorans* who is slowly brought to enlightenment by the patient teaching of his interlocutor. The *senior,* whose speeches are largely taken from Bonaventure's *Apologia* and Pecham's own *Expositio super regulam,* clearly enough represents the voice of tradition, authority, and wisdom. The Quaracchi editors are wrong, in my view, to say that the wise old man *is* Bonaventure, for the work does successfully capture in some degree that sense of the eschatalogical mystery of poverty so beloved by Ubertino and St. Bernard, which takes the discussion away from the arena of history. On the whole, however, the poetic cast of the *Canticum* works at counterpurposes with the predominately technical and controversial content of the argument. One has the impression that Pecham has tried to plow with ox and ass yoked together, and with somewhat indifferent results.

There is a much happier, if less ambitious, wedding of poetry and apologetics in a final poverty tract, the so-called *Defensio Fratrum Mendicantium,* a poetic dialogue in mono-rhyme quatrains. The *Defensio* claims a place in one of the traditional genres of medieval poetry, the *contrasto* or *débat,* such as those between body and soul, wine and water, winter and summer, and so on. But if the tune is old, the words are refreshingly new. The clever fiction of the *Defensio* is that of a plea in chancery in which "Mundus" (the World) seeks papal redress of grievances suffered at the hands of "Religio" (the Religious Life). Mundus is no mere straw man or stage villain like Worldly Goods in *Everyman.* Rather, he is the articulate spokesman of a lucid, coherent, and scripturally based critique of the whole idea of the religious life. His position with regard to the friars is a moderate one, outlining in various shades of gray what William of Saint-Amour and his friends could see only in terms of stark black and white. Indeed, so persuasive seem to be his philosophical objections against the priority of the contemplative life in general, and so damning his account of the empirical situation with regard to the various religious orders in particular, that it seems for a moment as if the Pope must rule in his favor. It is only Religio's brilliant summary defense, taking up some quarter of the entire poem and dealing as gracefully as the jogging rhythm will allow with such matters as Anselm's solution to the apparent conflict between free will and the vows of regulars, which saves the day.

Though it reveals the scholastic mannerisms of the academy and even touches of classical learning (Mundus, says Religio, is another "vile Thersites"), the *Defensio* is the work of a poet trying to reach and please an extended audience rather than the essay of a schoolmaster. The question of mendicancy is taken from the arena of capitular legislation and papal decretals to be put in the largest possible theological perspective. Mundus claims to have been redeemed by the cross of Christ; Religio shows to what extent that claim is valid, and to what extent not. And in the course of the debate the relationship of the friars, gray and black alike, to the holy men under the Old Law and the religious orders under the New is tactfully yet emphatically made. Pecham views the fraternal orders as the legitimate heirs and, in a sense, the logical extensions of both the Old Testament prophets and the variegated religious life of a millennium of Christianity. Though subliminal and without any explicit Joachimism behind it, the idea is more elegantly present in the *Defensio* than in the *Canticum pauperis,* and more important to the nature of the argument.

Academic writings devoted to the poverty question are very numerous, for few Franciscan theologians of rank associated with the university from the time of William of Saint-Amour on failed to address the issue directly in a *quaestio* or obliquely in a larger theological context. No synoptic study of all the literature, some of which is still unpublished, has ever been undertaken, but most of it is at least touched on in the general histories of the poverty contest. Parochial in its context and repetitive in its content, a good deal of the minor controversial literature will be of interest mainly to the specialist. There are, however, a few minor apologetic essays written by officers of the Order, or by others called upon for one reason or another to act as formal spokesmen for Franciscan teaching. An example of the genre, and one which commanded an enthusiastic if narrow readership during the years of controversy, is the little tract of Hugh of Digne, the close friend of John of Parma, called *De finibus paupertatis.*[7] The *De finibus* sketches quite clearly the line of argument which would be taken up first

[7] *De finibus paupertatis,* ed. Claudia Florovsky, *AFH,* v (1912), 277-290; reprinted, with the Rule commentary, by Alessandra Sisto, *Figure del primo francescanesimo in Provenza* (Florence, 1971).

by the Spirituals, then by the *fraticelli.* All institutions of religion, Hugh says, aspire to a peculiar and defining form of excellence. That of the Friars Minor is the practice of apostolic poverty. The man who has solemnly taken a religious vow is not at liberty to abrogate it and is, furthermore, obliged to do all the specific things necessary for the attainment of the principal vow—in the case of the friars, the vow of poverty. Hugh lists ten outward and visible signs which reflect the perfection of poverty practiced, among which are the *usus pauperis,* coarseness of garment, bare feet, the refusal to use money, simplicity of speech, and a number of other practices which made up the litmus test of the true Franciscan observance as administered by the rigorists. Most of them show up, in negative refraction, in the character of Friar John in Chaucer's "Summoner's Tale."

It is not at all surprising that most of the formal documents in the poverty debate, taken as a whole, share the usual weakness of literary polemic, a sometimes unhappy extravagance both of argument and of prose style. Even so careful a theologian as Thomas Aquinas, backed into a corner by William of Saint-Amour, would argue in the *Contra impugnantes* that the fruition of Christian perfection lay in the practice of evangelical poverty—a view modified in the *Summa,* but not before an adversary was able to scoff, "Faith, hope, charity, but the greatest of these is poverty!" Many of the Franciscan apologists seemed at times to agree, though in a different tone of voice, and there is a perceptible line of tradition which links the poverty tracts of the 1250's to the time of the heresy of the *fraticelli.* That heresy took many different forms, but its central error was the establishment of the "rule of poverty," unmediated and unglossed, as the final earthly authority for the ordering of the Christian life.

For the Franciscan *fraticelli,* the *Rule* of the founder would become a supreme authority on earth. Such a position may have been a misrepresentation, to put it mildly, of the point of view even of the Leo sources, but the *fraticelli* would be able to point to texts there, and in the *Sacrum Commercium,* and in Pecham, and Hugh of Digne, which, wrenched from their poetic or polemical contexts, would make up a plausible patrology of absolute poverty.

Another important source of poverty literature is to be found in commentaries on the *Rule,* some of which have already been mentioned in passing. It is in no way shocking that, at one level, Franciscan writers of the thirteenth century looked upon their founder's rule as having something of the authority and inviolability of Scripture. Much of Franciscan legislation is taken from the Bible, either word for word or in close paraphrase; all of it is deeply imbued with biblical teaching. The problem of the *Rule* arose—as did, in other contexts, the problem of the Bible itself—not over the authority of the document, but over the validity of its interpretation. Francis himself, at the time he wrote the *Testament,* considered both the language and the intent of the *Rule* plain and simple, and he commanded his followers to abstain from exegesis. Yet it was not to be so, and in the complex literary history of the poverty debate it is this "plain and simple" document which is the object of thousands of pages of *explication de texte.* The papal pronouncements which began with Gregory IX's *Quo elongati* in 1230 and did not end with the declarations of John XXII, which effectively sealed the doors of the Church to the weary cause of the rigorists, have been sufficiently studied by three generations of Franciscan scholars. Quite as important, in terms of the larger literary picture, are the formal commentaries to the *Rule* during the thirteenth, fourteenth, and fifteenth centuries, either by partisans in the dispute or its mediators or heirs. Among the best-known commentaries are those by Olivi and Clareno; Pecham's commentary (to be distinguished from the long tenth chapter of his *Tractatus pauperis,* which also deals with the *Rule*) is a dignified and impressive document which deserves to be better known.[8] In it we see more of Pecham the pastor and spiritual master, less of the lawyer and debater. Among the others there are at least three which merit attention.

The first of these, indeed the first formal commentary to the *Rule* we have, is the *Exposition of the Four Masters,* dating from 1241-1242.[9] The "four masters" (Alexander of Hales, John of Rupella, Robert of Bascia, and Eudes Rigaud) constituted an international commission of famous Franciscan theologians, established to clarify points of discipline and practice which were already, at that early date, receiving differing emphases and interpretations along the two broad lines of tendency which would later be known as the Community and the Spirituals. It is not, therefore, a complete commentary, but rather an anthology of carefully worded answers to vexing questions. On the vexing question of poverty the four masters proved somewhat sibylline, drawing a distinction between imperfect poverty (proprietory dominion over the modest necessities of life) and perfect poverty (the *usus pauperis,* or mendicancy). While it is the

[8] *Expositio super Regulam Fratrum Minorum,* mistakenly attributed to Bonaventure in the Quaracchi *Opera,* VIII, pp. 391-437; Bonaventure's (genuine) *Sermo super Regulam Fratrum Minorum* will be found *ibid.,* pp. 438-448; David Flood has edited *Peter Olivi's Rule Commentary* (Wiesbaden, 1972). Angelo Clareno's *Expositio Regulae Fratrum Minorum* has been edited by L. Oliger (Quaracchi, 1912).

[9] *Expositio Quatuor Magistrorum super Regulam Fratrum Minorum,* ed. L. Oliger (Rome, 1950).

latter which is "the poverty of the Friars Minor," the four masters reveal no hostility to those lines of reasonable accommodation necessary for the governance of the Order and for the establishment of such institutions as the *studium* at Paris. The *Expositio* is thus an important early indication of the kind of moderate, or Bonaventurean, line of interpretation which would become the majority position of the Community.

Two other commentators, writing two centuries later, are eloquent witnesses to the vitality and literary fruitfulness of the *Rule*'s teachings on poverty in the fifteenth-century revival of Franciscanism, long after the *fraticelli* had ceased to be a current issue. Nicolas of Osima (d. 1454) wrote two separate commentaries, one on the *Regula bullata,* another for the rule of the Poor Clares.[10] Nicolas' prose is spare and telling, and his simple doctrine gained a very wide audience through St. Bernardino of Siena, the most famous preacher of the Italian *quattrocento.* Finally, St. John of Capestrano (1386-1456), the "reformer of the Order," wrote eloquent glosses to the rules of both the first and second orders, which in their spiritual clarity and their distance from the rancor of controversy deserve to find a place among the minor monuments of Franciscan spirituality.[11]

The most flamboyant, but also the sombrest, chapter in the history of the poverty debate is that which treats of the tribulations of the Spirituals and the rise of the heresy of the *fraticelli,* and from this unhappy period in the Order's history we have a number of literary documents of enduring importance. Here we are confronted with a certain problem of terminology. The word "Spir-

[10] *Tre operette volgari di Frati Nicolo da Osimo,* ed. G. Spezi (Rome, 1865).

[11] *Esposizione della Regola dei Frati Minori,* ed. A. Ghinato (Rome, 1960).

itual" is often used rather casually, as I have so far done in this book, to refer to the unorganized "party" within the Order whose vision of Franciscan life was tied to a literal interpretation of the *Rule* and strongly influenced by the stock literary images of the Leo sources. We shall of course do well to remember that at no time, even under the quasi-formal leadership of Angelo Clareno, was this "party" a recognizable and coherent group. The Spirituals cannot, in general, be identified either in terms of administrative organization or in terms of their special "doctrines" or "teachings."[12] They are most accurately thought of, instead, in terms of certain major tendencies which to greater or lesser degree they share. The most important of these tendencies include a preference for rural eremitism over urban conventualism, a deep-seated anti-academicism, and the conviction that the essence of Franciscanism lay in the strict observance of the unmediated *Rule* and the *Testament* of the founder. There is also, in several Spiritual writers, a marked strain of the apocalypticism which was generally endemic in thirteenth-century Europe, and a marked interest in the immediate application of the teachings of Joachim of Fiore to the contemporary history of the Church. The origins of the very term "Spiritual" are obscure. It seems to have been first used by the people of the Midi to describe, with approbation, the observant friars in their conflict with their adversaries within the Order and at the papal court. Joachim's term "spiritual men" *(viri spirituales),* which he used to prophesy a new order of religious within the Church, probably also influenced at least certain thinkers, like Ubertino da Casale.

The term *fraticelli* is likewise vague, and under it were grouped those heretics who, in the fourteenth century,

[12] See the article "Spirituels" by L. Oliger, *DTC,* XIV, cols 2522-2549.

chose the path of separatism and sought to live a life of "Franciscan" poverty outside the Order and outside the sanctions of the Church, and whose teaching with regard to the absolute poverty of Christ and the Apostles, though it had abundant and authoritative precedent in the thirteenth century, was in direct contradiction to that of Pope John XXII. There was a dominant Franciscan tradition among the *fraticelli,* but among those condemned under the name were Vaudois, Beghards, Beguines, and assorted other fanatics of poverty.[13]

The history of the Spirituals is a complicated one, which it would be imprudent to attempt in brief compass, but in terms of the literary history of the poverty debate among the Spirituals, one may safely identify three writers who, in quite different ways, exemplify the rigorist doctrine of absolute poverty during the Order's most trying years of controversy and schism: Peter of John Olivi (c. 1248-1298), Angelo Clareno (died c. 1323), and Ubertino da Casale (1259 - c. 1338).

The last of these, Ubertino, will claim our attention in a later chapter. Though his whole life was, in a way, a monument to the doomed doctrine of absolute poverty, his great work, called the *Arbor vitae crucifixae,* one of the true, neglected masterpieces of medieval spirituality, reveals a poetic design and mystical theology which transcend its immediate connections with the poverty controversy; it is most appropriately considered in connection with the mystical works of Bonaventure, the *De compositione exterioris et interioris hominis* of David of Augsburg, the *Meditations on the Life of Christ,* and other works of ambitious schematic design. There is nothing at all like it to be found among the works of the Spirituals' unofficial saint, Olivi.

[13] See the article "Fraticelli" by Clement Schmitt, *DS,* V, cols 1167-1188.

Olivi was a Frenchman who joined the Order as a child in Narbonne.[14] He studied at Paris under Pecham and other luminaries in a university still vibrant to the memory of Bonaventure. Though he never completed his formal degree requirements, he was an acknowledged and accomplished theologian. If we knew nothing more of him than his writing, we should judge him a schoolman pure and simple. His scholastic writings on the poverty question can be credited with some share of the protracted success of the Spiritual cause in the later thirteenth century, but they are for the most part stylistically uninteresting and devoid of the poetic vision by means of which other controversial documents in the debate exercised some real influence on the wider literary world. His postils on the Apocalypse, rich in influence from Joachim as any such commentary of the time was virtually certain to be, are another matter; so are one or two brief essays in mystical and ascetic theology. On the whole, however, Olivi was not a remarkable writer. What was remarkable about him, apparently, was the quality of life, at once saintly and charismatic, which left its impress literally upon thousands but which is but faintly hinted at in the written page. Hence it is that Olivi's greatest literary importance is, in a sense, as a character rather than as an author. He was widely honored as a saint, and his tomb soon became the site of a popular cult dangerous to the Community, which, for a time, rivalled that of the Portiuncula itself. In the pages of Clareno and Ubertino, Olivi lives not so much as an academic authority as a kind of human icon of latter-day Franciscan poverty, a reproof to backsliders and a comfort to the persecuted.

[14] See the article "Olieu" by F. Callaey, *DTC,* XI, cols 982-991.

Olivi was a forerunner, an elder, a prophet. When he died in full vigor in 1298, his vision of Franciscanism, though increasingly a legal fiction, still enjoyed at least lip service from important princes of the Church. During the pontificates of Boniface VIII and John XXII all that was changed and, in the end, the dogmatic basis from which the Spirituals justified their practice, the doctrine that neither Christ nor the Apostles either as individuals or in common "owned" property, was declared to be noxious heresy. In the poetic language of the *Sacrum Commercium,* Poverty had been joined by her sister, Persecution. It is from this period in Franciscan history that there emerged one of the most extraordinary personalities of the Middle Ages or of any time, Angelo Clareno.[15]

Angelo's life was as melodramatic in fact as any of the imagined martyrdoms of his contemporary, Ramon Lull. Its controlling images are the prison gate and the stony road. Almost constantly either in prison on charges of heresy and schism or in the furtive exile which alone left him free to preach and practice the Franciscan vocation to which he dedicated his life, he died discredited, banished from the Order in which he had been professed. A man of apparent contradictions, he has remained a controversial figure in the Order's history to this very day. A branded schismatic, he never denied prelatical authority or acted in disobedience to its command. An avowed despiser of the vanity of the academy, he was a great admirer of the intellectual achievements of Bonaventure and had the signal distinction of being one of the major translators of Greek texts in his age.

[15] An excellent introduction to Angelo will be found in L. Berardini, *Frate Angelo da Clareno alla luce della storia* (Osimo, 1964).

Under different circumstances Angelo might have been one of the honored luminaries of the Church, and a writer of a very different sort from what he was. Certainly his circle of admirers was not limited to the Spirituals, and he counted among his close friends the Augustinian hermit Simon of Cascia, one of the greatest spiritual writers of the fourteenth century. In one or two of his own minor writings, such as the *Breviloquium super doctrina salutis ad parvulos Christi,* we have a glimpse of his abilities as a writer of popular and affective theology.[16] He was to have scant time for such efforts, however, and his major works were destined to be his commentary on the *Rule,* a spirited *Apologia* in which he defended himself as a Catholic, and an extraordinary *Cronaca* of the history of poverty within the Franciscan Order.

The *Apologia pro vita sua* was addressed, indirectly, to the Spaniard Alvaro Pelayo, who, in two carefully thought-out letters, had attacked Angelo.[17] Though it covers a good deal of ground, it is mainly a refutation of four "lies" uttered by Pelayo: that Angelo had left the Franciscan Order, that he had written "from his own heart and not in the spirit of Jesus," that he was a schismatic, and that he was disobedient to and disrespectful of prelates. Of all these charges, which Angelo of course denies, the most revealing is perhaps the second, that his prose is too elegant and impressive to be the spontaneous expression of one poor in spirit. Angelo was credited even by his opponents with being an effective writer, and he is nowhere more impressive than

[16] Ed. N. Mattioli, *Il Beato Simone Fidati da Cascia dell' Ordine Romitano di S. Agostino* (Rome, 1898), pp. 471-487.

[17] *Angelus Clarinus ad Alvarum Pelagium Apologia pro vita sua,* ed. V. Doucet, *AFH,* xxxix (1946-1948), 63-200.

in his most "literary" work, the history of the seven tribulations of the Minorite Order.

The *Cronaca (Chronicon seu Historia septem tribulationum Ordinis Minorum),* written in the calm of Angelo's sojourn with the Benedictines of Subiaco, is a reflective work of history which traces the fortunes of the Franciscan Order from its foundation at the command of Christ to its trials under John XXII. Given the author's major premises, it is a scrupulous and careful piece of work which, in recent years, Franciscan scholars have recognized as a document authoritative with regard to many of the complicated details of the Order's history during the period which it covers. For the modern reader these premises give the work a somewhat lurid cast, for Angelo not only assumes the Spiritual cause essentially without argument, but is also convinced of the present and apocalyptic machinations of the mystery of iniquity. Accordingly, the *Cronaca* is something of an anthology of heroes and villains. The chief villain of a large field is Brother Elias, the Judas to whom Francis turned over the government of the Order after his debilitating missionary tour. The heroes include John of Parma, the great Minister General, and of course Olivi. Angelo is no Abelard, and his own role in the history he recites is for the most part a minor one. Indeed one has the impression that human characters altogether are subtly subordinate to the mystery of a grander design, when there is war in heaven, and Michael and his angels fight against the dragon.

For Angelo the Spiritual conception of apostolic poverty was an eschatological imperative, and perhaps what he and other Spiritual writers most happily learned from the Abbot Joachim was a lively sense of poetic expectation and prophecy. He is a typically "Franciscan" historian insofar as he sees the realities of the gospel given new and tangible life in the history of his own times, and pointing to even more dramatic truths in the future. The book ends with neither the resignation nor the recrimination characteristic of the memoirs of a deposed political leader, but with a vindicating prophecy of the victory of poverty. "But then all those will stand confounded who, counting Saint Francis of little worth, have depended upon their own prudence, and adored the idols of worldly wisdom, and built up altars to their useless knowledge. For Christ will show to His own poor ones those secret and mysterious teachings of His wisdom, and they will hear the words of His mysteries from His own mouth. . . . Satan will not have the victory over them, but will be trampled beneath their feet; and they shall have for their teacher God (the Father), Jesus Christ, and the Holy Ghost, for ever and ever. Amen."

Before leaving the Spirituals, we must briefly consider the man whose accusations of sectarianism stirred Angelo to write his *Apologia.* Alvaro Pelayo, lawyer, diplomat, papal penitencer, was an important member of the Franciscan "establishment" which saw the Order through its worst days under John XXII. It would not, however, be just to let Angelo play Newman to Alvaro's Kingsley, for this Spanish legist and bishop is a moral and literary figure of considerable stature in his own right. He is an important and neglected commentator on the question of Franciscan poverty as viewed from within the Community, who demonstrates how dangerous it would be to accept the rather Manichean formulation of a good deal of Spiritual literature in which the majority of the Order are painted as backsliding sybarites hungry for the fleshpots of Egypt.

Alvaro wrote important works of popular apologetic and exemplary literature, but his greatest work is the massive *De statu et planctu Ecclesiae*, written in two redactions after he had left Avignon around 1340.[18] It is a work with few analogues in medieval literature, at once a moral encyclopedia which reflects its author's training as a canon lawyer, and a comprehensive and on the whole pessimistic analysis of the state of the fourteenth-century Church. The form of the work is that of a threnody, in which Pelayo laments with the voice of a medieval Jeremiah the unworthy state of the new Israel. His Latin style is often rather elaborate, and he shares with many of the other cultivated authors of Avignon a penchant for difficult words. The general effect of the book is impressive if at times startling in its rhetoric. A major section of its second part is given over to a discussion of the Franciscan Order, and questions relating to the practice of poverty show up recurrently elsewhere as well. In his excoriating denunciations of corrupt friars and the general erosion of ancient observance within the Order, we hear the voice of a "primitive" Franciscanism as impassioned and authentic as any Spiritual, sharing the same vocabulary, could have wished.

There is little in the way of surviving literature of the *fraticelli*, and still less which can claim place in a general survey such as this. There is, however, one anomalous text which must be mentioned in connection with the poverty debate, and that is the prose history of the trial and execution of the *fraticello* Michael of Calci, burned at the stake in Florence in 1389.[19] The *History*

[18] *De statu et planctu Ecclesiae* (Ulm, 1474; Lyon, 1517; Venice, 1560).

[19] *Il Supplizio di fra Michele da Calci,* ed. Giuseppe de Luca in *Prosatori Minori del Trecento,* I (Milan, n.d.), pp. 213-236; *Storia di fra Michele minorita,* ed. Francesco Flora (Florence, 1946).

of Fra Michele is a fourteenth-century passion play in prose. The anonymous author was an eyewitness to most of what he describes, though he admits, with a kind of naive candor which is the work's authenticating mark, that some of his details are second-hand. It matters little, for the whole of the action is refracted through the prism of the Scriptures. The episcopal tribunal is the Sanhedrin, the Florentine mob the rabble of Jerusalem thirsting for the blood of the Messiah. The procurator of the episcopal court is the *principe dei farisei,* and Fra Michele dies with Christ's last words on his lips. Yet the imposition of the scriptural view is not theologically self-conscious, as it often is with Celano and the other hagiographers of Franciscan tradition, let alone as elaborately typological and mystical as it is with Bartholomew of Pisa. Rather, for this brilliant and understated apologist of the *altissima poverta,* the execution of this obdurate fanatic can be seen in no other terms than those of the life of a Christ *povero e crussifisso.* It is Fra Michele's crime, in the vivid pages of the Florentine martyrology, to maintain the teaching with regard to the *usus pauperis* which had been the official teaching of the Church "as determined by the decretal *Exiit qui seminat.*" If the appeal to the text of a papal brief seems banal in a history claiming something of high tragedy, it is nonetheless natural. For the *History of Fra Michele* projects a view of the world for which the central moral problem is that of an attitude toward apostolic poverty, even as the central political problem is the posture of the Franciscan Order toward the primitive teachings of its golden age. The author underscores with particular rhetorical emphasis the moment in the *via dolorosa* in which Michele and his tormenters pass by the Franciscan church of Santa Croce.

The *History of Fra Michele* must be regarded as something of a museum piece in the history of Franciscan literature, for there is no evidence of its publication or influence beyond a narrow circle of discredited Italian *fraticelli*. Yet it remains a vivid example of the extraordinary literary power of the vision of poverty even most narrowly and polemically considered. In its quiet mastery of the humble style, its sure sense of drama, its economical use of scant but telling narrative detail, above all in the immediacy of its rhythms and patterns of real dialogue, the *History of Fra Michele* is not surpassed even by those acknowledged masters of the fourteenth-century *novella* with whom its author must necessarily be compared. And if, in its purely literary strategies and impact, it is closer to Sacchetti or Sercambi than to Olivi or Angelo Clareno, it remains one of the purest documents in the literature of Franciscan poverty, as clearly focused in its vision of the Franciscan life as the *Sacrum Commercium* itself.

There is one further topic which must be touched upon. The spiritual lyric, the most conspicuous gift of the Franciscan movement to the literature of medieval Europe, will be a major concern of the next chapter. Yet it would be impossible to complete even a spare sketch of the literature of Franciscan poverty without mentioning the extraordinarily rich development of the poverty theme in the Franciscan lyric. From the famous *laude* of the Cortona confraternity to the "Franciscan" poems of the Scottish poet William Dunbar in the fifteenth century, an impressive and varied lyric school, both within the Order and outside it, would sing the praises of *ma donna povertà,* and preach the vanity of human wishes to the music of lute and gittern.

We have already seen how the *Sacrum Commercium,* using the sexual imagery of the Canticles and a rich monastic tradition of mystical marriage, creates a vivid and dramatic image of espousal. That Poverty was Francis' "bride," a bride whom he loved with all the passion and abandon of a bridegroom, is an idea which already finds its charming statement in Celano (*Vita prima,* I, 7) and in the *Legend of the Three Companions* (ch. 3). Here poetry becomes the handmaiden of theology, for we shall find no clearer indication in any of the academic commentaries of the thirteenth century as to the defining characteristics of Franciscan poverty, those subtle but crucial emphases which distinguish it from contemporary spiritual movements with which it shares so much. For Francis and the Franciscan "poets," poverty is neither principally an ascetic technique nor an effective evangelical posture, but the very locus of the closest possible union with Christ, Christ "a pauper, crucified."

It is a paradoxical vision which sees the culmination of both Christ's dominion and His love in His poverty, and which finds its most satisfying expression in what can be called without captiousness the love poetry of the Franciscan troubadours. Jacopone da Todi (c. 1230 - 1306), the most famous of them, has one poem (*Povertat' ennamorata*) which quite knowingly and skillfully manipulates one of the stock *formulae* of secular love poetry in the service of the Franciscan ideal.[20] Poverty, "beloved poverty," is said to be greater than the kingdoms of the world—named with some geographical exhaustiveness—greater than the created world and its bounty, greater than "the moon, the sun, heaven and

[20] For bibliography on Jacopone, see note 71, p. 184. The two poems discussed here are numbers 47 and 36 in the *Laude,* ed. Franco Mancini (Bari, 1974). On Jacopone as a poet of poverty, see Carla Cadorna, *Il Cantore della Poverta* (Florence, 1923).

its stars." By the end of the poem, the beloved identified as Poverty in the first line has been fused with a more familiar ideal of thirteenth-century poetry, *cortesia*:

> Poi el mio voler a Dio data, possesor so d'onne stato,
> en loro amor so transformato, ennamorata cortesia!

Among the many "lauds" of Jacopone written to celebrate the beauty of the Franciscan bride is the lovely *O amor de povertato,* a poem much admired by St. Bernardino, and the specific object of his felicitous remark that Jacopone was a "second David."

The other great poet of poverty who must at least be mentioned in this context was Brother Ugo Panziera (c. 1265 - c. 1330), in some ways a more polished and accomplished technician than Jacopone.[21]. Ugo develops the epithalamic convention with melodic dignity and theological effectiveness in a number of his *laude,* but with a particular haunting beauty in *Poverta terrena . . . vita del mio core,* which ends with a striking image of poverty as a fragrant flower, the eternal perfume of Christ. Discussions of Franciscan poetry in the age of Jacopone usually underscore its "naive" and "simple" qualities. They are there, to be sure; but we should not let them make us lose sight of the boldness and, in its context, the freshness of the major metaphors of Franciscan poverty in the lyric poets. It is no lapse on Dante's part that in the solemn and glorious moment in the eleventh canto of the *Paradiso* in which Thomas Aquinas narrates the history of Francis of Assisi, it is the legend of the "mystical marriage" from the narrative imagination of the *Sacrum Commercium* and the Franciscan troubadours which is retold in the flawless *terza rima* of the master.

[21] *Le Laudi,* ed. Virgilio di Benedetto (Rome, 1963), pp. 75-76.

4

Preachers, Teachers, Apostles, and the Jugglers of the Lord

Pope Innocent III opened the solemnities of the Fourth Lateran Council in 1215 with a discourse on Luke 22:15, "With desire I have desired to eat this passover with you before I suffer." The Passion text was apt, for the Church was in many ways gripped in an agony apparent only to some. Christendom shrank from external attack; and in the European heartland, the *corpus Christianorum* trembled with the chill of an imperfectly diagnosed fever. Innocent's pontificate had witnessed the powerful reassertion of Islam and the sordid degradation of the crusading ideal in the sack of Constantinople. He tried now to promote another holy war in the East against the phalanxes of the infidel. Closer to home, the enemies of the Christian community were not the great beast of the Apocalypse, but the wilier "little foxes" of the Canticle, the heretics who with stealth and cunning spoiled the vineyard of the Church. Standards of clerical education and moral witness were at best uneven, and often notoriously scandalous. Religious men and women thirsted for a truly "apostolic life" and the living fulfillment of the Scriptures; but among those who preached the word were many who sowed cockles among the wheat. In the council's elementary program of "church reform"—directed to the competent teaching of Catholic truth, the preaching of the word, the regular administration of penance, and the visible rectitude of religious life—the bishops sketched the agenda which would become the special province of the mendicant orders. One important chapter in Franciscan literary history is the history of the literary implications of the Lateran constitutions.

Neither the program of clerical erudition which they suggested nor their specifically pastoral motive was new. Indeed they found their classic and authoritative statement in the standard medieval handbook of Christian rhetoric, St. Augustine's *On Christian Doctrine.* There, in a famous passage, Augustine had defended the Christian use of a pagan liberal learning redeemed and appropriated by Christian revelation. The learning of the Gentiles was "Egyptian gold"—those gilt and silver ornaments looted from Pharaoh's people by the Hebrews in the Exodus. This literary "expropriation of the expropriators," as we may wish to think of it, is justified not because of the intrinsic value of the antique treasury of letters, but because of the help it can bring to the study of Scripture. It is this exegetical enterprise which is foremost in Augustine's mind. "Just as certain scholars have interpreted separately all the Hebrew, Syrian, Egyptian, and other foreign names and words that appear in the Holy Scriptures without interpretation, and just as Eusebius has written a history because of questions in the divine books which demand its use, so that it is not necessary for Christians to engage in much labor for a few things, in the same way I think it might be possible, if any capable person could be persuaded to undertake the task for the sake of his brethren, to collect in order and write down singly explanations of whatever unfamiliar geographical locations, animals, herbs and trees, stone and metals are mentioned in the Scripture."[1]

In Augustine's thought, all "theology" was encompassed by the plenary understanding of the Bible; hence it necessarily implied a useful knowledge of humane letters and "natural science" as well. This attitude was a commonplace of the twelfth-century schools, and it was a working assumption of the Lateran delegates in 1215, who in a sense intended through their decrees to make available in the pastoral situation, "for the sake of the brethren" as it were, much of the more useful kind of work being done in the schools. What makes the council's "program" of major literary importance is not its novelty (for it was not novel) but the vigor with which it was frequently carried out by diocesan bishops, the rising tide of authentic religious renewal with which it became associated, and the complex social shifts and movements with which it coincided.

My aim in this chapter will be to describe the kinds of "Lateran literature" which became an important part of the mendicant mission, and particularly that of the Order of Friars Minor and the Order of Preachers, the dove and the raven of thirteenth-century apocalyptic expectations, the two great luminaries newly come into the world to shine the light of truth into the darkest corners of ignorance and error. Theirs was an apostolic mission of word and sacrament, of preaching the kingdom of God and the necessary implication of the kingdom, penance; and the books which they wrote and

[1] *De doctrina christiana,* II, xxxix, 59; *On Christian Doctrine,* trans. D. W. Robertson (New York, 1958), p. 74.

compiled, edited and translated, were the ancillary tools of their offices as preachers and confessors.

The thirteenth century saw a remarkable proliferation of miscellaneous materials, often commissioned or encouraged by local bishops, designed to improve the spiritual efficacy of preaching and the administration of penance, and to make available to as wide an audience as possible the vast spiritual riches of the Bible. These materials included exegetical aids of every kind, dictionaries, encyclopedias, collections of exempla from history and the world of nature, joke books, preachers' cribs, sermon collections, penitential handbooks. Such was the library implied by the Franciscan mission; what might be called the Franciscan method implied as well the appropriation of secular story and song, the creation of a vigorous vernacular hymnody, and the fullest exploitation of the affective and dramatic potential of sacred history.

Though it would be difficult to exaggerate the importance of the Franciscan contributions to this literature, it is not altogether impossible to do so; and we must always remember that what we are witnessing is the efflorescence and enrichment of certain literary traditions, some of them very ancient and all of them lively in the twelfth century, rather than unprecedented inventions. Just as mendicant religion is itself both old and new in the thirteenth century, an institutional reformulation of certain ascetic aspirations as old as the gospel itself, marked by the unique spiritual genius of a remarkable man, so also the literature of the mendicant movement takes its place in the great tradition, both continuous and ever changing, of the broad stream of medieval religious literature. What is new in the "Lateran literature" of the Franciscans is not primarily novelty of literary conception or form, but a new spiritual emphasis, a new style which it encouraged, and a new audience of which it was part creature and part creator.

The apostleship of evangelical preaching was absolutely fundamental to Francis' concept of religious life, a "life according to the holy gospel," and provision for preaching will be found in all the early legislative documents of the Order. Yet what is clear in principle becomes less distinct in practice. What did Francis of Assisi mean by "preaching"? The question has as yet received no authoritative answer, but we do have at least two kinds of useful evidence, the religious context of early Franciscanism and the witness of the primitive *vitae* to Francis' own preaching techniques.

A more or less undifferentiated obligation to preach was a commonplace expectation of the "common life" movements of the eleventh and twelfth centuries, which had responded, as Francis would, with a literal immediacy to Christ's command to "preach, saying, the kingdom of God is at hand" (Mt. 10:7). We shall find abundant evidence of this expectation among reformers and heretics in particular. Unauthorized lay preaching was a common practice among the suspect groups of Lombardy and Provence, and the common apostolate of preaching had been one of the points on which Valdesius ("Peter Waldo"), the founder of the Poor Men of Lyon, had proved intractable. One of the longest and most ponderous of the Lateran constitutions, *Excommunicamus et anathemizamus omnem haeresim,* insisted that any preacher must have the authorization of the Pope or his local bishop before he mounted a pulpit.[2]

[2] The Lateran constitutions are published in the *Conciliorum Oecumenicorum Decreta,* ed. J. Alberigo et al., 3rd ed. (Bologna, 1973), pp. 230ff.

The Church was clearly faced with a practical dilemma, for it had at once to affirm the apostolic nature of the office of preacher and to establish effective controls for its exercise. The establishment of the Order of Preachers, from its very inception an intellectually elite group with strong papal loyalty and backing, gives evidence of these concerns. So does the language about preaching in the Franciscan rules, which is markedly cautious and regulatory. The *regula non bullata* begins a long chapter (17) on preaching thus: "No friar may preach contrary to Church law or without the permission of his minister. The minister, for his part, must be careful not to grant permission indiscriminately. All the friars, however, should preach by their example."[3] The Rule of 1223 is more explicitly aware of the ecclesiological implications which were indeed to be raised by mendicant ministry: "The friars are forbidden to preach in any diocese, if the bishop objects to it. No friar should dare to preach to the people unless he has been examined and approved by the Minister General of the Order and has received from him the commission to preach."[4]

The phrase "to the people" (*populo*) in the Rule of 1223 is revealing, for it clearly suggests a vernacular audience. The essential "newness" of mendicant preaching, like other aspects of mendicant ministry, was its conjunction of religious profession with the pastoral mission to the secular world. The kind of preaching which Francis inferred from the gospels, and which he assumes in his rules, is that of Valdesius rather than that of Guerric of Igny. The friars "should aim only at the advantage and spiritual good of their listeners, telling

[3] *Omnibus,* p. 44.
[4] *Cap.* 10; *Omnibus,* p. 62.

them briefly about vice and virtue, punishment and glory, because our Lord himself kept his words short on earth."[5]

In this injunction we find some suggestion of preaching method, but on the whole the evidence of the rules, though clear enough with regard to the general vocation of Franciscan preaching, is imprecise in terms of its specific content and techniques. Here we must turn to the *vitae,* though even the vignettes we have of Francis as a preacher are in some ways difficult to assess. One of the chief aims of medieval hagiography, not always shared by modern biography, is to record the remarkable rather than the banal. It is extraordinary to preach to a flock of birds, less so to an assembly of farmers. Even so, there is extremely valuable evidence around the edges of the narratives of Thomas of Celano as to Francis' own preaching techniques. It is in the first place notable that Thomas dates the beginning of Francis' religious ministry with his beginning to preach. From the very start his theme was penance, the theme of John the Baptist, and the appropriate theme of the voice crying in the wilderness and the herald of the Great King. "From then on he began to preach penance to all with great fervor of spirit and joy of mind, edifying his hearers with his simple words and his greatness of heart."[6] Primitive Franciscan texts, including the legislation, insist on the rhetorical simplicity of evangelical preaching, probably revealing a contrast with the highly articulate, structured sermon of monastic tradition. What seems to be implied is the absence of mechanical order as well as a limited and familiar range of vocabulary. The contrast clearly does not refer to any blandness in

[5] *Omnibus,* p. 62.
[6] I Celano, I, x, 23; *Omnibus,* p. 247.

the *manner* of delivery, and it was the manner of delivery quite as much as the emphasis upon such specific themes as penance, poverty, and peace which defined the distinctive Franciscan preaching style.

The most explicit contrast between Francis' own preaching and that of contemporary expectation comes in a famous passage in Thomas' second life which deserves to be cited in its fullness. It is the well-known story of the effect of one of Francis' sermons on a physician. "Although the evangelist Francis preached to the unlearned people through visible and simple things, in as much as he knew that virtue is more necessary than words, nevertheless among spiritual men and men of greater capacity he spoke enlivening and profound words. He would suggest in a few words what was beyond expression, and using fervent gestures and nods, he would transport his hearers wholly to heavenly things. He did not make use of the keys of philosophical distinctions; he did not put order to his sermons, for he did not compose them ahead of time. Christ, the true Power and Wisdom, gave to his voice the voice of power. A certain doctor, a learned and eloquent man, once said: 'While I can retain the preaching of others word for word, only the things that St. Francis speaks elude me. If I commit any of them to memory, they do not seem to be the same that dropped from his lips before.' "[7]

All these features of an unorthodox homiletic style Thomas of Celano is disposed to call "simplicity," a term which had already become a kind of code word for the rigorous Franciscans by which they denominated the primitive values of their Order, now threatened, in their view, by growth in power, influence, and intellectuality. A further demonstration of *simplicitas* for Thomas

[7] II Celano, II, lxxiii, 107; *Omnibus*, p. 450.

is the fact that Francis preached to a single person as he did to a mob of thousands and that, presumably unlike other medieval preachers and certainly unlike modern ones, he was quite aware that he sometimes had nothing to say. "Out of the purity of his mind he provided for himself security in preaching a sermon and, without thinking about it beforehand, he spoke wonderful things to all and things not heard before. When he did give some time to meditation before a sermon, he at times forgot what he had meditated upon when the people had come together, and he knew nothing else to say. Without embarrassment he would confess to the people that he had thought of many things but could remember nothing at all of them."[8] The word "security" here also bears a load, for "security" was what was promised by the writers of preachers' cribs and the producers of other mechanical homiletic aids, one of which would bear as its title *Dormi secure*!

Francis' actual sermons are reported by Thomas of Celano only in a reconstructed or summary form; it is nonetheless clear from numerous passages that Francis spoke familiarly, conversationally, but also emotionally and dramatically, and that he used exemplary materials suited to the level of his audience. We may suppose that he frequently used pseudo-scriptural parables of the sort preserved at some length in a unique passage of the *Vita secunda*. There Francis addresses the Pope beneath the light veil of an allegory of the poor woman in the desert, an allegory notable neither for the originality of its metaphoric language nor the coherence of its texture, which would not be out of place in the *Gesta Romanorum*.[9] This, too, would have been a kind of *simplicitas*!

[8] I Celano, I, xxvii, 72; *Omnibus*, p. 289.
[9] II Celano, I, xi, 16-17; *Omnibus*, pp. 376-77.

We must remind ourselves that the *vitae* of Thomas of Celano are works of polished literary artifice, and that the fabric of his narrative, both in terms of its "stories" and its language, is woven from the thread of the Scriptures and of a rich hagiographic tradition. Even narrative clichés, however, can and do express historical truths; and there are two features of Thomas' accounts which are particularly suggestive. The first is the spontaneity of delivery, here held up not merely as an evidence of extraordinary sanctity but as an explicit alternative, in its freedom from the wonted structural constraints of the academic sermon, to the sort of preaching familiar to the "learned and eloquent" physician, or to the learned and eloquent biographer, for that matter. The second is the implication of vigorous bodily movement, the "fervent gestures and nods" which elsewhere excited Thomas to the happy if derivative phrase that Francis "made a tongue of his whole body" when he preached. There are repeated indications that Francis' "fervor" took corporal expression, that his preaching was characterized by a good deal of kinetic energy, rhythmic movement, emphatic gesticulation. When he spoke to the curia "he moved his feet as though he were dancing," and his friend and protector Hugolino was on tenterhooks, fearing that his prelatical colleagues would think Francis a ridiculous buffoon.[10]

Once again it is difficult to define with sufficient accuracy the historical context which would do justice to both the traditional and the novel in Francis' conception of preaching. The vast body of surviving medieval "sermon materials" or "pulpit literature"—circumlocutions which confess the exasperation of criticism before a large body of texts nearly miscellaneous in nature and baf-

[10] I Celano, I, xxvii, 73; *Omnibus*, p. 290.

flingly complex in their interrelationships—is an *embarras de richesse.* While the patient yet exciting work of a long line of distinguished scholars—in particular Lecoy de la Marche in France, G. W. Owst in England, and, most recently, J. B. Schneyer in Germany[11]—has given us some kind of map to what is in effect an unexplored literary continent, it has also taught us to be shy of convenient generalization about "medieval preaching" or "medieval sermons," which actually display astonishing variety. It is accordingly important to make the explicit confession that the aspects of "Franciscan preaching" to be considered in this chapter are highly selective, and approached from an oblique angle. The interests of the literary historian in the preaching of the thirteenth and fourteenth centuries will focus on the vernacular or popular sermon, on its literary qualities and techniques, and upon the kinds of literature from which it derives and to which it is related. Such considerations are of course not entirely outside the purpose of the systematic student of Christian homiletics either, but they are by no means the question which receive his most emphatic attention.[12]

The general term *sermo,* or sermon, is in fact a rather ambiguous one as it was used in the Middle Ages, and it describes a variety of at times distinct literary genres. Before we can assess the importance of Franciscan pulpit literature to the popular culture of late medieval

[11] My discussion depends upon the work of these scholars: A. Lecoy de la Marche, *La Chaire française au moyen age* (Paris, 1886); G. R. Owst, *Preaching in Medieval England* (Cambridge, 1926) and *Literature and Pulpit in Medieval England,* 2nd. ed. (Oxford, 1961); and Johann Baptist Schneyer, *Geschichte der katholischen Predigt* (Freiburg, 1969).

[12] For a full but uneven discussion of Franciscan preaching see Anscar Zwart, "The History of Franciscan Preaching and of Francinscan Preachers (1209-1927): a Bio-Bibliographical Study," *The Franciscan Educational Conference,* IX (1927), pp. 242-587.

Europe, it will be necessary to distinguish between some of the kinds of medieval *sermones* which have, in one form or another, survived. It is important to realize, in the first place, that most early medieval sermons known to the late Middle Ages had either been cast in or had taken on a severely "literary" character, and they implied an actual preacher and congregation only by historical suggestion. Such is the case, for example, with the classical repertory of homiletic texts from the patristic period—particularly the sermons of Augustine, Gregory, Caesarius of Arles, Peter Chrysologus, and a few others—which are the foundations of the sermon literature of the first Christian millennium. They represented a highly respected and influential literary genre, a genre we might call the "closet sermon," still very much in vogue in the twelfth century. It has been a subject of scholarly controversy, for example, whether Bernard's famous *Sermons on the Canticles,* certainly the greatest of the Cistercian homilaries, was ever actually preached at all. Such works of course made a very great cultural impact, but they did so within the context of the literate world of readers and writers. Bernard would be "vernacularized" only by the fraternal poets.

Furthermore, most sermons which actually were preached were confined to a capitular or academic setting which closely circumscribed their audience and strongly influenced their character. The liturgical and exegetical sermons of the Benedictine tradition, or the theological sermons and "collations" such as those of St. Bonaventure, represent different aspects of the religious sermon, or *sermo ad cleros,* the one deeply scriptural, the other speculative and scholastic, but both intended for a learned and professed audience.

None of this should suggest that popular or evangelical preaching was foreign to the patristic and monastic traditions typified, for example, by St. Ambrose or the Carolingian missionaries ("intus monachi, foris apostoli"), who converted large parts of Germany. Peter Damian and Bernard of Clairvaux, both of them the products of a learned and austere spirituality, were nonetheless enormously successful popular preachers. In fact, what the mendicant movement did with preaching, as with other aspects of church ministry, was to channel many of the spiritual resources which had been the near monopoly of the cloistered religious into the secular world of parish life. The questions concerning preaching which occupied the Lateran delegates had been of two sorts. The one, suggested by their concerns with clerical education, had to do with the quality, frequency, and efficacy of ordinary parish preaching. The other, underscored by their concern with authority, pointed to a fear of the popular successes of heretical groups for whom "apostolic" preaching was a major and essential aspect of authentic Christian life. That such preaching found a receptive audience there can be no doubt, but in order to find it and capture it the Church had to launch a broad and effective popular campaign. It is in the greatly increased sense of preaching mission that the "literary" importance of Franciscan sermons is to be found.

For the vast majority of ordinary men and women of the late Middle Ages, public preaching provided the richest and most familiar "literary" experience of their lives. The arts of the pulpit, especially as refined by the mendicants, exposed them to a wide range of verbal and histrionic artifice and invited their vicarious mental and emotional participation in an endlessly varied sacred history. In sermons they found not merely a vivid presentation of the Bible, the fundamental book behind most of the genres of medieval literature, but also a thick mélange of jokes, riddles, popular science and pseudoscience, history, practical technology, and exotic narrative which would have entered their cultural consciousness in no other way. For every person who heard the *Divine Comedy* or the *Romance of the Rose* (and we must bear in mind that by and large medieval "literary" experience was the experience of *hearing* a text read, by oneself or by another) a hundred would have known the excitement of an ambitious metaphor and the conspiratorial pleasure of a biting satire through the medium of a sermon. It is in some ways unfair that Gregory's fine term "biblia pauperum" has been exclusively usurped by the visual representations of sacred history which could allow the illiterate in some measure to read. They were also *read to,* dramatically and with feeling, from that copious anthology of vernacular letters so inadequately summed up as "sermon literature."

Though formal sermons of one kind or another were undoubtedly the chief medium of popular religious instruction, neither the content of medieval preaching nor the context of its delivery was so austerely "religious" as we might be inclined to assume by looking at a few selected homilaries. The work of the friars permanently raised the level of parish preaching by the secular clergy, both in terms of its frequency and in terms of its ambition, over the course of an extended period of time; but its most obvious and immediate impact would be seen in the various kinds of special preaching missions which they undertook. These missions included what were in effect evangelical "revival meetings," the special Lenten preaching of the *Quadragesimale* and, at various times and places throughout Europe, the preaching of Peter's Pence, the advertisement of Crusades and other special enterprises, missions against heretics, harangues against Jews, pilgrimage sermons, and a variety of other undertakings in which the sacred and profane were inextricably mixed. The atmosphere surrounding such events might be festival, lugubrious, or sinister, depending upon the occasion, but it was seldom traditionally ecclesiastical. Often there was a markedly secular, even a circus air about the proceedings, where the preacher of a "hot" gospel competed with the vendors of hot pies for an audience hungry for both. By no means everyone attended such affairs out of an attitude of unmixed devotion. Chaucer's Wife of Bath, hardly a picture of cloistered medieval piety, loved to go to "preching" resplendent in her scarlet hose, "for to se and eek for to be seye of lusty folk." Christ had sent His Apostles *into the world.*

Furthermore, the conventions of the medieval sermon, which accommodated the boredom or disagreement of auditors, put the preacher on his mettle and encouraged him to use his wits and all the aids at his disposal. In the monastic tradition, formal interventions of disagreement were commonplace.[13] The eulogist of the Cistercian abbot, Ailred of Rievaulx, advances as one of the proofs of his sanctity the fact that he suffered even "inappropriate" interruptions of his sermons patiently and charitably. The academic *disputatio* of the scholastic period, in which a reputation could be made or lost in an afternoon's debate, is in some ways simply the logical conclusion of the kind of banter characteristic of the livelier monastic chapters. Laymen—and women—

[13] The following examples come mainly from Lecoy de la Marche, *La Chaire française,* pp. 216 ff.

also upon occasion could feel free to object or simply to kibbitz. St. Louis, that marvelous man, resolved a theological debate excited by a sermon in his presence by sending out for a copy of Augustine's *Commentaries on John,* which testified in favor of the preacher. The Dominican Nicholas of Gorran, author of a widely respected sermon book called the *Fundamentum aureum,* was called down "in the middle of a sermon" by an irate feminist who could not support his accusation that Pilate's wife tried to intervene on Jesus' behalf only because she wanted to frustrate the work of Redemption.

Preachers to the humbler sort were usually, though not always, on safer ground. Franco Sacchetti, the Florentine novelist of the late fourteenth century, tells the story of a friar with academic inclinations who chose the subject of usury as an appropriate one for his Quadragesimale mission to some poor wool workers, one of whom interrupted him and told him to preach on something relevant![14] But there could be other distractions, including sudden shifts in the weather or the appearance of a competing attraction. Dogs and other animals wandered at will around their makeshift pulpits, and more than one unlucky evangelist was drowned out by the bleating of a literal flock or the inattentive chattering of a metaphoric one. Even Francis himself, the preacher to birds, once had to demand silence of a flock of swallows that he might be heard by his human auditors![15]

The context of "popular" preaching was astonishingly varied. In a small parish church in England, on one of the great feast days of the year, a rustic curate with small English and less Latin might deliver a timely and rhe-

[14] *Trecentonovelle,* no. 100; in Franco Sacchetti, *Opere,* ed. Aldo Borlinghi (Milan, 1957), pp. 320-322.

[15] I Celano, I, xxi, 59; *Omnibus,* pp. 278-79.

torically respectable sermon from a handbook like the *Festial* of John Mirk (one of the books which would be printed by Caxton). In a great piazza in a central Italian town a friar might lead a vast throng of thousands of people, most of them weeping profusely, in the solemn recitation of simple penitential prayers. In crusade rallies, litanies against the plague, or in "preaching Christ crucified" from the uncovered pulpit of a market cross —as well, of course, as in the more commonplace "postils" and "divisions" of a Sunday sermon—preachers found the opportunity to display, and congregations the opportunity to be moved by, what was in effect the spectacle and technique of dramatic experience. "For centuries," writes G. R. Owst of Chaucer's England, "the sacred episodes had been declaimed with a freedom and dramatic intensity unknown to mere liturgical recitation." He is speaking specifically of the dramatic presentation of scriptural materials in sermons which, long before the composition of any of our known Corpus Christi cycles, "had already set forth in true and satisfying combination the colloquial, the proverbial, the jovial, and the religious."[16]

The ambition and degree of this "pulpit" drama of course varied considerably. Francis himself could move his hearers to inexpressible religious experience with "fervent gestures and nods." Two hundred years later St. Bernardino, not usually given to frivolous behavior, was preaching the gospel of Christ, *povero e crocifisso,* with "the keys of philosophical distinctions" moderated by jokes, the raucous imitations of birds and animals, stage voices, and catchy songs. We can only imagine the dramatic excitement of the major German missions of

[16] Owst, *Literature and Pulpit,* pp. 473-74.

Berthold of Regensburg.[17] So vast were his audiences, according to Salimbene, that he preached from a curious kind of portable tower, festooned with bright pennants which, as they flapped in the wind, showed his eager audience their best position to hear him. Early Franciscan history records many episodes, some miraculous and some merely extraordinary, which testify to the thick emotional atmosphere surrounding the friars' scaffolds.

We shall consider some evidence of formal connections between Franciscan preaching and the miracle plays when we come to speak of the drama. Less ambitious than a full-scale play or even a brief dramatic tableau was the homiletic use of pictures and other "props." In the mission of the "Twelve Apostles" to Mexico in the early sixteenth century, large "Bible pictures" were very widely used, and only in part as a response to problems of language. Our evidence for medieval Europe is unfortunately fragmentary, but there are many suggestions of the homiletic exploitation of visual art. Owst has excerpted from the sermon books of England a wealth of information showing the preachers' defense of the utility of images. Preachers often held up crosses or crucifixes in the pulpit, and in the Lenten missions displayed material emblems of the Passion. They probably also exploited the mural and window decorations of the churches in which they preached, which, as we know from the friars' critics, were often regarded by some as excessively elaborate and ornate. One English poem satirizing the Franciscans, dated 1382, taxes the friars with lying about St. Francis and scoffing at God "When thai hangen him on hegh on a grene tre,

[17] *Berthold von Regensburg: Vollständige Ausgabe seiner Predigten,* ed. F. Pfeiffer, 2 vols. (Vienna, 1862-1880).

with leues & with blossemes that bright are of ble."[18] What is being described is of course a painting of the *Lignum Vitae,* that picture of the fruits of Christ's sacrifice which St Bonaventure asks the contemplative reader to picture in his mind's eye and which Francesco da Volaterra or Taddeo Gaddi actually painted in the refectory of Santa Croce in Florence. The poem catalogues other specifically Franciscan icons with sufficient clarity to allow us to identify them with confidence. They must once have decorated the walls of some forgotten English church, where they may have provided a visual text for a friar's sermon.

The elements of drama, spectacle, and vicarious emotional life which popular preaching could bring to its audience were not secular encroachments on the sacred office of the pulpit but parts of the broad religious strategy, widely subscribed to by the Franciscans, of "indigenizing," of adapting the form of the evangelical message to its most appropriate cultural expression for a specific audience. As we shall see, it was this attitude above all which accounts for the complex Franciscan involvement with vernacular poetry, with song, and with the mystery plays. The strategy in fact has clear patristic precedent; Cardinal Newman took it to be one of the most important factors in the triumph of Christianity in the antique world.

There were of course many famous preachers among the fathers of the Church, but the great patristic homiletic theoretician (if we may use that word) was Gregory the Great. In his *Cura pastoralis* he had distinguished between no less than thirty-six special "cases" which demanded of the preacher versatility, flexibility, and a

[18] *Historical Poems of the XIVth and XVth Centuries,* ed. Rossell Hope Robbins (New York, 1959), p. 163.

careful knowledge of his audience. It is not the same to preach to men as to women, to the rich as to the poor, to the young as to the old. The spiritual medicine applied for sins of carnal excess is different from that prescribed for cases of avarice or envy. The office of the preacher, therefore, required far more than rhetorical skill and a training in dogmatics. It required as well great sagacity, vigor, power, and courage. In another famous book, the *Moralia in Job,* Gregory had extolled the preacher's office with a metaphoric vocabulary which, however bizarre it may seem in modern ears, captured the permanent respect of the Middle Ages in its suggestions of the preacher's force and animal energy. Preachers are teeth; they are also horses. The weathervanes on old country churches may remind us that, for Gregory, preachers were cocks. That they were dogs explains the wit behind the Dominican pun, *Domini canes.*

The apostolic office brought with it the apostolic injunction to "be all things to all men," and much of the literary richness which surrounds the medieval Franciscan pulpit can be explained in terms of a desire to identify and accommodate the tastes and expectations of different kinds of audience. The learned English "humanist" friars of whom Beryl Smalley has written sought one audience; the friars in charge of the noviciate in Palma of Mallorca, who composed and acted out a sermon-play about the life of the founder and the duties of a brother, sought a different. But both sought to speak, in appropriate and effective ways, of virtue and vice, heaven and hell.

In the earliest history of the order there is some evidence of an unacknowledged conflict between two desired ends: simplicity and spontaneity of preaching on the one hand, and efficacy on the other. Francis, the imitator of Jesus Christ, sent his apostles into the world as lambs among wolves, and the initial missionary ventures had a tragi-comic dimension. The naiveté with which the first generation of friars looked for the collapse of Islam before the face of an apostolic preaching in Occidental tongues, a recurrent motif in Francis' own biography, may seem to us remarkable. Certainly it seemed so to Jordan of Giano, the earliest historian of the Franciscan movement, who reports, not entirely without a grim humor, the shipwreck of the apostolic vessel against the sharp rocks of Babel in 1219. Five friars were butchered in Morocco (called Spain by Jordan). In Hungary, shepherds set their dogs on the uncomprehending missionaries, and beat them until they surrendered their meager clothing, down to and including their underwear. The history of the first German mission could have come from a medieval jest book. Giovanni da Penna and some sixty other Italian friars, "perhaps even more," moved across the snowy Alps knowing only a single syllable of German, *Ja*. This served them well enough so long as they were asked whether they would like something to eat and somewhere to spend the night, but it proved disastrous when they were asked whether they were the Lombard heretics of whom one had been hearing so much!

These are precious memories in the history of Franciscanism, but they probably teach us more about the emblematic imagination of Francis and his immediate circle than they do about Franciscan preaching. The preparations for subsequent missions were more careful. When Julian of Spire preached to the Germans in his mother tongue, people listened. When Conrad of Saxony and Berthold of Regensburg preached, they listened by the thousand. And if Islam in fact never collapsed, it was not because the friars of Spain and the eastern missions were ignorant of the languages and religious traditions of that great force which curved around the bottom of European Christendom like a crescent.

I have already alluded to the Mexican mission of the sixteenth century. That enterprise, though removed from our immediate purposes by some two and a half centuries and some thousands of miles, may strangely enough give us some of our most valuable evidence about those Franciscan attitudes of "indigenization" which interest us.[19] The evangelization of New Spain was, by special papal commission, given over to the holy Friars of the Observance, twelve of whom (in literal imitation of the gospels) arrived in the New World in 1524, just three centuries after, though in a world now much larger, the first friars had crossed the Channel to England. The evangelization of New Spain, so redolent of the spiritual atmosphere of primal Franciscanism, has left behind a vast body of documentation of the sort that is simply lacking for the Middle Ages. Although conditions were vastly different from those in the Old World, the friars instinctively turned to their tested repertory of spiritual techniques and materials. The first Mexican catechism, the *Doctrina cristiana breve* of Alonso de Molina, could as well have been written for peasants in the Aquitaine in the thirteenth century as for Indians in the Valley of Mexico in the sixteenth.

Indigenization did not mean, of course, toleration of the practices, temples, or "idols" of the antique religion, and a strong faction among the missionaries was particularly zealous in the destruction of these visible monuments of native religion. But there was another side to

[19] Robert Ricard, *La "Conquête spirituelle" du Méxique* (Paris, 1933), pp. 55ff.

the enterprise, reflected in the remarkable work of Bernardino de Sahagún, which sought to find the key to successful evangelization in the closest possible knowledge of indigenous culture. Bernardino's *Historia general de las cosas de Nueva-España* is one of the signal monuments of early ethnography, based as it is on years of patient inquiry into the language, society, religion, mythology, and customs of the Indians among whom he worked. Fray Bernardino would probably be shocked to know that his life's work is now prized as a unique encyclopedia of pre-Columbian anthropology. For him, it was the *materia medica* for the physicians who set out to cure the spiritual pest of the ancient gods.

For the purposes of this book our interests focus on the medicine rather than the disease. What was the "basic Christian doctrine" which Franciscans like Alonso de Molina set out to expose in their preaching? Here we have an enormous amount of evidence, both in the theoretical pronouncements of bishops and chapter meetings and in the dozens of medieval books of elementary religious instruction which have survived, particularly from the fourteenth and fifteenth centuries. We may wish to look first at the simplest level of all, in works designed for children, and in fact the first known series of catechetical sermons for children would indeed seem to have been that of a Franciscan, Markward of Lindau, a Bavarian provincial of the late fourteenth century. This is, however, already a late date, and we have much earlier and much more interesting evidence—though admittedly not in sermon form—in the *Doctrina pueril,* one of the early works of the Catalan genius Ramon Lull.[20]

[20] *Doctrina pueril,* ed. M. Obrador, in *Obras de Ramon Lull,* I, pp. 1-199 (Palnia, 1905); the medieval French version, *Doctrine d'Enfant,* ed. A. Llinarès (Paris, 1969).

Written about 1280, this work enjoyed a vernacular circulation both in its original form and in a contemporary French translation. As its title suggests, it aims to provide the basic materials necessary for the education of a child. It would be a mistake to ask whether these are or are not "religious." Given Lull's life-long preoccupations with the problems of effective missionary apologetics, popular mysticism, and encyclopedic science, it is hardly surprising that the *Doctrina pueril* includes in its simple but unifying vision elements of the social and the dogmatic, the pedagogic, and the homiletic. The book actually was used, certainly in fiction and probably in fact, as a catechism for the young. The hero of Lull's famous "novel" *Blanquerna* is, at the age of eight, put to work on it by his father in order to learn the articles of faith, the two commandments of the New Law, the seven sacraments of the Church, the capital virtues and vices, "and the other things which the book contains." The "other things" are by no means without interest. They include the major feasts of the church year, the names of the disciplines of the *trivium* and the *quadrivium,* the orders of society, and the eschatological realities of heaven and hell, described, within the confines of an intentionally simple prose style, in a fashion which would not have embarrassed Dante Alighieri.

This kind of "literary" catechism was of course not a Franciscan invention, and Lull's *Doctrina* takes its place in a venerable tradition best represented in twelfth-century France by the *Elucidarium* and its vernacular reworkings in its own and subsequent centuries, in poetic progeny like the *Poeme Morale* and the pilgrimage allegories of Guillaume de Deguilleville. In its more severely ecclesiastical moods the impulse turned not to poetry but to the formal didacticism of the handbooks on the virtues and the vices, the Ten Commandments, the gifts of the Holy Spirit, the seven sacraments, and so forth, which account for so many of the "best sellers" of the incunabula period. Their shared characteristic is an emphasis on *moral* instruction, usually viewed from an openly practical point of view. They are nowhere truer to their Franciscan relationships, whether they be of adoption or of generation, than in their focus on "vice and virtue, punishment and glory."

The literary history of the catechism, if it were ever to be written, would doubtless provide us with answers to some of our most persistent questions relating to the emergence of a truly vernacular European culture in the late Middle Ages. Its doctrinal topics, mechanically displayed as they are in their mnemonic families of threes and fours and sevens and tens, determined the psychological clichés to which poets and painters turned no less habitually than preachers and confessors when they sought to speak of the complexities of human moral behavior. What such a history could not give us would be a complete picture of all "sermon literature," which reflects a program of clerical study far broader than the specifically doctrinal.

Around the middle of the thirteenth century the Dominican Humbert of Romans, himself a famous preacher, compiled for his brethren a book called *De eruditione praedicatoris.* The scope of the book is rather larger than its title might suggest for it is concerned with the whole spiritual formation of the preacher. Humbert does, however, enumerate nearly a dozen specific "sciences" which the preacher must master. A number of these involve matters of tact and judgment, of when and how to preach, and what approach to take with what audience, but several of the others constitute a kind of academic syllabus for a preacher's *studium*. A preacher must first have a knowledge of the Scriptures, since all preaching should expound Scripture. Secondly, he must have a knowledge of creatures. "God has shown forth his wisdom in all his works, which is why Blessed Anthony says that creatures are a book." He must have a knowledge of exemplary stories (*scientia historiarum*). "There are many stories, not only among the faithful but also among the unfaithful, which are very useful for the purpose of edification in preaching."[21]

I think that we shall not too greatly misrepresent matters if we see in this "syllabus" for preachers a major program of mendicant letters, shared with varying emphases and local variation by Dominicans and Franciscans alike. It was a program which encouraged the enormous output, throughout the thirteenth century and into the fourteenth, of Bible "aids" of various kinds, of collections of *exempla* and simple "stories," and of encyclopedias of science. These genres were seldom totally distinct, and one writer borrowed or added to the work of another with a frequency which has encouraged scholars to write of their books as though they were not literature at all but large and uninviting balls of twine, sources, and influence. Yet, though strong men blench before this vast forest of doggerel and old wives' tales, we shall find in its secret, shadowed paths the major highways of the popular literary culture of pre-modern Europe.

The aims of scriptural study in the Middle Ages had been established long before the friars began their work, and we shall seriously misunderstand their contribution if we confuse a certain originality of mendicant emphasis and style with a novelty in substance. Those aims were

[21] *Opera de vita regulari*, ed. J. J. Berthier (Turin, 1956), II, pp. 373 ff.

primarily practical, designed to uncover, unlock, open, reveal, disclose—such is the typical language of the exegetes themselves—a hidden "spiritual" sense of the Scriptures which lay beneath the surface of its "letter." This spiritual meaning, though conventionally categorized in terms of several "levels" of significance by the thirteenth century, was in the vast majority of actual exegetical situations a moral meaning. The techniques and tools which exegetes used in exposing this moral meaning, or "tropological sense" as it was sometimes technically called, were of course not those of modern scriptural criticism, though they were at times related to them. They were instead those useful sciences proposed by Augustine in *De doctrina christiana,* enabled by what was throughout the Middle Ages perhaps the most indispensable tool of all, a memory trained to capacities far beyond those with which most of us are familiar today.

In fact, medieval preachers and writers habitually cite the Scriptures, and often other texts as well, from memory. The first serious concordance to the Latin Bible was not even undertaken until the thirteenth century; it should not surprise us that it was then the work of a friar, Hugh of St.-Cher, O.P., working with a committee of five hundred of his brethren. Hugh's concordance—as also his own extensive serial commentary on the sacred text—reflects a common interest among thirteenth-century exegetes to make complete and synoptic catalogues which bring together, in modern and convenient form, the best work of the fathers, the Carolingian masters, and the schoolmen of the twelfth century. In doing so, of course, they often made substantial contributions of their own, frequently ones which reflected a quite personal sense of evangelical mission.

Such is the case, for example, with Nicholas of Lyra, the Norman friar who must surely be the most famous of all the many medieval Franciscan exegetes.[22] His copious *Postillae perpetuae in universa Biblia,* written in the 1320's, enjoyed the widest possible circulation; and the "doctor de Lyra" is one of the indispensable authorities for theological debate, on all sides, in the two centuries between the Black Death and the death of Luther. "Si Lyra non lyrasset," goes the old verse, "totus mundus delirasset"; but it would be difficult to say whether he has been more cruelly served by his detractors or his admirers. He has often been credited with a new and even revolutionary attitude to the text of Scripture, which rejected as speculative and unfruitful an allegorical grappling with the spiritual senses and concentrated instead on an empirical historical and philological study of the letter.

The grounds for this misapprehension, demolished by Henri de Lubac, would seem to be in part Nicholas' derision of fanciful interpretations without a warrant in the literal text, and in part his insistence on serious philological preparation for the Christian exegete.[23] Both of these attitudes are, however, anything but new in the fourteenth century, and they clearly reflect both the precept and the practice of Augustine, Jerome, Gregory, and other famous doctors. The insistence is, to be sure, "Franciscan." Francis' *dictum* that the burden of preaching be simple and moral—that is, practical—reflects it; so does the statement of Diego de Estella in his *Modus Concionandi* (sixteenth century) that the preacher of idle allegories would better spend his money on *Amadis de Gaula* than on Augustine!

[22] See "Nicolas de Lyre, frère mineur," in *HLF,* xxvi (1927), pp. 355-400.
[23] Henri de Lubac, *Exégèse médiévale* (Paris, 1961), II, ii, pp. 344-367.

Serious philology, too, had an ancient pedigree in Christian exegesis. Jerome, the midwife of the Vulgate itself, had been a serious student of languages. Certainly it was by no means usual in the fourteenth century for a Christian scholar to know Hebrew, as Nicholas did, but Nicholas belonged to a "party" within his order which was strongly touched by some of the ideas of Joachim of Fiore, particularly those concerning the conversion of the Jews.

The general idea of the concordance or spiritual collation of various parts of the Bible, made famous by Joachim's book on the *Concordance of the Old and New Testaments,* was one which had captured the imagination of Nicholas of Lyra. It is also a controlling motif in the work of that model of all Franciscan "doctors," St. Anthony of Padua.[24] St. Anthony of Padua actually came from Lisbon, where he was far advanced in the spiritual progress of the Augustinian common life when the bones of the Franciscan martyrs from Morocco were translated to Portugal. The life of plenary apostleship represented by these relics thrilled him with its promise and its dangers; and he eagerly traded his white scapular for the drab tunic of the brothers. He had a scant decade left before an early death robbed the Order of its second great saint, and the uncertain charcoal sketch of his biography was overwhelmed with the confident, panchromatic tempera of legend.

That Anthony was a remarkable preacher there can be no doubt. Gregory IX, flabbergasted by his eloquence, called him the "ark of the Covenant"; and Francis appointed him the first university lector from the Order. This testimony, however, speaks to his learning; all the

[24] Recent critical bibliography in Jacques Toussaert, *Antonius von Padua: Versuch einer kritischen Biographie* (Cologne, 1967), pp. 96ff.

early biographies agree that he had great popular success as well, with throngs running into the thousands, with heretics, and with the fish in the waterways of Rimini. We can only guess at the range of style and content of Anthony's popular sermons, but from what evidence we have it appears likely that he commanded a whole repertory of styles and that he freely included in his sermons elements of the ludicrous and the oblique.

That evidence is largely made up of the surviving sketchbook of liturgical sermons—he actually called them *Concordances*—which, though learned and Latin, probably reveal his most consistent mental habits. The "concordance" was a homiletic essay which sought to link together the liturgical "propers" for a given Sunday according to common themes arrived at through rapid allegories and etymologies. For example, the sermon for the Fourth Sunday in Lent links the epistle text from Galatians 4 (the allegory of Abraham, Sarah, and Hagar) with the gospel pericope from John 6 (the story of the feeding of the five thousand). The passages are coaxed, through the processes of "concordance," to yield a unified spiritual meaning. The five loaves are the Pentateuch, the two fishes intelligence and memory, the two condiments needed to relish the scriptural feast. But they are also Moses and Peter, respective heads of Synagogue and Church; the Synagogue and Church, in turn, are signified by Sarah and Hagar.[25]

Such exegesis, which is always trivialized in summary, required more than quick wit and an inventive imagination. It demanded a profound and detailed knowledge of the sacred text itself, and of its internal resonances and rhythms, themes and counterpoints. Furthermore, the

[25] *Les Sermons de St. Antoine de Padoue pour l'année liturgique,* trans. Paul Bayart (Paris, 1944), pp. 110-114.

exegete must have a thorough command of a tradition of interpretation, which in the case of the lectionary readings was often particularly copious. Some etymology is called for, and also the gift of the literary critic to see deep similarities in texts which are superficially quite unlike each other. The name Moses means "pulled from the water." To know that much required no rabbinic study greater than the memory of the second chapter of Exodus. But Peter too was both fisher and fish, pulled from the water by Christ both figuratively and literally (Mat. 14:31).

Above all, the preacher-exegete must have the clarity of vision to tie together the various strands of spiritual meaning into one firm knot of moral purpose. Neither here nor elsewhere does Anthony leave his hearers puzzled over an abstruse allegory; he points the allegory toward a useful "tropological" meaning. In this case it involves the proper hierarchy of the reason and the passions, one of the favorite topics of medieval psychologists.

This final exegetical skill, that of spiritual tact and imagination, was not one which the handbooks could hope to teach. What they could and did provide the preacher was a reference library of the raw materials of his art, in lists, charts, catalogues, dictionaries, "picture" books, running commentaries—the lumber and raw plaster out of which he must fashion an edifice of exegetical argument. The sheer variety of such aids is astonishing, and their quality, on balance, surprisingly high. They range from argumentative scholastic commentaries on the Apocalypse to the Anglo-Norman Holkham Bible in word and image; and from Jacob van Maerlant's *Rijmbibel* to the famous commentary on the Book of Wisdom by Robert Holkot, O.P. In the most general possible terms, these works were intended to provide preachers with exemplary materials for their sermons, with handy catalogues of specific "instances" in which the moral truth of a scriptural text could be brought home to the preacher's congregation.

The extent to which a preacher should go beyond the text of the Bible itself for such moral emblems was a matter of controversy. We have already adduced the testimony of Humbert of Romans to the effect that even the stories of the infidel were charged with a high moral purpose for the Christian preacher. Indeed the extent to which preachers were likely to turn elsewhere than the Bible is suggested obliquely in another sermon of St. Anthony in which he says that scriptural preaching, not "sweet fables," is what reaches the ears of God. The contrast certainly must imply some real experience, perhaps with someone like Friar Hugh Paucapalea ("Smallstraw"), whose forensic triumphs Salimbene of Adam applauded with enthusiasm. Friar Hugh confounded the self-styled astrologer Guido of Furlivio, a vocal opponent of the friars, in a disputation full of "proverbs, fables, and examples . . . all of which he reduced to a moral meaning."[26]

One man's meat is another man's poison. What Salimbene praises is sharply condemned by the fourteenth-century English satire, *Pierce the Ploughmans Crede.* The author, possibly a Lollard but more likely simply a secular opponent of the mendicants, accuses the friars, among other crimes, of dazzling the people with "jests of Rome." This is a specific accusation, for he means the book called *Gesta Romanorum,* a famous collection of little narratives and their moral "reductions," probably put together by friars and, as their critic rightly maintained, certainly used by them in their preaching.

[26] Salimbene de Adam, *Cronica,* ed. Giuseppe Scalia (Bari, 1966), I, p. 239.

That book, though particularly famous, is merely one of dozens and perhaps hundreds of surviving books of *exempla* materials intended for the use of preachers; and *exempla* anthologies, after the Bible "helps" themselves, form a second major genre of "sermon literature." Thanks to the classic work of J. T. Welter half a century ago, we are in a position to speak with some confidence about these books.[27] Welter has shown that, though the homiletic *exemplum* is an ancient form, its common use became current only in the revival of preaching in the twelfth century. The publication of the *exempla* books themselves is a phenomenon of the thirteenth and fourteenth centuries, and it is in general closely connected with the mendicant missions. Probably the most famous preachers' exemplaries, if we may invent a term, are those of Etienne de Bourbon and the Englishman John Bromyard, author of the celebrated *Summa Predicantium,* but the specifically Franciscan contributions are probably more numerous.

An *exemplum* was a narrative vignette, fact or fiction, or a scientific *datum,* real or imagined, capable of and to a greater or lesser degree actually suited for, moral application. Very few of the oblique strategies of the pulpit can escape this definition. The Bible itself, particularly in the parables of our Lord, is replete with fully "medieval" exempla. The good Samaritan, the "Prodigal Son," the pearl of great price, the house built on a sand foundation—such are the very models for what might be called the "historiated" *exemplum.* But an *exemplum* might also be enshrined in a pithy saying, solemn or risible. "A man can cut himself with his own knife," says Chaucer's good parson, "and he can

[27] J. T. Welter, *L'Exemplum dans la littérature religieuse et didactique du Moyen Age* (Paris, 1927).

commit a sin with his own wife." Or the preacher might find a moral emblem in observations drawn from nature. "A dog returns to its own vomit."

The range of literary texts to which medieval moralists could turn was nearly as large as the history of antique literature itself, and a writer's chief limitations were those of learning and the availability of texts. The use of sacred history for the exemplary demonstration of moral truth, particularly by a Christian Church profoundly self-conscious of its relationship to the "old Israel" and convinced of its own unique historical meaning, was implied by the very nature of the Scriptures themselves. From the most ancient time Christian literature, following the mode of the sacred text, uses the "stories" of the Bible for exemplary moral purposes. Yet the profane historians of Antiquity, too, by and large shared a moral vision of their enterprise which sought to find in the notable deeds of men of the past admonition and encouragement for those of the present. Such an attitude is, for example, inescapable in the Roman history of Livy, and it helped to make that work one of the indispensable volumes in the library of medieval humanism. The patristic age created its own epitome of ancient history, particularly in Augustine's magisterial *City of God,* a work which would prove endlessly fascinating to medieval readers and which became the richest mine from which the friar humanists of the fourteenth century dug and chiselled the gleaming ore for their sermons and manuals.

The observed or invented world of natural science, and particularly the habits and qualities, real or imagined, of birds and animals were another treasure house of *exempla,* and the lessons of the bestiary had a natural and appropriate authority in an agricultural world in which animals were the familiar and omnipresent extensions of human community. The ancient *Physiologus,* source of the medieval bestiary tradition, had been used extensively if somewhat cautiously as an exegetical tool by the fathers of the Church, and its animal allegories had become permanently imbedded in the Visigothic and Carolingian encyclopedias which were standard reference works of the pre-vernacular period. In the Middle Ages they were true commonplaces, and some of them are still current with Shakespeare and Donne. In the thirteenth and fourteenth centuries, bestiary *exempla* found a wide diffusion both in prose and poetry, and often in forms which involved considerable literary sophistication, wit, and learning. The Italian *Moralized Bestiary* from Gubbio, in the Franciscan heartland, is in effect a sonnet sequence celebrating exotic beasts and their mythic moral properties. The poem on the beaver, for example, is built around a slightly ribald Romance pun, *castor/castrator.* The beaver, when pursued by a hunter, severs his sinful members to make escape lighter and quicker. The hunter is the devil, the beaver mankind, the moral ascetic.[28]

I have already mentioned the *Gesta Romanorum,* which is usually but not quite fairly taken as the representative of "popular" exemplary literature. The summary form in which the stories have been written down, and the iron apparatus of moral reduction in which they are encased, too often gives them a confused and mechanical tone which would almost certainly disappear with their presentation by a skilful preacher. Most of them concern Roman "emperors"—usually, but not always, figures for God—in various episodes of real or contrived history. It is by no means easy to point to exem-

[28] *Poeti del Duecento,* ed. G. Contini (Milan, 1960), II, p. 316.

plary *exempla,* but one of the stories concerning the emperor "Polemius" (or Polenius) has a number of the distinctive features of the collection: exotic possibility, incomprehensible motivation, a vivid moral point, and a touch of the grand guignol.[29] Polemius was married to a Spanish princess, who gave birth to three sons. One day when the boys were well grown the wife told Polemius that he was the father of only one of them, but she would not tell him which one. On his deathbed, Polemius called the three to his side and showed them a precious ring which, he said, was his legacy to his legitimate son. Then he died. In order to avoid unseemly quarrels, the youngest son proposed that the matter of adjudication be taken to a certain "wise king" in the vicinity. This king's judgment was as follows: "You must take your father's corpse from the grave and tie it to a tree. Then each of you will shoot an arrow into his heart. He whose arrow sinks deepest shall have the ring." The first man shot, and the second shot deeper; but the third refused to participate in such a sacrilege "for all the goods in the world." It was he, of course, who was judged the true son, and it was he who won the precious ring. The emperor is God, the wise king Holy Church. The three sons are, respectively, the Jews and the Saracens, the false Christians, who are worse than either by far, and finally the "true Christians." The ring is heaven.

Not all the *exempla* books are collections of fully developed stories. Some of them reveal a bibliographic habit of mind which refers the reader to other works wherein "blessed Augustine has a wonderful example of pride," or where there is another story, and one *valde pulcher,* concerning Turpin, Archbishop of Reims. Others still have something of the character of a journal or

[29] *Gesta Romanorum,* ed. H. Oesterley (Berlin, 1872).

informal diary, a commonplace- or scrapbook in which some prudent preacher has squirrelled away his pile of pulpit acorns against the winter. Some of these characteristics are evident in the *Tabula exemplorum secundum ordinem alphabeti,* compiled by a Franciscan in France in the thirteenth century and published by Welter in his "Thesaurus Exemplorum" series.[30]

The *Tabula* is in effect a catalogue of moral metaphors and story "ideas," sometimes developed into finished vignettes but more often than not left in the form of raw material; as its title would suggest, these nuggets of pulpit wisdom are distributed alphabetically among key-word topics, some hundred and fifty in all, ranging from *accidia* to *Xristus*—an orthographic eccentricity which helps give fullness to the alphabetical scheme. The compiler of the *Tabula* has a lively sense of the apt simile in both its brief and its extended forms, and also a winning, whimsical wit. In order to make green wood burn, one must place it on the blazing flame of a dry old log. Just so the devil, when he sets out to ignite youthful fornication, uses the incendiary help of a creased and withered *vetula*: an observation which our friar's contemporary, Jean de Meun, was making in a different way. Readers of Shakespeare ("What's in a name? A rose by any other name would smell as sweet . . .") might be disconcerted by another story in the collection, much more in the spirit of Oscar Wilde. "*Item*; remember the story of the beautiful daughter of the blacksmith, whom many barons and nobles wanted to marry because of her beauty, but when they asked her name lost interest, because it was a low-class name. So her father changed her name and called her Rosa, and immediately a great

[30] *La Tabula exemplorum secundum ordinem alphabeti,* ed. J. T. Welter (Paris, 1926).

man married her." He has a good little joke about St. Bernard, faced with the difficult social situation of his father's late retirement to a monastery. What must Bernard now call his father? Not *pater,* since such was not the custom of the order. But certainly not *frater* since he was in fact "pater." So he said, "Musart, musart, tu viens trop tart!"

Many of the *exempla* collections are of course the work of the apparently indefatigable medieval "anonymous hand," but we do know at least one Franciscan fabulist, through his work rather than through the specific help of an external biography, well enough to get some sense of his literary temperament. Nicholas Bozon was an English friar whose literary career belongs to the generation immediately preceding the Black Death.[31] He may have had connections with the famous family of Bohun (Boone) which played an important role in the aristocratic life of England in the later Middle Ages and which had some connections with Geoffrey Chaucer. His work has received less attention than is its due partly for the accidental reason that he wrote in Anglo-Norman, a language in declining fortunes even in his day and one which was destined to be regarded by several of the editors of the *Histoire littéraire de la France* as though it were a perverse and demeaning parody of French. In fact, his literary career is of unusual interest, though it could probably best be studied in that context of mendicant humanism evoked for us by Beryl Smalley rather than in one of philological curiosity.[32]

Nicholas was an uneven, but ambitious, poet, and he shows an explicit awareness of the "secular" poetic tra-

[31] See "Nicole Bozon, frère mineur," in *HLF,* xxxvi (1927), pp. 44-424.
[32] B. Smalley, *English Friars and Antiquity in the Early Fourteenth Century* (New York, 1960).

dition in French which includes the *lais* of Marie de France and the *Roman de la Rose.* His considerable poetic *oeuvre* has not yet been brought together, but it includes pieces of varying originality and skill. There are saints' lives, versified "sermons," poetic *exempla,* several difficult and important spiritual allegories, a fine collection of *proverbes de bon enseignement,* and some conventional but sprightly *débats.*

His poetry had some popular success. Some of his works are to be found in multiple manuscripts, and at least part of his book of *proverbes* was translated into Middle English.[33] But his slender fame today rests upon his collection of preachers' *exempla* which he apparently called the *Tabula metaphorarum* and which his modern editors have helpfully renamed the *Contes Moralisés.*[34] The 145 "moralized stories" in the collection come mainly, though not exclusively, from the observed world of natural science. In a very brief prologue Nicholas says that the reader will find in his little book "many beautiful *exempla* of different kinds through which he may learn to avoid sin and embrace virtue"; and he goes on to paraphrase a text from Job (12:7-8) which was a favorite of the bestiary encyclopedists. "But ask now the beasts, and they shall teach thee; and the birds of the air, and they shall tell thee. Speak to the earth, and it shall answer thee: and the fishes of the sea shall tell."

Examined in their catalogue forms, the actual moral lessons of geology and zoology are predictably miscellaneous and often enough banal and contrived. Yet that is to miss the literary possibilities of the *exemplum,* which was not a sermon in itself but rather a decorative

[33] *Les Proverbes de bon enseignement de Nicole Bozon,* ed. A. C. Thorn, *Lunds Universitets Arsskrift,* XVII, 4 (1921).

[34] *Les Contes moralisés de Nicole Bozon, frère mineur,* ed. L. Toulmin Smith and Paul Meyer (Paris, 1889).

detail which could be used with greater or less good sense and aesthetic tact in the construction of a whole moral argument. The first *exemplum,* from Isidore of Seville, is that of the magnet stone. The magnet stone can have two meanings, one bad and one good. Readings *in bono* and *in malo,* typical of the Augustinian exegetical tradition, are common enough in the *exempla* collections as well. In an evil sense the magnet's force is like the attractive power of Adam's sin; in a good sense it is like the power of Christ which attracts men to salvation. However "naive" we are disposed to judge such similes, they clearly had more practical utility for an untrained audience than did refined concepts of the *primus motus concupiscentiae* or "cooperative grace." The elephant, who scrunches up his ears against annoying "noseeums" (clearly the best translation for *wibetz*) is an example of the wise man who blocks from his ears the rumor of gossip and ill report. The crow and the fox are great friends and colleagues, says Nicholas, who had not had the opportunity to read La Fontaine. Their friendship typifies the collusion of sinners. Nicholas' stories sometimes have a social point. The sheep and the goat, he says, graze in different manners; the sheep *"en reposant"* and the goat *"ens passant."* The latter typifies the rapacious rich, who wander about devouring the poor.

Medieval *exempla* collections vary considerably in nature, ambition, imagination, and literary sophistication. The genre has its masterpieces, such as the *Speculum Laicorum* and the "anecdotes" of Etienne de Bourbon, but also its dross. The controlling factors, as with any other piece of written work, include the capacities and aims of the author and specific didactic purposes of the collection. It is nonetheless possible to make certain generalizations about the contents of *exempla* books, especially in terms of their diffusion of popular religious narratives. They call upon a wide range of learning and lore, from popular saws to learned vignettes from the fathers, and it is hardly adequate to dismiss them as one scholar would, as "anthologies of folk receipts and old wives' tales."

In fact their most remarkable feature may well be that their origins are far from "popular" in any obvious sense. They are on the contrary narrowly clerical. Their single most important inspiration is the literature of antique eremitism, the *Vitae Patrum,* the "paradise of the Fathers," and the letters of Jerome. In their pages flagpole saints and thaumaturgical abbots abound. The Syrian desert commands an audience among the pine woods of the north, and the refined asceticism of desert troglodytes presents itself as a moral norm for bakers and bachelors of arts. Of the fathers, it is Gregory the Great whose works are most assiduously mined. This is hardly surprising. He is by far the most anecdotal of the four doctors of the Latin Church, and his strong pastoral concerns make him something of a friar before the letter. From those writers who were in effect their immediate or near contemporaries the exemplarists also chose their favorites. They included Peter Damian and Jacques de Vitry, a chatty preacher and a chatty historian, and as a master of the marvelous, Caesarius of Heisterback, the Cistercian compiler of the *Dialogus miraculorum* and a close contemporary of Francis of Assisi.

Such writers provided the repertory of materials to which compilers of the *exempla* books most frequently turned, but their potential range of source materials was of course much wider, as wide indeed as the oak shelves of chapter libraries. Almost anything was grist for their mills, including the local and the personal, elements of which often add surprising charm to a genre derivative in its very nature. Two large but representative collections from the late Middle Ages, put together by ambitious compilers knowledgeable about the major resources for such a task, can perhaps suggest both the breadth of available source material and the varying emphases with which they could be presented. The first of these is the Catalan anthology, probably dating from the late fourteenth century, ordered alphabetically from *abbas* to *ypocrita*—not always so large a leap in medieval letters.[35] Altogether, this *Recull de Eximplis* cites well over a hundred different works. These include classical moralists and historians such as Æsop, Cicero, Orosius, and Seneca, nearly all the major fathers of the Church, a significant range of popular saints' legends (including some not to be found in the *Legenda aurea,* the authoritative hagiographical catalogue for most of the later *exempla* books), and the wit and wisdom of more obscure moderns. Even granting that the compiler of the *Recull* would for the most part have been sifting through earlier collections rather than poring over primary texts, his editorial achievement alone is impressive. The book is clearly intended for clerical reference use, and its alphabetical rubrics (sometimes in contrast to the Catalan catchwords) are in Latin.

A markedly different kind of work was the famous *Speculum exemplorum,* compiled in the incunabula period, probably by the Carthusian monk Gillis Goudsmid.[36] It was first printed at Deventer, and its greatest popularity would seem always to have been in the Low

[35] *Recull de Eximplis e miracles, gestes, e faules,* ed. M. Aguilo y Fuster, 2 vols. (Barcelona, 1881).

[36] See Juliane Matuszak, *Das Speculum exemplorum als Quelle volkstümlicher Glaubensvorstellungen des Spätmittelalters* (Sieburg, 1967).

Countries and Germany. Though it has recently been studied as a repertory of folk theology, its actual composition is considerably more "clerical" than is that of the Catalan collection. It relies very heavily on the *Vitae Patrum* and other eremitic texts, and it almost systematically uses the biographical dictionaries of the religious orders—including the Cistercians, Franciscans, Dominicans, and Augustinian hermits—which were available to Goudsmid. For his miracle stories Goudsmid used Bede, always popular for such purposes, as well as the inexhaustible mine of Caesarius' *Dialogus miraculorum*. For natural history he had that part of the encyclopedia of Thomas of Cantimpré called the *Bonum universale de apibus*.

The *exemplum* from authority—from the life of "a certain holy abbot," or from Isidore, or *Physiologus*, was one thing; the eyewitness account another. From the literary point of view, one of the most important features of the *exempla* collections is their accommodation of the local, the personal, and the autobiographical. Personal authorial witness, generally rather pale and formulaic in the hagiographic literature, takes on a convincing immediacy when its "locale" moves from the Syrian desert to a hamlet in Warwickshire or a tannery in Bruges, and there is a suggestive continuum between the first-person narrative of Gothic *exempla* books and the narrative techniques of an increasingly exemplary Gothic fiction as we find it in the pages of Boccaccio or Chaucer. Salimbene's *Chronicle*, sometimes faulted for a want of an explicitly "Franciscan consciousness," is at moments a kind of *exempla* collection set to history.

We must remember, too, that many medieval friars who were in no way academicians were nonetheless men of considerable and cosmopolitan practical education, often well-traveled, fluent in foreign languages, conversant with the customs of different regions and lands, in close communication with a truly international fraternity. It is little wonder that many bishops and local parish priests feared them as modern *gyrovagi* and fast talkers, for many of them could and did speak with a captivating authority of first-hand experiences quite as exotic in their way as the marvels of the pilgrim books and the chronicles of crusaders.

The author of the *Liber exemplorum ad usum praedicantium,* published by A. G. Little, the earliest of the specifically Franciscan collections of which we know, was an English friar who had studied at Paris and spent his active ministry mainly in Ireland.[37] His book is everywhere thickened, enriched, vivified by his own personal experiences and those narrated to him by the friars with whom he lived and worked over the years. He tells a miracle of the Virgin which he heard with his own ears from an Italian friar in Paris. A brother from Denmark had told him once of the deplorable custom in his rustic home according to which a woman in childbirth is encouraged by her women neighbors with bawdy songs, dances, and high-jinks with a straw doll. Nicholas of Aachen, the *visitator* of the Hibernian province, told the friars at Cork a lovely story about one of *his* local saints, the emperor Henry II.

The literary appetites excited by the exemplary methods perfected in fraternal preaching and writing could be satisfied in other ways, and we can perhaps judge the extent to which *exempla* could add richness to works of secular literature by considering briefly the *Roman de la Rose* of Jean de Meun (c. 1290) and the *Canterbury*

[37] *Liber exemplorum ad usum praedicantium,* ed. A. G. Little (Aberdeen, 1908).

Tales of Geoffrey Chaucer a century later, both of them seminal works in the history of Gothic fiction.

At the point at which Jean de Meun appropriated the "story" of the *Roman de la Rose,* the poem's central "character," the Lover, stood languishing before the prison which separated him from the "rose," the object of his extravagant and irrational passion.[38] Jean's strategy is to reintroduce the character Reason, who conducts a long and one-sided conversation with the Lover in an attempt to dissuade him from his folly and to point out a correct course for him. Her task is in effect to play "Good Angel" to the Lover's "Lively Vices," not an enviable one in terms of its traditional dramatic difficulties, and her long speech is in effect a secular sermon. One of the chief means by which Jean de Meun invests this abstract lady with a degree of authority, dignity, and "reader interest," almost altogether lacking in her delineation by Guillaume de Lorris, is through her effective, versatile, and witty use of *exempla.* These include materials both from Christian (i.e., Boethius) and from pagan writers, from poets and historians, from ancient authorities and from what is the thirteenth-century equivalent of the daily newspaper. Homer, Ovid, Plato, Seneca, Croesus—all are called to the stand to witness against the Lover's folly. And even though Jean de Meun is one of the most learned of medieval poets, it is clear enough that he is borrowing his classical materials not from a random and eclectic reading of his own but from exemplary anthologies specially constructed for his purposes.

Geoffrey Chaucer, who set himself to school at the feet of Jean de Meun, makes brilliant and witty use of formal literary *exempla* throughout the *Canterbury*

[38] Guillaume de Lorris and Jean de Meun, *Le Roman de la Rose,* ed. Félix Lecoy (Paris, 1965-70), I, pp. 130 ff.

Tales. One instance is of particular "Franciscan" relevance, for it comes from the "Summoner's Tale," one of Chaucer's finest and one of the most devastating of the dozens of medieval satires against corrupt friars.[39] In the "Summoner's Tale" a certain friar, actually motivated by transparent greed but pretending spiritual solicitude for the wealthy and infirm burgher to whose house he has come to beg, delivers an inspired sermon on wrath. The theme is appropriate in every way, for wrath is certainly the man's controlling vice. The comedy is enriched and complicated by the fact that the friar, too, will be exposed as a child of wrath, and by his ludicrous but evident inability to see the true spiritual meaning of the splendid sermon he has so ably mouthed. The preacher vividly points out the evils of wrath with a series of learned *exempla,* mainly from the *De ira* of Seneca. One of them is the story of Cambyses, a drunken ruler who was once reprimanded by a virtuous retainer who held that drunkenness was a vice particularly abhorrent in a prince, since it impaired both the ability to think and the ability to act. In a sodden rage Cambyses ordered the man's young son to be brought before him. He took aim with his bow and killed him with a single arrow to the heart, saying, "See, drink has not made my aim unsteady!" According to the friar's interpretation, the lesson of this *exemplum* is that while it is proper to reprimand a poor man for his vices, it is by no means prudent to do so to a powerful one!

> To a povre man men shold his vices tell,
> But nat to a lord, thogh he sholde go to helle!

In this instance the irony is capped by the likelihood, recently and persuasively argued, that Chaucer's friar

[39] *The Works of Geoffrey Chaucer,* ed. F. N. Robinson, 2nd ed. (Boston, 1961), pp. 94 ff.

actually came by his Senecan *exempla* in the *Communiloquium* of John of Wales.[40]

The friar could hardly have turned to a more convenient source. John of Wales is in many ways typical of the second- and third-generation friars who, at Paris and elsewhere, actively combined demanding academic careers with a full apostleship of service to the Order and popular evangelism.[41] John's known writings (and some are lost) cover a wide range. Some of them, as we would expect from a *magister,* are technical and even arcane. He was a careful student of Olivi's doctrines, and he himself wrote some remarkable *postillae* on the Gospel of St. John and an outward-looking book about the errors of Mohammed.

Much of John's learning, however superficially displayed, is used in his only popular book, the *Communiloquium.*[42] In addition to the scriptural and patristic *sententiae* which provide the real meat of the work, an extraordinary list of Latin authors, many of them rarely mentioned outside of the academy in the thirteenth century, is summoned to defend Christian commonplaces. We shall find not merely Cicero and Valerius Maximus and Boethius, but altogether rarer and more "learned" doctors, Trogus Pompeius, Quintillian, and Aulus Gellius.

The *Communiloquium* is a handbook for "the evangelical preacher or teacher," who, John tells us, "has an obligation to the wise and the unwise alike." His clarity of purpose shapes the brief prologue; in it John explains that the preacher must follow the apostolic injunction to be all things to all men—that is, he must be acutely con-

[40] R. A. Pratt, "Chaucer and the Hand that Fed Him," *Speculum,* xli (1966), 619-642.

[41] See Smalley, *English Friars and Antiquity,* pp. 51-55.

[42] *Communiloquium* (Strassburg, 1489; reprinted London, 1966).

scious of the nature of his audience, their level of sophistication, and their tastes and expectations. Furthermore, he maintains that the formal homily is by no means the most effective medium of instruction for all sorts and conditions of men. Many people are more likely to respond to informal or intimate conversation, even to table talk, and the evangelist, something of a spiritual opportunist, must be able to seize such off-the-cuff chances and exploit them.

The structure of the *Communiloquium* reveals its author's practical ambitions for his book. Its seven unequal parts are organized not around abstract theological categories, as we might expect, nor even around the schema of the capital vices and virtues, categories which medieval people seem to have found a practical and descriptive way of talking about complex personal experience. Rather, the work's controlling themes are insistently social. The first, long section is devoted to the civil state, its composition, and governance; the next deals with what we would call "interpersonal relationships," considered, in true medieval fashion, not merely in social and economic terms but also with regard to such spiritual realities as the natural law and sacramental grace. Further parts of the book are devoted to those accidents of fortune observable in the human situation; to the Church and its right ordering; to the nature and aims of education; to questions involved in the religious life, and particularly the life of poverty; and, finally, to the Christian's necessary preparation for death.

Taken as a whole, this scheme presents a kind of encyclopedia of "conversations" organized in a way which is immediately relevant to the social complexities of mendicant apostleship. The friar, reading John's handbook, is instructed in the appropriate level and mode of address for prince and pauper, in the techniques of appealing to the local concerns of artisans and draymen, in the tested repertory of evangelical gambits successful with women and the young. John of Wales places a very high value on "relevance." The *homo evangelicus* who would preach to blacksmiths and armorers must know the lingo of the trade, and thus forge and burnish the irons of gospel truth. Soldiers will the sooner understand faith in Christ if it is described to them in terms of obedience to military superiors; when the weaver understands that spiritual raiment, like his woolen shirts, must be carded, spun, woven, and dyed, he will the sooner set about preparing for himself a glorious garment.

This kind of spiritual "accommodation," of which we have seen repeated examples in Franciscan pastoral literature, has a long history. Medieval friars themselves sometimes pointed out that it characterized Christ's own method of teaching in agricultural parables. Its subsequent literary history has not been an entirely happy one; the celestial railroads of the nineteenth century have their bathetic analogues by the dozen in the viscid spirituality of the medieval twilight. John's general approach is of course totally consistent with the major evangelical thrust of the mendicants, and in particular of the Franciscans, to translate the Church into a vernacular and one might even say a secular context. What was remarkable about the *Communiloquium* and other handbooks like it, however, was not merely that they legitimized for sophisticated literary use an empirical iconography of daily life in the markets and shops but that they combined this appeal to felt experience with a real flair for *haute vulgarisation* of learned and classical texts, popular science, and exotic tales from the East. The rhetoric they developed was one with an appeal to prelate and peasant alike.

The synoptic and practical intentions of the *Communiloquium* were typical, as well, of the two most ambitious genres of "Lateran" literature, the encyclopedia and the confession manual, which between them provided the literate world of the late Middle Ages and the Renaissance with its accepted commonplaces concerning the material universe and the nature of human behavior. Like most of the other sorts of books discussed so far in this chapter, the moral encyclopedia can trace a history back through the patristic period to Antiquity. The literary culture of the twelfth century, as has frequently been remarked, shows an articulate tendency toward encyclopedism of various sorts—in dictionaries, catalogues, lists, "trees," *summae,* and other ambitious attempts to present large bodies of sacred and profane science schematically in their wholeness. The *Didascalicon* of Hugh of St.-Victor can represent the genre in its most learned and elegant forms, as can the so-called *Speculum universale* of Raoul Ardent its practicality or the *De naturis rerum* of Alexander Neckham its scientism.

What the mendicant scholars of the thirteenth century brought to this tradition was not a novelty of conception but a startling quest for the inclusive and the definitive. This tendency is particularly marked among the Dominican encyclopedists, always the more self-consciously "intellectual" of mendicant scholars. From a literary point of view, the truly extraordinary feature of the *Summa theologiae* of Thomas Aquinas is not that it "Christianized Aristotle" or "reconciled faith and reason," as we are forever telling undergraduates, but that in it St. Thomas has devised a peculiarly clear and practical literary structure capable of addressing *all* of sacred doctrine. In a similar vein, William Peraldus had set out in his massive *summae* of the virtues and the vices to present a complete and schematic moral theology in lively, exemplary form, and Vincent of Beauvais, in what is justly the most celebrated encyclopedia of the entire Middle Ages—the *Speculum Majus* or "Great Mirror" —had set out to codify all knowledge, period.

The medieval encyclopedia was a "tool," a reference book, but its actual practical utility varied greatly, depending upon its mode of organization and the degree to which its author imagined a specific audience for it. The definitive was sometimes at war with the practical, and it takes no mean muscle to manhandle the folios of Vincent of Beauvais. Furthermore, all the books mentioned above, even though each of them in its own way penetrated the vernacular cultures of the Gothic period—and particularly those of Peraldus, as we shall see—were explicitly learned; and to appreciate more fully the truly pastoral possibilities of the genre we should probably turn to what are amusingly called the "minor" encyclopedias of the thirteenth century, meaning, presumably, works of a mere thousand pages or so.[43] The two most important of these were both written by friars, Thomas of Cantimpré, O.P., and the Franciscan Bartolomeus Anglicus, "Bartholomew the Englishman." Thomas' encyclopedia, like that of Neckam, simply called the *De naturis rerum,* was especially designed as a preachers' aid, and it circulated widely, especially in Dominican circles. Part of it—including its celebrated moral apiary which supplied many of the *exempla* in Goudsmid's *Speculum exemplorum*—enjoyed something like a real vogue, but it is still searching for its publisher.

[43] P. Michaud-Quantin, "Les petites encyclopédies du XIIIe siècle," in *La Pensée encyclopédique au Moyen Age,* by Maurice de Gandillac and others (Neuchatel, 1966), pp. 105-120.

The real masterpiece of the "minor encyclopedia" is the *De proprietatibus rerum* of Bartholomew the Englishman, scholar, lector, preacher, and missionary, finished about mid-century.[44] Bartholomew states his ambitions for his work in a brief prologue. With characteristic and winning self-effacement, he says that he has undertaken a task "useful to myself and perhaps to others," as an aid to understanding the Scriptures. In the pages of Scripture, images from the world of nature are the lexicon of a mysterious language of enigma and allegory. I think we can best understand the nature of the *De proprietatibus* by giving this preface its full weight. Bartholomew has sometimes been written about as though his role were dimly to prefigure a modern scientific consciousness; he himself saw matters differently. The fifth book will deal with "the human body and its individual members *which are mentioned in the Scriptures.*" We are still some way from Gray's *Anatomy,* and very much nearer to the *Repertorium Morale,* the Bible wordbook of the fourteenth-century monk Pierre Bersuire.

The spiritual program suggested by the prologue is that of Dionysian ascent as in the most famous of all manuals of Franciscan mysticism, Bonaventure's *Itinerarium.* The mind rises to the understanding of the invisible divine nature by degrees; the first degree, of course, is the observation of "those things that are made," in St. Paul's famous words in Romans 1:20, cited by Bartholomew along with the *Angelic Hierarchies* of Dionysius. Such an invocation of the hierarchy of contemplation suggests the purposes for which the book was made

[44] *Bartholomaei Anglici de genuinis rerum coelestium, terrestrium et inferarum Proprietatibus libri XVIII* (Frankfurt, 1601; reprinted Frankfurt, 1964).

rather than its skeletal structure, which is one of emanation rather than of progression. Bartholomew begins actually with those things unseen—God, the angels, the soul and its properties—to each of which he devotes a book, before moving to the visible world, beginning with a book on the four elements of material creation and the four humors of animal life. The very first words of the encyclopedia proper are the Catholic definition or assertion of God's nature which had introduced the credal statement *Firmiter credimus,* the first of the constitutions published by the Fourth Lateran Council. The citation is appropriate in more than one way, for Bartholomew's encyclopedia was without question one of the thirteenth-century works most widely used by those who set out to implement the council's program of Church renewal.

There are nineteen books in the encyclopedia, of differing length and scope. The three "theological" books already mentioned, while largely speculative, do contain a certain amount of purely practical information as well, for example, about demon possession or the physiological bases of the five senses. Book Six deals with the "ages of man" as well as with much else, including familial relationships, nurses, midwives, meals, dreams, and bodily exercise. The seventh book records in sixty-nine lugubrious chapters the various medical disorders to which the human body is subject. Book Eight moves outside man to describe the earth and the heavenly bodies. The ninth is devoted to times and seasons, calendrical and liturgical, and the tenth to the elements, fire, smoke, sparks, and ashes. Book Eleven treats the "air," its winds, clouds, and weathers. The remaining books fit more comfortably into the genres of medieval natural science. Two are in effect bestiaries—Book Twelve, on birds, and Book Eighteen, on animals. Three are geographical (Thirteen, on rivers; Fourteen, mainly on biblical mountains; and Fifteen, on "regions and provinces"). The sixteenth book is a lapidary, the seventeenth an herbal. The nineteenth and final book claims to be on "accidents," understood in the scholastic sense, the colors and smells of things, their weights and sounds. That it in fact deals at length with eggs and musical instruments, and ends with a discourse on the mysteries of the "number *sexquealterus,*" will scarcely be disconcerting to the readers by now experienced in Bartholomew's unflinching organizational logic.

Bartholomew the Englishman can hardly be credited with, or accused of, an experimental attitude toward the natural sciences, and the statement with which he concludes his prologue—"I have put little or nothing of my own here, but took everything from the authentic books of saints and philosophers"—is a boast rather than an apology. For him, as for his intended clerical readers, the quality of his own work was guaranteed by the impressive list of authorities "briefly" digested there, a list in a literal sense, appended, almost by way of advertisement, to the manuscripts and early printed editions. The book is all but overwhelmed with authority—from Antiquity, from the Age of the Fathers, from the more recent brilliance of the twelfth century. Isidore and Hrabanus Maurus, pioneers of the Christian encyclopedia, take on new life in Bartholomew. Friars far from "humanistic" in their leanings could find in his pages safe and convenient gobbets of Plato, Aristotle, Ovid, and Persius. Hard science is by no means lacking, and most of the authorities from whom Chaucer's physician learned his medicine—Avicenna, Constantine, Galen, Haly—are liberally anthologized. So, too, are the moralists, Boethius, Cicero, and others. And everywhere, and on practically all subjects, the curious reader can find an apt citation from the great St. Augustine.

The *De proprietatibus* was enormously successful in the same sense that Webster's and the Britannica have been successful. We may doubt that many read it cover to cover, but it became a *sine qua non* for preachers, teachers, and poets, providing most if not quite all of what they knew of the workings of the digestive system, the antiquities of the Bible, the habits of crocodiles, and the properties of the jasper stone. Salimbene of Adam, somewhat startled by his own report of Frederick II's war elephant, is happy enough to direct his readers to the first book of Maccabees and to the *De proprietatibus,* where Frater Bartolomeus had sufficiently written of such matters.[45] Bartholomew's editorial work did a great deal to popularize exemplary natural science, and it was but a short further step to the vernacular versions which made his book available to a lay audience in the major languages of Europe. It was repeatedly translated or adapted in the two centuries following its Latin publication, often by men of real literary distinction: Vivaldo Becalzer in Italy; Jean Corbichon, OESA, in France; John Trevisa, Chaucer's contemporary, in England.[46] By the time of the Renaissance, "Bartolomaeus" has himself taken on the aura of an ancient and powerful authority. Shakespeare learned much of his curious lore from a book which now brings joy only to graduate students of English literature, *Batman upon Bartholomew.*

If we read of such matters at all, we will read that the encyclopedic tradition died out at the end of the thir-

[45] *Cronica,* ed. G. Scalia, I, p. 134.

[46] *On the Properties of Things: John Trevisa's Translation of Bartholomaeus Anglicus De Proprietatibus Rerum,* ed. M. C. Seymour and others (Oxford, 1975-).

teenth century, to await a triumphant resurrection and a glorified body only in the eighteenth century with Denis Diderot. We can believe this, however, only by ignoring several fourteenth-century books of very great potential importance to the literary historian. I have already mentioned in passing the name of Berchorius (Pierre Bersuire). It is also necessary at least to mention that of Francesc Eiximinis, author of the greatest of all Franciscan encyclopedias, the Catalan *Crestia,* which he composed in serial stages during the final quarter of the fourteenth century.[47] Eiximinis divided his materials somewhat unevenly into four major books. The first of these was devoted to dogmatic theology and the second to the sciences of the spirit and ascetic discipline. The fourth book was an ambitious mirror for princes, much in the style of the *Speculum Regum* of his fellow Iberian Alvaro Pelayo in an earlier generation. It is the third book, the *Terc del Crestia,* the only part of the encyclopedia to enjoy modern publication, which is the largest and, from the point of view of the interests of this chapter, the most important of its sections.[48] The *Terc del Crestia,* for the most part devoted to "those things that are made," is a vast and neglected storehouse of exemplary and scientific lore presented in fluent and fulsome vernacular narrative style which gives the finest articulation to the ambition to "teach delightfully," which was the literary testament of Ramon Lull.

It is hardly an exaggeration to say that in Catalonia the pastoral mission of mendicant religion was the single most formative influence on the history of an important

[47] M. de Riquer, *Historia de la literatura catalana* (Barcelona, 1964), II, pp. 133-196.

[48] *Terç del Crestia,* ed. Marti de Barcelona and Norbert d'Ordal, 3 vols. (Barcelona, 1929-1932).

vernacular literature. One can make the same claim in relationship to the emergence, at a slightly earlier date, of a vigorous popular literature among the Flemings. The career of Jacob van Maerlant, the "father of Dutch poetry" who flourished in the second half of the thirteenth century, gives vivid testimony to the vernacular triumph of the moral and encyclopedic traditions.[49] Though from the start of his fecund career Maerlant was interested in the didactic possibilities of poetry, his earliest surviving works come from the aristocratic traditions of twelfth-century France, and in particular from the *roman d'antiquité.* He did a version of Walter of Chatillon's *Alexandreis,* and also a Troy book. The rest of his substantial *oeuvre,* however, is "moral" poetry of a quite explicit kind, conceived in an intellectual style which was to define Netherlandish literature, and much Netherlandish painting, through the period of the Reformation. Maerlant produced a *Rijmbibel* from materials in Peter Comestor's *Historia Scholastica,* and wrote poetic redactions of a number of famous encyclopedic and scientific works. An early lapidary and a "somniary" or dream book have been lost; but we still have, and the courageous can still read, in their improbable Flemish couplets, *Der Naturen Bloeme,* an anthology "bouquet" from the natural history of Thomas of Cantimpré, the *Spieghel Historiael* from the encyclopedia of Vincent of Beauvais, and the *Hemelechede der Hemelijcheit,* from the *Secreta Secretorum.* Maerlant's biography is obscure, but he had strong Franciscan connections, evidenced both by the ideas in his own original poems and by his commission to make a poetic version of the *Legenda Major* of Bonaventure, the *Sinte Franciscus Leven,* in which he proposes that the

[49] See J. van Mierlo, *De letterkunde van de Middeleeuwen (Geschiedenis van de Letterkunde der Nederlanden,* I [Brussels, 1949]), pp. 302-324.

poverello of Assisi, rather than Tristan, Lancelot, or the other tired worthies of courtly romance, is the real hero of the age.[50] He also wrote a life of St. Clare, now lost. His literary interests in their mature form could almost serve as a paradigm of the unofficial literary "program" of the mendicant orders.

St. Francis dated the birth of his own new life and hence in a sense the birth of his new Order from that day "when he began to do penance," and the insistent invitation to a radical reformation informed practically every document he has left us and practically every sermon his biographers report. When, as he began to write his *Testament,* he sought a single concept which could characterize the new life which he had taken on, it was the concept of penance which alone could serve. "This is how God inspired me, Brother Francis, to embark upon a life of penance."[51] In terms of the inner life of the friars and of the emergent religious style of the Order, the emphasis placed upon penance was very profound. The ascetical dimension of radical poverty exercised, as we have seen, a formative influence on the modes of thirteenth-century mystical *accessus* and on the Franciscan theology of the religious life. It likewise helps to explain a good deal of what was new in the Franciscan *Rule* and in the administrative structures and practices of the Order.

In another sense, however, Francis was merely following the high road of medieval religious life. Early ascetic literature abounds with flamboyant penitential precept and practice; and in legends of the desert fathers, the stylite saints, the Antonine hermits, the coracle *peregrini* of the Irish seas, one can easily find literary expressions of the "life of penance" quite as total and committed as

[50] *Sinte Franciscus Leven,* ed. P. Maximilianus (Zwolle, 1954), I, p. 36.
[51] *Omnibus,* p. 67.

that which Francis proposed for himself and for those who were his brothers. Much of the true originality of the penitential aspirations of thirteenth-century religion lay in their truly social nature. The image which Francis used to account for his withdrawal "from the world" in his *Testament* is that of the lepers. "When I was in sin, the sight of lepers nauseated me beyond measure; but then God himself led me into their company, and I had pity on them. When I had once become acquainted with them, what had previously nauseated me became a source of spiritual and physical consolation for me. After that I did not wait long before leaving the world."[52] This is an extraordinary statement which typifies the spiritual paradox of Franciscanism, at once an impulse of pure and withdrawn asceticism and a commitment to the fullest possible social engagement. Francis learns to "leave" the world only when he learns to love its most despised and terrifying members. As with so much else in the *Testament,* the pattern of thought and imagery here revealed suggests a larger truth about the Order as a whole.[53] For the truth is that the friars' greatest contribution to the development of the medieval theology of penance was social; it found its arena not in cloistered, private spiritual experience and in hermetic mystical tracts read only by a few, but in the hubbub of courts and country fairs, and in books which were among the best-sellers of their day. To oversimplify only slightly, the friars made penance popular, and transformed its sacramental practice from what one scholar has called "a rare, perhaps even a dramatic event in the life of a Christian" to a normal and habitual spiritual exercise faithfully performed by

[52] *Omnibus,* p. 67.
[53] See the illuminating discussion by K. Esser, *Das Testament des heiligen Franziskus von Assisi* (Münster, 1949).

millions of ordinary laymen. In the process they produced many books which were not merely important literary contributions in their own right but which had a significant influence on the formation of literary taste and topics in the high vernacular period.

The penitential constitution promulgated by the Lateran Council in 1215, *Omnis utriusque sexus,* specified that it was the obligation of the faithful to make a full auricular confession at least once a year, for the Easter Communion, to "their own priest"—a term which in time proved sufficiently vague to allow a bitter debate between the friars and the secular clergy over the power of the confessional.[54] Its more immediate effect was to accelerate the demand from bishops and others for materials which could help prepare penitents for confession and to instruct priests in the examination of souls. Hence the literary phenomenon of the penitential *summa* or "confession manual," which is one of the remarkable features of the religious literature of the thirteenth and fourteenth centuries.[55]

Penitential handbooks were not, of course, exclusively the work of friars, and there are several important ones which antedate *Omnis utriusque sexus.* St. Columban's penitential is one example, as is the *Liber poenitentialis* of Alain de Lille. Yet it was the mendicants who, increasingly concerned with the administration of penance both as the penitentiaries of the mighty and as the apostles to the poor, made of them a real specialty. The most widely read casuists of the period were not Franciscans but Dominicans, three or four of whose handbooks must be mentioned in any survey of the subject, however cursorily.

[54] *Conciliorum Oecumenicorum Decreta,* p. 245.
[55] See Pierre Michaud-Quantin, *Sommes de casuistique et manuels de confession au moyen age* (Louvain, 1962).

The first, and from the vantage point of legal history probably the most important, is the *Summa de casibus poenitentiae* by the Catalan Raymond of Peñaforte (Pennyfort), which first appeared in 1220-1221 and then in an expanded version in 1234. The original work was structured in three books devoted respectively to sins against God, sins against one's neighbor, and the special moral problems of those in holy orders. The fourth book, added in the redaction of 1234, deals with marriage; and it remains an absolutely fundamental source book for historians of theology and society alike.

Around the same time William Peraldus (Peyrault), a French friar-preacher, published an extensive treatise on the capital vices, the *Summa de vitiis,* which some years later he complemented with a *Summa de virtutibus.* I have already had occasion to mention the literary importance of this popular work. It gave authoritative form to the classification and the iconography of the capital vices and virtues and, therefore, to the ways in which medieval writers typically think about the delineation of "psychological" action, and it was beyond question one of the seminal repositories of the "allegorical imagery" of medieval and Renaissance poets and painters.[56] In the final decade of the thirteenth century, John of Fribourg composed a series of commentaries or keys to St. Raymond's *Summa* with the motive of making the work, already a classic, more accessible to the clergy and to students of the canon law. The most common version of John of Fribourg's work, usually called the *Summa confessorum,* "modernized" Pennyfort's classic by bringing to it the fashionable new theological distinctions of the famous Dominican doctors at Paris, especially those of

[56] Rosemond Tuve, *Allegorical Imagery* (Princeton, 1966), p. 81.

Thomas Aquinas. One must finally mention in passing a vernacular handbook designed more for the penitent layman than for the confessor, the *Specchio della vera penitenza* of the Florentine friar Jacopo Passavanti, who flourished in the generation after Dante and whose importance for the formation of an Italian literary language has plausibly been compared with his.

There were, of course, influential Franciscan manuals as well. We may take as their example the so-called *Formula Confessionum* of Fr. Jean Rigaud (d. 1323).[57] Like the Spaniard Alvaro Pelayo, Rigaud was papal penitentiary in Avignon and a member of the group of remarkably able Franciscan administrators and legists who adorned the papal court in the "Babylonian captivity" of the first quarter of the fourteenth century. Jean had a varied literary career. His best-known work is his *Life of Saint Anthony of Padua,* a model of hagiographic clarity, grace, and economy, if not always of the critical method, which remains to this day an inviting book to read.[58] His other writings have been unhappily neglected and are for the most part available only in manuscript. They include, in addition to the *Formula Confessionum,* a number of important sermons on a wide range of subjects. Rigaud was a versatile evangelist who typified his Order's broad conception of mission, and his confession manual, though written for a specific unnamed friend, enjoyed a fairly wide circulation during the fourteenth century.

After a brief dedication, Jean immediately defines the purpose of his work under five rubrics which explain systematically the nature and sequence of sacramental penance: what must precede it, what the sacrament it-

[57] See A. Teetaert, "La *formula confessionis* du frère mineur Jean Rigaud," in *Miscellanea . . . A. De Meyer* (Louvain, 1946), pp. 651-76.

[58] Jean Rigauld, *La vie de Saint Antoine de Padoue,* trans. Alexandre Masseron (Paris, 1956).

self involves in its performance, what follows from it. The author then lists the chapter divisions of his casuistic analysis, designed to help the penitent and the confessor to explore a conscience. He begins with the five senses, the carnal "windows" of the body through which concupiscent temptations enter. He then discusses, serially, the seven capital vices (the so-called "deadly sins") encouraging the penitent to remember them in order through the use of the mnemonic *saligia,* a word made up of their initial letters: *s*uperbia, *a*varitia, *l*uxuria, *i*nvidia, *g*ula, *i*ra, *a*ccidia. This in turn is followed by schematic discussions of the Ten Commandments, the works of mercy, the theological virtues, the sacraments, the cardinal virtues, the parts of penance, and a "form of confession" properly speaking.

A bald description of the *Formula* runs the risk of making it seem aridly scholastic and mechanical, but it is actually quite different. Although Jean's schema are conventional and academic, his motives are entirely practical; he seeks to instruct, but to do so delightfully and informally. In Jean's mind, preaching is closely connected with the administration of penance, and the form of penance should be brief, clear, and simple in conformity with the instructions to preachers in the *Regula bullata* that they "should aim only at the advantage and spiritual good of their listeners. . ."

The *Formula Confessionum,* without for a moment ceasing to be very serious in its treatment of the theology of penance, makes a distinctively literary appeal to its readers through the use of arresting metaphors, *exempla,* little narrative allegories, and the like. At the outset, for example, penance is called a "medicine" in an elaborate and studied medical metaphor which recurs throughout the work. The image is a medieval commonplace of scriptural origin, but in several of the confession manuals it becomes a real structural device, and it was also taken over by "literary" writers, such as Albertanus of Brescia, whose unassuming allegory, called the *Liber Consolationis et Consilii,* enjoyed considerable popularity—there is a version of it in the "Tale of Melibee" in Chaucer's *Canterbury Tales,* for example—and in Henry of Lancaster's *Livre de Seintz Medecines,* composed in England in the mid-fourteenth century.

England, indeed, perhaps because of a peculiar national penchant for sin or poetry or both, became the particular home of the "literary" penitential manual. It was there, apparently, that the first versified *summa* in Latin was composed, and certainly there that William of Wadington wrote the *Manuel de Péchés* in the late fourteenth century. This work was in turn translated into an English poem of nearly thirteen thousand lines, *Handling Sin,* by Robert Mannyng of Bourne, a religious of Sempringham Priory; and the English fourteenth century saw the unlikely proliferation of versified instructions on baptizing infants in breech births and warnings against masturbation.

The number of such works of indubitable Franciscan provenance is small, though it includes such an important book as the *Fasciculus Morum.* Mendicant influence is nonetheless clear in the pages of *Handling Sin,* or in such a pastoral masterpiece as the *Oculus sacerdotis* of the secular priest William of Pagula.[59] This latter work, an important example of the kind of handbooks which pastorally minded bishops could supply for their clergy, contains, like Jean Rigaud's *Summa,* an entire brief course in dogmatic theology structured around the apostolic

[59] See L. E. Boyle, "The *Oculus Sacerdotis* and Some Other Works of William of Pagula," *Transactions of the Royal Historical Society,* V, v (1955), pp. 81-110.

pastoral offices of preaching and shriving. In its various redactions, William's work had a very wide circulation in several English dioceses, and it was eventually versified by the hirpling muse of John Mirk in his *Instructions for Parish Priests.*[60] Its basic idea was by no means original to William of Pagula, and its clear source of inspiration was the so-called *Oculus moralis* of the Franciscan Peter of Limoges.[61] This was a work of extraordinary popularity—over eighty manuscripts have been identified—which exposed the materials of pastoral theology beneath an elaborate metaphor of ophthalmology. The priest is an eye doctor who must be expert in the physiology and pathology of spiritual sight. Beneath this somewhat unlikely conceit, Peter of Limoges sustained a real *tour de force,* bringing into his work exemplary materials from the Bible, the fathers, the classical poets, and such learned authorities as Alhazen (a real eye doctor), Bernard Silvestris, and the *Liber de commixtione elementorum.* The effect of such a work was at once to edify the clergy and to supply them with literary topics of potential usefulness for their own ministry. The *Oculus moralis* was flattered by a persistent medieval ascription to John Pecham, high praise indeed.

One final Franciscan casuist deserves brief mention, Nicholas of Osimo. Though his career falls well into the fifteenth century, he must be granted the same chronological easement we have on occasion afforded to Bernardino of Siena, his close friend and spiritual colleague. By the end of the fourteenth century there was something of an established repertory of penitential texts which included, in addition to the *summae* of Peraldus

[60] John Mirk, *Instructions for Parish Priests,* ed. Gillis Kristensson (Lund, 1974).

[61] On Peter of Limoges see *AFH,* xvi (1923), pp. 309 ff.

and Pennyfort, a work quite as well known as either of them in its own day. This compendium was sometimes also called the *Summa confessorum* but more frequently *Pisanella* after its Dominican author Bartholomew of San Concordio in Pisa. It was perhaps the aridly legal cast of this book that invited Nicholas of Osimo to "Franciscanize" it slightly in what he called diplomatically a *Supplementum* but what is in fact a partial recasting of the materials along more "literary" lines.[62] Nicholas followed the alphabetical headings of Pisanus from *abbas* to *zelus,* but he included not merely supplementary canonic opinion but a wealth of refurbished *exempla* as well.

The miscellaneous and uneven library of "Lateran literature" which has occupied my major attention in this chapter so far grew naturally and inevitably out of the major spiritual emphases of mendicant ministry, which was itself a reawakening and quickening of Church life rather than a beginning without conscious precedents and traditions. The sermon books and penitentials of the friars, their poetic catalogues of virtues and vices, their "pictures" from Pliny and Livy, their dictionaries and vast folio encyclopedias were for the most part different in degree rather than in kind from the pastoral literature of Christian antiquity. The program of clerical education which King Alfred had sponsored in the ninth century was little different in its aims or instinctive methods from that of the English bishops in the thirteenth.

What *was* new in the literary impact of the mendicant movement was the creation of a durable and long-lived edifice of intellectual clichés which dominated the imaginative fictions of the emerging vernaculars of Western

[62] Nicholas of Osimo's *Supplementum* was frequently published; I have used the edition of Venice, 1474.

Europe at a profound and sometimes subliminal level. Jean de Meun, in attacking the friars in the *Roman de la Rose,* does so in trenchant poetry enabled by the major features of "Franciscan" style. The Anglican Edmund Spenser, writing a Protestant epic in the near hysterical atmosphere of the Spanish Armada, instinctively uses the moral vocabulary of Dominican penitential manuals. It is this energy of medieval religious literature which gives it a catalytic importance quite beyond any question of its limitations of point of view or of the absolute aesthetic achievement of its products. The "Parson's Tale" has inevitably to be one of the most important in Chaucer's *Canterbury Tales.* No stratagem of the mason is more revealing than his choice of the quarry stone.

To use the more than faintly damning praise of "source" or "influence" is not necessary when we come to consider another major genre of Franciscan literature, lyric poetry. Here the achievement was absolute even in terms of the more conventional aesthetic expectations of literary criticism. The life of Francis of Assisi was alive with the music of pipes and timbrels, the songs of birds, and the ravishing and celestial melodies of unseen lutes. It was perhaps inevitable that his tuneful vision of divine grace would animate the mission of his friars. "When the sweetest melody of spirit would bubble up in him, he would give exterior expression to it in French, and the breath of the divine whisper which his ear perceived in secret would burst forth in French in a song of joy. At times, as we saw with our own eyes, he would pick up a stick from the ground and putting it over his left arm, would draw across it, as across a violin, a little bow bent by means of a string; and going through the motions of playing, he would sing in French about his Lord. This whole ecstasy of joy would often end in tears and his song of gladness would be dissolved in compassion for the passion of Christ."[63]

He was himself a poet and, if "critical attention" be the gauge of a poet's success, an enormously successful one. His one song, the *Laudes creaturarum* or *Canticle of Brother Sun,* is but thirty-three lines long, yet it has been the subject of many full-length books and shorter essays "too numerous to mention." The "critical attention" which he sought, however, was nothing less than a broken spirit and a contrite heart. When he had composed his canticle, according to the *Legend of Perugia,* "his heart was then full of so much sweetness and consolation that he wanted Brother Pacificus, who in the world had been the king of poets and the most courtly master of song, to go through the world with a few pious and spiritual friars to preach and sing the praises of God. The best preacher would first deliver the sermon; then all would sing the 'Praises of the Lord,' as true jongleurs of God. At the end of the song, the preacher would say to the people: 'We are the jongleurs of God, and the only reward we want is to see you lead a truly penitent life.' Then he added: 'Who are, indeed, God's servants if not jongleurs who strive to move men's hearts in order to lead them to the joys of the spirit?' When he spoke in this way of 'the servant of God,' he especially had in mind the Friars Minor who had been given to the world to save it."[64]

It is very probable, as David Jeffrey has recently suggested in his remarkable book, *The Early English Lyric and Franciscan Spirituality,* that the early and widespread Franciscan ministry of song reflected not only a characteristic spiritual spontaneity but also a conscious

[63] II Celano, II, xc, 127; *Omnibus,* p. 467.
[64] *Legend of Perugia,* 43; *Omnibus,* pp. 1021-22.

desire to exploit authentic modes of religious experience already becoming popular among groups of reform-minded laymen, including, conspicuously, the heretics of Lombardy and Provence.[65] We may recall that Valdesius, founder of the Poor Men of Lyon, was converted to a life of evangelical poverty by hearing a juggler sing a song of St. Alexis, and that the "teachings" of the Waldensians were recorded not in volumes of discursive theology but in simple songs with titles like "The Noble Lesson," "The New Comfort," and "The Scorn of the World."

The Franciscan contribution to the learned Latin lyric has long been recognized, but it is not inappropriate to recall that the *Stabat Mater,* the *Dies irae,* and the *Philomela* of John Pecham represent poetic achievement of the very highest order. But such poems, though they in a sense both came from the liturgy and returned to it, had limited missionary potential. We do have ample evidence, however, in the researches of Jeffrey and others, that the kind of connection between preaching and singing which made the phrase "God's jugglers" appropriate became a common and permanent feature of the mendicant missions. Berthold of Regensburg thought that simple folk songs would be the most effective vehicles for teaching Catholic truth and confuting heresy to a peasant audience closed to "the keys of philosophical distinctions." Bernardino of Siena, who cawed and whinnied from the scaffold, also sang from it. The Italian *laudesi,* and the mendicant confraternities throughout Europe, typically gave a lyric expression to their corporate spiritual aspirations.

That Francis should have sung *in French* has given rise to all manner of speculation, from the vaguely plausi-

[65] David L. Jeffrey, *The Early English Lyric and Franciscan Spirituality* (Lincoln, 1975), pp. 12 ff.

ble to the thoroughly fantastic. My own rumor would be that he sang in the *langue d'oc* because that was the language of the most admired poetry of his day, and he sought to reach out and exploit a secular tradition for sacred purposes. This is certainly what the Franciscans did with the *carole,* with what success we can perhaps gauge by the semantic journey the word has made between Francis' day and ours. The medieval carol was a dance, with song, which involved the participants' holding hands in a moving circle. Forms of it were popular with all levels of society—not merely with the "courtly" class—and it was frequently and roundly preached against by the kind of moralist whose life's most consuming interests would seem to have been the pedestrian frivolities and lecheries of the common man. The attitude of many Franciscan missionaries, especially in the British Isles, was very different. They accommodated the carol, making it their own by the old technique of *contrafactum,* thus "recycling" these old bottles for the new wine of a new song. There is a fourteenth-century English psalter (British Library Royal 2 B vii) which illustrates, quite without irony, the true spiritual joy of the just (Ps. 72:18 f.) with a picture of friars and sisters carolling. Even in their raw condition, popular songs could be used for a sermon; and we have an English homily by one inventive preacher on the text of some carol catch, "I found my lover at a wrestling match, and lost him at a stone-throwing contest."

This kind of literary freebooting was not so much authoritarian bowdlerizing as it was a frontal assault by the shock troops of the sacred against the stone keep of the profane. In the literary sphere the Franciscans sought to make religion popular, in part by making what was already popular religious, an old Franciscan habit.

A more clearly "invented" kind of poem and the most ancient and authentic form of the Franciscan lyric is the Italian *lauda,* the very name of which, pointing as it does to the imperative forms of *laudare,* "to praise," suggests the scriptural continuum of Franciscan song. Thomas of Celano spoke of Francis' *Cantico di frate sole,* the most famous of all *laude,* as a poem "in the manner of the prophet David"; and in its fullest development the genre engaged the full range of psalmodic ambitions: praise, prayer, penitence, meditation, imprecation.

Like the psalms, which had been the shared language of communal worship and corporate prayer throughout the rich history of Christian monastic life, the *laude* had from the start—which means from the time of Francis himself and of his spiritual forebears—an aspiration toward the double articulation of the personal and the liturgical. It is by no means surprising that we see them in common use in the religious revival of the first mendicant missions, in the civic life of the town centers, and in the powerfully emotive public religion of the penitential movements. Salimbene writes of a certain hermit, Brother Benedictus, called "the friar of the cornet," and "a great friend of the Friars Minor," who appeared with a large brass horn and apocalyptic attire before the gates of Parma in 1223 to lead the "boys" in antiphonal vernacular praises of the Trinity and the Blessed Virgin. This Brother Benedict, "a simple and illiterate man," may or may not be identical with Giovanni da Vicenza, "Brother J.," identified as a Franciscan by the Benedictine historian Richard of San Germano, who was an eye witness to the arrival of the Alleluia chorus to that town in June of 1233.

The religious arena in which the *laude* flourished, however, was not that of the eremitic wilderness but of the religious confraternities of the increasingly "urban" landscape of Italy and Provence.[66] These confraternities, which played a signal role in the development of sacred drama as well, multiplied very rapidly, not only on the Mediterranean littoral but in the north as well, often under the patronage of Franciscan or Dominican chapters. Though these social groupings were of the greatest importance in the formation of a truly popular spirituality in the vernacular period, there is much about them that we still must learn; for they provided their members a wide and superficially inconsistent range of spiritual and material services, from "round-robin" intercession to dowry loans and burial insurance.

The commanding spiritual themes of the specifically mendicant fraternities, as also of many others, were two: penance and praise, and particularly the praise of the Blessed Virgin Mary. In Italy the *laudario,* or hymn collection, of a local fraternity might be at once a shared service book and a trophy of the particular and local excellence of the native lyric muse. In its encouragement of the local and even the personal in stylistic expression, the tradition of the vernacular *lauda* established a certain immediate distance from that international and anonymous tradition of medieval Latin hymnody with which it is in some other respects continuous.

By far the most famous of the confraternal *laudari* is that from Cortona, an ancient town midway between Assisi and Siena. This precious manuscript, which almost certainly belonged to the confraternity of Santa Maria della Laude at the church dedicated to St. Francis, is one of the great treasures of thirteenth-century letters in

[66] See the excellent introduction in *Laude Dugentesche,* ed. Giorgio Varanini (Milan, 1972), pp. ix-xlv.

Italy.[67] Its early if imprecise date and the extraordinary range of its lyric inventions and experimentation, together with the rare musical notation which it provides for many of the lyrics, make it a unique witness to the vitality and varied beauty of a new kind of popular hymnody whose chief characteristics are affective piety, the sensuous exploitation of mystical metaphor, bold but versatile rhapsodic cadence, and at times an insistently personal voice. Its hymnody is as different from that of Fortunatus or the Ambrosian school as are the *Considerazioni sulle stimmate* from the *Orationes* of St. Anslem. Its pages open an important new chapter in the history of Western lyric poetry.

The Cortona *laude* are casually liturgical in their organization, the subjects of the poems being roughly divided *de tempore* and *de sanctis.* The major feasts of the Christian year from Christmas to All Hallows have been provided with appropriate hymns. The lyric "calendar" of the saints is rather less systematic, though it includes many of the most popular cults of the twelfth century, such as those of St. John the Evangelist, St. Michael, and the Magdalene, along with the "founding" saints of the Order, Francis and Anthony. Many of the best poems are dedicated to the Virgin—an observation which would hold true of the Franciscan lyric in all languages—and many are devoted not even in a formulaic sense to an historical object or feast or saint, but to a spiritual mood or theme, particularly that of penance. One of the manuscript's most remarkable features is its inclusion of four songs by a named author, a certain "doctor Garzo" who has in each case signed his work in the concluding stanza,

[67] "Laudi cortonesi del secolo XIII," ed. Guido Mazzoni, *Il Propugnatore,* II, ii (1889), 205-270, and III, i (1890), 5-48; good selections in Contini, *Poeti del Duecento* and Varanini, *Laude Dugentesche.*

and who presents his praises, at once deeply personal and liturgically anonymous, to Our Lady:

De la dolcore ke 'n te e tanta
lingua ne core non po dicer quanta.
Garço doctore di voi, donna, canta,
virgene sancta, cum tutto honorança.

Garzo was by no means the only Franciscan poet to "sign his name," and with the Franciscan lyricists we begin to move out of the world of poetic anonymity. A poem, no less than a sermon or a *summa*, could be proudly passed on as the work of a certain *frater* or *magister*. I have already mentioned in an earlier chapter Ugo Panziera, one of Lady Poverty's troubadours. In England we find the beautiful and ambitious "love rune," written in the full self-consciousness of courtly tradition and in part with its stylized erotic language, "a song which friar Thomas of Hales of the Order of Friars Minor composed at the request of a girl consecrated to God."[68] In the same province of Anglia flourished Friar William Herbert, who vernacularized, in the sense both of translation and of adaptation, a number of the most splendid Latin liturgical hymns, and, in the fifteenth century, James Ryman, an uneven but prolific poet, whose spiritual subject matter lies scattered across the whole spectrum of Franciscan life.[69] At this same late period on the Continent we might single out, among many others, Friar Iñigo de Mendoza, author of the *Coplas de vida Christi*.[70] But the greatest of all the Franciscan lyricists

[68] *English Lyrics of the XIIIth Century*, ed. Carleton Brown (Oxford, 1932), p. 68.

[69] Some hymns of Herbert (Herebert) are published by Carleton Brown in *Religious Lyrics of the XIVth Century*, 2nd ed. (Oxford, 1957), pp. 15 ff.; "Die Gedichte des Franziskaners Jacob Ryman," *Archiv für das Studium der neueren Sprachen und Litteraturen*, lxxix (1892), 167-338.

[70] See Julio Rodríguez-Puértolas, *Fray Iñigo de Mendoza y sus "Coplas de Vita Christi"* (Madrid, 1968).

was also one of the earliest, the Umbrian Jacopo Benedetti, known in religion as Brother Jacopone da Todi.[71]

Jacopone from Todi, that most magnificantly understated of the "hill towns," carved from the very rock of its foundation, was one of the purest spirits of his age and the most versatile lyric poet of medieval Italy; yet his spiritual greatness has been clouded by the stormy controversies of the poverty debate and his essential poetic genius undervalued by a critical tradition mesmerized by the enamelled and often vacuous elegance of the *dolce stil nuovo.* His life was an emblem of the creative power of love which was the Franciscan agony. Like his master Francis, whose memory never dimmed in his mind or in his songs, Jacopone was a young man of parts, with money, prospects, good connections, and the fine opinion of the world. All this he threw over, under dramatic and moving circumstances, for the love of holy poverty, *"Povertate poco amata,"* that bride whom he could share with Christ and Francis, and to whom he remained always true, whether on the green and pleasant slopes of La Verna or in the damp cellars of the Pope's dungeons.

The *laude* of Jacopone are immensely rich, nuanced, varied, personal. He makes of the rustic rhythms of the *ballata* a vehicle of astonishing versatility, appropriate for the simplest kind of catechism or the boldest and most abrasive forms of satire. He is capable of accommodating unprepossessing doctrine to the catchy rhythms of the popular song, or of investing the same simple melodies with complex felt experience and the ecstasies of the spirit. His song is both the intuition and the expression of the authentic experience of love:

[71] The edition of the *Laude* by Franco Mancini (Bari, 1974) superseded earlier work and contains full bibliographical information.

O iubelo de core
che fai cantar d'amore[72]

or

Amor, devino foco
amor de riso e ioco,
amor, no dai a poco
cà e' ricco esmesurato.[73]

Jacopone is the poet of many voices and is, indeed, one of the earliest poets in any language to develop such a diversified repertory of "personal" lyric experience. His bitter attacks on Boniface VIII, his and Dante's *bete noire,* have commanded a wide interest in our own day, an age of vituperative "confrontation," but his brittle moral self-confidence, only a step away from self-righteousness, hardly represents the best even of his darker moods. For that we must turn to a piece like *Que farai, fra Iacovone?,* a meditation upon his imprisonment in which the specific material circumstances of his bondage —a stinking latrine, a meal of onions—become the powerful metaphors of penitential energy.

Though his themes are often personal, his own experience is never the final subject of any poem as it is so often with the worldly lovers of the Sicilian School. Instead, his poetry is always exemplary, pointing to an external and objective moral universe which demands, explains, qualifies, and finally redeems the sufferings of the poetic voice. His greatest theme is love, then penance and poverty. They all come together in the sorrows of Christ and His Mother, emotionally, to a degree "realistically," yet finally supernaturally imagined in a manner shared with St. Bernard and the author of the *Meditationes vitae Christi.* His most famous lyric, *Donna de*

[72] *Laude,* ed. Mancini, p. 35.
[73] *Laude,* ed. Mancini, p. 108.

Paradiso, takes the form of a dramatic dialogue distributed among the figures of a Gothic Crucifixion by Giotto or Simonetti. The stately, almost ceremonious disbursal of the dialogue into four-line stanzas of the *ballata* keeps the literary imitation of the Passion at a certain liturgical distance, but in the studied and pathetic colloquialism of the language Jacopone has already fully developed the visceral power to make sacred history quake and weep which we associate with the great masterpieces of the Corpus Christi drama a century and more later. "O mamma, o' n'ei venuta?" cries out the Christ to His Mother; and she answers in the template images of the Pietà:

> Figlio bianco e biondo,
> figlio volto iocondo,
> figlio, per ché t'ha 'l mondo,
> figlio, così sprezzato?[74]

The vernacular religious lyric of the thirteenth, fourteenth, and early fifteenth centuries is perhaps the most explicit witness to the emergence throughout Europe of a pervasive and durable "Franciscan" style in which the conscious manipulation of vicarious emotional experience has become an important element.[75] We shall find in this extraordinary, international outburst of song a full repertory, developed with an almost unbelievable completeness of detail, of a verbal iconography of the Cross, the Passion, the Man of Sorrows, the *pietà,* the *Mater dolorosa*—large and gripping pathetic images, painted with the panchromatic vivacity of rouged bruises and carmined blood, images always pointed to

[74] *Laude,* ed. Mancini, p. 205.

[75] See Luciano Canonici, "La Passione di Cristo nei poeti francescani" in *La Passione di Gesù Cristo nella Spiritualità francescana* (Quaderni di Spiritualità francescana, 4 [Assisi, 1962]).

an affective piety of penance. When Christ's Mother swooned weeping to the ground, when Christ Himself addressed sinners from His bloody cross or, as in the brilliant English lyric "Lullay, lullay, little child, why weepest thou so sore?," the Christ-child wept in His cradle in anticipation of the Passion, singers and hearers too might share in the hot, salt tears that were, according to the famous penitentiaries of the Orders, the condiment of true contrition.

To call this style "realistic," as is sometimes done, is both inaccurate and inadequate, for though it encouraged to a point the development of an intermittent visual verisimilitude, its principal aim was never the depiction of what from a medieval point of view we so laughably call "real life" but the arresting engagement of the visceral and the emotional, in the classical manner of the Bonaventurean *accessus,* to begin a spiritual assent beyond the realm of sensory experience. In its artistic condescension to the tactile and visual, and in its expression in the hand-clap rhythms of peasant dances, Franciscan spiritual style raised the suspicions both of the elite ascetics of the Benedictine tradition and of the iconoclastic reformers of the Conciliar period; but within its own cultural limitations, it greatly enriched the aesthetic possibilities of ordinary men and women in Gothic Europe, and became the indispensable medium, during a protracted and vital period of Western art history, of serious attempts to render the true and the beautiful.

One further implication of this style can bring an end to this tentative chapter by suggesting, tentatively, a topic which must certainly engage the close attention of students of Franciscan literature in the future. That implication is latent in the style's dramatic character, its typical exploitation of the verbal and visual evocations of an anachronistic sacred history which simultaneously "was" and "is." The "dialogue" of the *Donna de paradiso* is, in fact, more complex, more inventive, and far more theatrical in its assumptions than is that of the *Quem quaeretis* trope, or the *Processio prophetarum,* or the other purely "liturgical drama" from which the mystery plays were once thought to have evolved through the severe editorial process of Darwinian natural selection. The pictorial *tableaux* of the Franciscan lyric, particularly in their detailed and didactic exploration of the Passion, are in effect often dramatic "scenes" which in their lack of narrative wholeness at times insistently point to a larger frame of "plot" or "story," accessible to their audiences but absent from the naked printed page.[76]

There is considerable if scattered positive evidence linking the Franciscans to the production of religious drama in the fourteenth century. The "sacred representations" of Italy, the dramatic *laude,* combining often highly emotional public processions with scriptural "histories," have clear Franciscan associations. We know from Lecoy de la March and others that preaching frequently accompanied, or explained, the performance of the religious drama in France. David Jeffrey has gathered an impressive dossier of evidence which documents the specific connections between Franciscans and religious theater in England.[77] I have seen with my own eyes, as Thomas of Celano might say, an ancient nativity play, *Los Pastores,* "brought from Spain many years ago" by Franciscan missionaries, in the words of the prologue spoken by a player dressed as a friar, and per-

[76] Rosemary Woolf, *The English Religious Lyric in the Middle Ages* (Oxford, 1968), p. 45.

[77] David L. Jeffrey, "Franciscan Spirituality and the Rise of Early English Drama," *Mosaic,* viii (1975), 17-46.

formed with minstrelsy in a church in Las Cruces, New Mexico in 1975.

Does this evidence argue for a "Franciscan origin" of the mystery plays? Perhaps not, though, like much of the evidence adduced by the most distinguished work on medieval drama in recent years, it certainly can argue against the hope of finding a single and simple "source" for a spiritual and literary phenomenon which was neither single nor simple. It also clearly demonstrates what we would have in any case to expect, that the friars found in this carnal reenactment of the history of salvation the appropriate resource of an evangelism which had as its commanding ambition the most vivid and effective extension of the Incarnation, wherein the invisible God, for the salvation of His people, had taken on the flesh of a very man.

5

Bonaventure and the Themes of Franciscan Mysticism

The Franciscan life is a life of double movement, of an outward journey and an inward one. In the last chapter I attempted to suggest some of the literary implications of the Franciscan sense of the *vita apostolica* which in the century following the founder's death made a mission field of antique Christendom itself. The Franciscan literature of the interior journey is scarcely less diverse, though by its very nature it may be somewhat more hermetic and difficult of access. The special features of Franciscan mysticism, to use the inevitable but not entirely happy word, are closely associated with the particular spiritual emphases of the Order, especially Franciscan poverty, and with the troubled spiritual history of the second half of the thirteenth century. These distinctive features cannot alone characterize the riches of the Franciscan mystical "school," which looks back beyond Francis to the classical sources of Christian asceticism, but they are defining pecularities.

In the first place, no major spiritual movement of the Middle Ages had been so intimately associated with the personality of its founder. The relationship between

Gregory the Great and Benedict of Nursia in the sixth century is closely analogous to that between Bonaventure and Francis in the thirteenth. In each case a younger man, still a child at the death of the elder, lived his life under his spiritual influence and became his "official" biographer. But in Gregory's life of Benedict in the *Dialogues* we shall find none of the absolutely personal quality of the *Legenda major,* let alone that of Thomas of Celano and the Leo sources. Most early Franciscans were convinced not merely of the spiritual greatness of their founder, but of his positive uniqueness in the history of salvation. Their attitude was often born of an overtly Joachimist view of history, in which the advent of the Order was itself a sign of apocalyptic significance; and sometimes, as in the case of Gerard of Borgo San Donnino and his "introduction" to the *Everlasting Gospel,* it descended to a vulgar and shocking heresy. In its most noble expression, as we find it in the *Sacrum Commercium* for example, the belief in the unique quality of Franciscan spiritual life becomes itself poetic energy.

Of course no religious movement springs into the world totally without roots, traditions, influences, and implied or acknowledged models, and Franciscanism, for all of its "newness," inevitably shared much in common with the "evangelical" and "apostolic" movements of the eleventh and twelfth centuries, particularly those of the south of France and of Lombardy. Unlike the Dominicans, who though they developed their own particular "constitutions" had simply appropriated the *Rule of St. Augustine,* the "common life" of the canonic reform, the Franciscans from the start *did* have their special and quite novel legislation. Yet they also had important spiritual bonds with the established orders, and particularly with the reformed Benedictines, the Cistercians. Bernard of Clairvaux, a great master of affective piety, was a friar *avant la lettre.*

It is not my intention in this chapter to offer a synoptic biography of Franciscan "mystics" or even a survey of the themes of Franciscan "mysticism." That has been done often enough and certainly well enough by others.[1] I shall presume, however, to introduce two or three Franciscan masters of the interior life and to suggest some ways in which their commanding ideas, and their characteristic styles of expression, indelibly marked the literary history of medieval Europe.

The discussion of medieval Franciscanism in almost any of its varied facets must return again and again to the same name, that of St. Bonaventure, the polymath genius whose influence upon the Order was so powerfully profound as to win for him the just title of "Second Founder." Minister General of the Order of Friars Minor, Cardinal of the Roman Church, Seraphic Doctor, saint, one of "those who were truly great," Bonaventure of Bagnoreggio was a man whose intellectual and moral achievements would have marked him out in any age for contemporary admiration and for the veneration of posterity. The central decades of the thirteenth century, however, were not "any age" but a golden age—of the medieval university, the springtime of the Franciscan Order, and the great heyday of an exuberant Gothic style in art and life. Bonaventure's extraordinary importance to the history of Franciscan literature cannot be understood adequately outside the broader context of his life and times.

Bonaventure's Franciscanism was neither accidental nor external, but profound, radical, essential to his reli-

[1] Cf. the bibliography in the *Omnibus,* pp. 1726 ff.

gious formation. His life overlapped that of the founder by the better part of a decade, and his primary education was at the feet of men who had walked the dusty roads of Umbria with him. Bonaventure was linked to his spiritual master by even more intimate ties, as he tells us himself at the end of the *Legenda minor.* "All over the world God's gifts are still being bestowed in abundance, through Francis' intercession; I who have written this life know this from my own experience. When I was still only a child, I became seriously ill and my mother made a vow to St. Francis, so that I was snatched from the jaws of death and restored to perfect health and strength. I remember it well and I put it on record now, for fear that I might be condemned for ingratitude, if I failed to mention such a favor."[2]

At Paris he studied with Alexander of Hales, the first and in some ways the finest of the major scholastic philosophers to wear the gray habit. Their relationship was one of mutual admiration, and Master Alexander once said of his disciple, "When I look at him, I see no evidence that Adam ever fell." As the official and appointed legislator of the Order and its official biographer —the editor of the Constitutions of Narbonne and of the *Legenda major*—Bonaventure was to have a crucial role in defining the nature and history of medieval Franciscanism. "Second Founder" is hardly hyperbole.

One is never fearless when approaching a giant, but St. Bonaventure has been well served by his *alumni,* and there is no major medieval thinker who has been made more accessible to modern scholars than he. The great edition of the *Opera Omnia,* prepared by the Quaracchi Fathers and published from their presses between 1882 and 1902, achieved a standard of critical excellence which

[2] *Legenda minor,* VII, 8; *Omnibus,* p. 830.

was revolutionary in its own time and is inspirational in ours. Beside its splendid pages the format of the Vienna Fathers seems dull and that of the *Corpus Christianorum* worse than dull. Such an edition is only now coming into being for Bernard, is still a distant prospect for Augustine, and has barely been dreamed of for Jerome or Ambrose. The Quaracchi edition and its lavish indices have made possible not merely a rich secondary literature of unusual quality but also a number of extremely helpful *guides de lecture* and reference works, the most important of which are E. Longpré's classic article "La théologie mystique de S. Bonaventure," J. Guy Bougerol's *Introduction à l'étude de St. Bonventure,* the *Lexique S. Bonaventure,* and the *Thesaurus Bonaventurianus,* a computer concordance now in progress.[3]

Bonaventure's written works are numerous and diverse, for they reflect not merely the fluent articulation of a restless spiritual imagination but the public pronouncements of a busy career as teacher, preacher, and statesman of the Order of Friars Minor. I of course do not intend to discuss, or even to mention, all of this vast *oeuvre,* but it is not possible to suggest Bonaventure's contribution to the literature of mystical piety without at least mentioning the larger context from which it grew.

From Bonaventure the teacher we have, first, the expansive commentary on the *Sentences* of Peter Lombard. The *Sentences*—an anthology of *setentiae* or authoritative scriptural and patristic opinions on theological matters —was the standard "set text" for theology students at the university. Its structure, four books divided into a

[3] E. Longpré, "La théologie mystique," *AFH,* XIV (1921), 36-108; J. Bougerol, *Introduction à l'étude* (Tournai, 1961); *Lexique Saint Bonaventure,* ed. Bougerol (Paris, 1969); *Thesaurus Bonaventurianus* (Louvain, 1972-); to these should be added the *Bibliographia Bonaventuriana,* ed. Bougerol (Quaracchi, 1974), which is the fifth volume of *S. Bonaventura 1274-1974.*

large number of "distinctions" and subdivided into seemingly innumerable chapters, is at best an ambiguous victory for twelfth-century order. There are indeed meandering paths through that forest, but they are hardly obvious to the stranger who steps for the first time into the heavy shadow of the wood. Yet no book aside from the Bible itself is more fundamental to the formation of academic theology in the thirteenth century, and its scholastic explication was the principal medium for the publication of theological ideas until the time of the Reformation and even beyond. Most scholastic commentaries on the *Sentences,* however "important" or exciting their ideas, make dreary reading. Bonaventure's is hardly light, but it does combine authority, eloquence, and imagination in a way which can remind us of the fundamental meaning of the word "magisterial."

It was also as a teacher that Bonaventure composed his exegetical works, few in number but powerful in effect. His commentaries on Ecclesiastes and the Book of Wisdom are among the finest treatments of the sapiential literature of the Old Testament before the great Wisdom commentary of Robert Holkot, O.P., in the fourteenth century. He wrote as well on the Gospel of John, but his great exegetical masterpiece is the thick commentary on Luke, which is copious, learned, mellow, and studded with some of the finest prose ornament in all of the doctor's work. It still towers beside the work of Ambrose, which it reverences but never apes, as one of the greatest of all medieval expositions of the third evangelist. To the professorial corpus must be added as well a number of theological *questiones disputatae,* at least some of which are of literary interest, and some theological sermons on such subjects as the Trinity, the Kingdom of God, and the sacramental Body of Christ.

The vocation of the teacher was closely associated with the office of the preacher, and we have from Bonaventure's pen several series of sermons, including sermons *de tempore* (for the Sundays and certain other special days of the liturgical year), sermons *de sanctis* (for the festival days of saints), and sermons *de Beata Virgine Maria* (for the Marian feasts). They are of a learned and indeed explicitly academic character, but they do not altogether lack the affective impulses of a Berthold of Regensburg or a Bernardino of Siena. Likewise the famous collations—which were in effect a specialized genre of sermon or perhaps "seminar"—should be mentioned in this connection. Bonaventure has often been credited with a series of interesting collations on the Gospel of John, one of the books to which he devoted a formal commentary, but these are probably the work of John of Wales. Of undisputed authorship are his collations on the Ten Commandments (1267), those on the seven gifts of the Holy Ghost (1268), and, the greatest of them all, the collations *In Hexaemeron,* which were unfinished at the time of his death in 1274.

All of Bonaventure's collations have a peculiar theological importance which grows out of the university setting in which they were composed, but the *Collationes in Hexaemeron* combine a maturity of thought with an unfaltering justness of style which make of them, in Bougerol's words, "the testament of a theologian solely preoccupied with leading minds and hearts to the knowledge and love of the sole teacher of wisdom, Christ."[4] The context which explains Bonaventure's dominant concerns in the *Hexaemeron* collations was the Parisian climate of Averroistic speculation, a climate made known to us most prominently by the condemnations of 1277.

[4] Bougerol, *Introduction a l'étude,* p. 186.

The work's medieval subtitle was the *Illuminationes Ecclesiae,* the "Lights of the Church," the seven levels of mental and spiritual illumination which begin with the intelligent perception of the world of nature and go on, or were meant to, to the Beatific Vision itself. Against the errors of the academicians, Bonaventure constructs an insistently Augustinian argument. Christ, the unique demonstration of human moral perfection, is likewise both the beginning and the end of human wisdom. The edifice of wisdom cannot be built upon the foundations of folly, and Bonaventure is particularly scornful of the vacuity of academic "metaphysics." The "true metaphysician" is the earnestly searching Christian who will see God articulated in his Verbum, the Word made flesh, and who, illuminated by the spiritual rays of divine emanation, will follow them back to their source (I, 17).[5] The mode of argument, exemplarism, is a peculiar characteristic of Bonaventure's thought. Its relevance to literary study is considerable, and we must return to it in a moment.

Bonaventure was elected Minister General of the Order of Friars Minor in 1257, and from that time until his death seventeen years later he had few moments which were truly his own. The greatest monument to his administrative career will of course not be found on the written page but in the spirit of the Order as it grappled with difficult and unforeseen problems of growth in the third quarter of the thirteenth century. Nonetheless, several of the books connected with Bonaventure's political career are of notable importance. I have already discussed in earlier chapters his biographies of Francis, works which will maintain a freshness and urgency as long as Francis of Assisi makes a claim on men's minds

[5] *Opera,* II, p. 332; trans. José de Vinck, p. 10.

and hearts, and the *Apologia pauperum,* the finest literary defense of mendicancy ever written.

The felicity of Bonaventure's style is quite distinctive, and it lies neither in an austere classicism nor in a remarkable lucidity. On the contrary, his Latin is often syntactically adventurous, meandering, and difficult to construe with confidence. His prose lacks the concentrated vigor of Jerome and the control of John of Salisbury. Yet it has special qualities—qualities both of the mind and of the heart—which guarantee for Bonaventure a permanent place among the great stylists of the golden age of medieval Latinity and which continue to exert their diverse attractions upon his readers today. After reading the *Collations on the Hexaemeron* or the *Mind's Road to God,* one will find Anselm puzzlingly cautious in his use of language and St. Thomas positively drab. Bonaventure's style is eminently Franciscan in that it combines an academic authority grounded in Ciceronian rhetoric with the varied *tempi* of the evangelical spirit: languor, laud, mystery. Bougerol writes of this style: "The simple art of St. Francis in the Canticle of the Sun becomes more learned with St. Bonaventure, but he still maintains that freshness of the fountain where, definitively, he found his most profound inspiration."[6]

This is, as Fr. Bougerol knows, to put the matter somewhat inexactly; for of course the real "fountain" for St. Bonaventure was not St. Francis alone, but *his* fountain, the Holy Scriptures, which are at once his constant literary inspiration, his rhetorical guide, and his authorial model. The Scriptures, a perfect symphony of letter and spirit, present the codified treasury of Christian wisdom adorned with the true eloquence which should always be the aim of Christian letters. Bonaventure states this

[6] Bougerol, *Introduction à l'étude,* p. 97.

idea with characteristic eloquence in a beautiful medley of the nineteenth collation on the *Hexaemeron*: "He who would learn," writes the Seraphic Doctor, "let him go to the fountain, that is, to the Bible, for in the philosophers there is no knowledge of the remission of sins, nor even in the Summae of the theologians, except insofar as they are based on the patristic sources which are themselves grounded in the Bible."[7] The Scriptures are a *school* in which the whole range of human *scientia* is available. At this school, children begin to learn their ABC's before proceeding to the more advanced aspects of grammar and composition, and long before attempting matters more difficult still. Those difficult matters, the aim of literary study and its reward, lie in the full spiritual sense of the Scriptures and the mystery which breathes beneath and through their letter. He illustrates his point with an exegetical idea taken from St. Gregory concerning Christ's first miracle, the miracle of the wedding at Cana. Why, he asks, did Christ, when He set out to perform the miracle, first ask that the empty firkins be filled with water? Why did he not merely say, *Fiat aqua,* or else make the wine *ex nihilo*? In the letter of the text we shall find no answer, but in the spirit we learn that the passage is, curiously, a passage about itself. It is only when we are filled to capacity with the "water" of elementary scriptural study—its ABC's, to revert to Bonaventure's image—that the spiritual miracle can take place within us, only then that we can hope to be given the Scriptures' hidden sense. In this sound principle of Augustinian hermeneutics Bonaventure offers his readers the key to understanding the foundation of his own mystical writings. In the same passage he says that the "entire Scriptures are like a *cithara,* in which the base

[7] Collatio XIX, 7; *Opera,* II, p. 421; trans. de Vinck, pp. 286-87.

chords do not sound by themselves, but only in reaction to the others." In like manner, each scriptural passage depends upon other passages, "each place with a thousand others."

There is a wonderful justness about this musical image, itself taken from patristic exegetical tradition, for it describes not merely the literary operations of the Scriptures but those of Bonaventure's works as well. His writing is never without the rigorous sense of extrinsically imposed form which we associate with the scholastic method; yet it never surrenders itself entirely to its mechanical divisions, subordinations, distinctions, and symmetries. Some medieval scholastics write as though they thought that language could be espaliered and whittled into verbal topiaries, like privets and plum trees. Our word *dunce*, derived from the name of a great Franciscan scholastic, hints at a literary truth beyond the malice of etymology. The true structural beauty of Bonaventure's work, taken as a whole, will be found in its qualities of harmony and counterpoint, internal rhythms both of thought and prosody, the establishment of a distinctive and privileged poetic vocabulary, and the imaginative juxtaposition of ideas.

It has often been said that the broad task of scholastic theology was to construct a continuum between the unseen God and the world of the material creation, or, again, to "reconcile faith and reason." Stated thus generally and imprecisely, the idea is unexceptional, but it fails to account for an important, indeed a crucial, motive which animated Bonaventure and many other thinkers. In some ways, St. Thomas Aquinas was what we might today call an "intellectual"; at least he would have understood the term. Bonaventure was emphatically not one. Nowhere in the thick volumes of the Quaracchi edition, not even in the most limited theological *quaestiones,* will we find legitimate evidence that theology is for Bonaventure a closed mental system, a mathematics, a dead language, a game or any of the other intellectual opiates of the medieval and modern Averroists. For Bonaventure the aim of theology is intensely (and to some, perhaps, offensively) practical. Its aim is to know God not as a distant and abstract category of philosophy, but as the active and loving Creator of material and spiritual life and the legislator and judge of human acts. Knowing God has consequences of a dramatic nature in terms of spiritual dynamism and moral growth.

In the metaphoric language of spiritual life in the Augustinian tradition we can see this truth. Knowledge of God involves a quest, a journey, a pilgrimage; the human capacity ascends by ladder rungs or spiral ramps or simply by the steep and stony trail to the divine presence. In Bonaventure's most famous spiritual work—*The Mind's Road to God*—there are metaphors of both horizontal and vertical movement, of walking and climbing. St. Bonaventure's "mystical theology" is his attempt to describe in practical terms the ways in which the human consciousness can know God and love Him, and it is in this context that he develops the language of "exemplarity" or "exemplarism" (neither of them particularly comfortable English terms) which is so useful in thinking about various kinds of medieval literature.[8]

There is no single Bonaventurean "doctrine" of the *exemplar,* and to speak of the matter briefly is to invite a certain amount of superficiality. Bonaventure uses the word *exemplar* in several different senses, cognate but by no means interchangeable, and it is important for our purposes to distinguish between at least two of

[8] See the article "Exemplarisme" by Albert Ampe, *DS,* IV, cols. 1870-1878.

them. In the first place, an *exemplar* is any model of a thing or act; such is the *exemplar* from which a secondary manuscript might be copied. Secondly, we should note that there is a special relationship in Bonaventure's vocabulary between the words *exemplar* and *image.* In his commentary on the *Sentences* (I, d. 31, part 2, art. 1) he explains that the *exemplar* is active, the *image* passive. The image, that is, is the reflected or imitated form of the *exemplar.* Now in Bonaventure's thought—closely akin to that of Augustine—God is the *exemplar* or defining model both of the created cosmos and of the real but incorporeal world of moral beauty. Jesus Christ, the uncreated Word, is at once and uniquely *exemplar* and *image.* That is, He is the model by which the moral world defines itself and the image by which God expresses and knows Himself.

The most succinct statement of this mystery comes in a surprising place, in the *Defense of the Mendicants*: "We should understand that since Christ is the Word both Uncreated and Incarnate, there is in Him a twofold principle of exemplarity, the one eternal and the other temporal. By the eternal, I mean the principle according to which He is the brightness of the Father's glory, and the image of His substance, and also the refulgence of eternal light, the spotless mirror of the power of God. In this mirror all things shine forth in their exemplarity, and they are produced, in their spirit and in their matter, from the beginning of the creation of the world until its end, for the perfecting of the entire universe. It is in this sense that Christ is the Uncreated Word, the intellectual Mirror and the eternal Exemplar of the whole fabric of creation. But insofar as He is the Incarnate Word, in the actuality of His assumed humanity, He is also the mirror of all graces, virtues, and merits; and therefore the dwelling of the Church Militant should be set up at this example, the dwelling of which Moses mysteriously says: See that you make it according to the pattern shown you on the mountain."[9]

Bonaventure's great theological works stand today like massive monuments in stone or bronze, great public works which commemorate the glories of a certain moment in the history of Christian thought. For them he will always be remembered and honored; but he will be read for his work as an artist in cameos, an incisor of ivory and carver of cherry and walnut. He is one of the masters of the theological "novel," but he is *the* master of the theological "short story." What are usually called his "mystical *opuscula*"—and in particular three of them, the *Itinerarium Mentis in Deum*, the *De triplici via*, and the *Lignum vitae*—are among the most beautiful and most influential of all the hundreds of spiritual books of the Middle Ages.[10]

Each of these three books made important contributions to the popular vocabulary of religious experience in the late Middle Ages. The *Mind's Road to God* is at once Bonaventure's most explicitly "Franciscan" spiritual manual and the simplest demonstration of his ideas of exemplarism in practice. Like Petrarch's *Ascent of Mount Ventoux* in the next century, Bonaventure's spiritual ascent begins with a physical one, a climb up Mount Alverna, where Francis had received the stigmata. Francis' vision of the six-winged seraph, recollected, becomes the structuring metaphor of the entire work. "In my meditation, it was at once clear to me that this vision represented not only the contemplative rapture of our

[9] *Apologia Pauperum*, II, 12; *Opera*, VIII, 242-243; de Vinck, *Defense of the Mendicants*, pp. 29-30.

[10] All three works are published in the first volume of de Vinck's *Mystical Opuscula*.

father, but also the road by which this rapture is attained."[11] The work then sketches, with a simplicity somewhat disguised by an exuberantly Gothic facade of symbolic symmetries, the steps by which the human mind can progress in the knowledge of God as illuminated in the physical and moral landscapes.

The *Lignum vitae*, mentioned in an earlier chapter in connection with the *Liber Conformitatum* of Barthelmy of Pisa, demonstrates the pleasing harmony of the visual and verbal imaginations in Bonaventure's pastoral writings. It imagines the life of Christ in terms of a tree, and encourages its readers to picture it in their imaginations. The imagined picture of the *lignum vitae* actually appears in a number of the surviving manuscripts, and it was painted in a stunning mural on the walls of the refectory of the Franciscan house of the Holy Cross in Florence in the second half of the fourteenth century. Either of these works—or for that matter several others so far not even mentioned, such as the *Breviloquium*, the *Soliloquium*, the *Vitis mystica*, and the *De Sex aliis Seraphin*—would repay a detailed analysis of imaginative conception, metaphoric vocabulary, and literary structure. But that would become a book, or at least a chapter, on the literary art of St. Bonaventure. For representative purposes the work which most clearly and simply exposes the major contours of Bonaventure's mystical system within its indispensable ascetic context is the *De triplici via*, a work of pamphlet length which takes up a scant thirty pages of the Quaracchi edition. Its influence has been enormous, and any student of medieval literature, interested in the processes of the movement of ideas from the

[11] *Itinerarium*, Prologue, 2; *Opera*, V, p. 295; de Vinck, *Mystical Opuscula I*, p. 6.

realm of the high culture to that of the people, will find few more instructive examples than this work.[12]

The mystical significance of numbers plays a large part in Bonaventure's literary imagination. Three's and seven's, and the multiples of three's and seven's, so dear to Franciscan and to medieval thought generally, he uses both as the supporting beams and the decorative panels of his literary edifices. The metaphysical wit of numerology, which so often becomes trite and mechanical in other writers, is seldom oppressive in Bonaventure's works, however, for the structuring principles they supply are no extrinsic afterthought but a radical part of the man's mind and art. Bonaventure is profoundly immersed in an Augustinian anthropology which sees God's image and similitude indelibly stamped in human nature in a radical trinity of memory, will, and understanding. This basic fact has for Bonaventure wide empirical and spiritual verification, and it is repeatedly revealed by mystery in the Scriptures.

The difficulty which a text like the *De triplici via* presents to modern readers does not reside in an obvious surface complexity but in a somewhat misleading simplicity. Words like "soul," "prayer," "contemplation," and so forth have for St. Bonaventure and for most medieval spiritual writers a specific, technical content which cannot be suggested by their rather pale and imprecise modern reflexes. Furthermore, it is too easy to characterize the work as "mystical" or "spiritual" in nature without seeing what its author and certainly many of its readers and imitators surely saw as an essential practicality.

[12] A particularly useful edition for students of literature is that of V. M. Breton, *La triple voie de saint Bonaventure* (Paris, 1942).

Some hint of the scope of Bonaventure's ambition for *multum in parvo* will be found in the scriptural text which he takes for his little book: "Behold I have described to thee three manner of ways, in thoughts and knowing." The text comes from one of the most beautiful sapiential medleys in Proverbs; specifically, it is a poetic exordium from the mouth of Divine Wisdom encouraging men to love and follow her. The full context of the passage is poetically very rich, and it includes clear suggestions of ascetic discipline, of the active reformation of morals and the practice of charity, and of the spiritual understanding of things unseen.

In reading the *De triplici via* it is particularly helpful to perceive that the work is grounded in what was for Bonaventure and his audience a functionally viable "psychology," poetic in its structure as indeed are our own popularly credited psychological systems, but nonetheless true to empirical experience. In fact Bonaventure begins constructing his argument at the level of *scientific* observations. Since "every kind of knowing shows forth a relationship with the Trinity" (*cum omnis scientia gerat Trinitatis insigne*) it is far from unexpected that the triple way itself submits to a triple explication.[13] It has a meaning with regard to the understanding of Holy Scripture, another with regard to the tripartite hierarchy of the soul's faculties, and a third with regard to spiritual discipline. As it applies to the Scriptures, the triple way points to the three "senses" of the sacred text which in conventional medieval exegesis lie behind its letter. Bonaventure here calls them the *moralem,* the *allegoricum,* and the *anagogicum.* This codification of aspects of biblical meaning was commonplace by the thirteenth century, but Bonaventure here presents them in analogy

[13] *De triplici via,* I, 2; *Opera,* VIII, p. 3; de Vinck, p. 64.

with the hierarchical operations of the soul: *purgatio, illuminatio,* and *perfectio.* Purgation leads to peace, illumination to truth, and perfection (to be understood as the active process rather than the static state) to charity. The *modus exercendi* with regard to the triple way is of course also triplex; it consists of reading and meditation, prayer, and contemplation.

The enduring fame of the *De triplici via* resides in the spiritual profundity and poetic economy with which Bonaventure elaborates the schematic materials outlined in the prologue. Before we consider the development of the argument, however, it may be well to stress an aspect of Bonaventure's thought which has sometimes been misunderstood even by informed commentators. The "trinities" of the *De triplici via* do not reflect conflicting or even alternative ways of knowing God; they are rather communal participants in a complex unity. In this regard it is of considerable significance that Bonaventure calls his book *The Triple Way* rather than *The Three Ways.* The tropological or moral meaning of a scriptural text, for instance, is not at odds with or radically different from that text's allegorical or anagogical meanings. They are all a complex unity of meaning which can be viewed from the perspective of various special concerns. In a similar manner, what are often called the "three ways" of purgation, illumination, and union are actually hierarchical aspects of a single triplex way—Jesus Christ, who said *"Ego sum via, veritas et vita."*

Hence it is that all three aspects of the triple way are unitively and simultaneously operative; furthermore, although the hierarchy of purgation-illumination-union rightly implies stages or degrees of growth toward perfection, there are all of the three traditional classes of "spiritual men"—beginners, proficients, and experts—at all the levels of the book's teachings. The *De triplici via* is not, therefore, like an academic course, with a spiritual diploma for its alumni, but a continuing and self-consuming program of pilgrimage. It is a book for all sorts and conditions of men, and a book for all seasons. Its subject is the subject of all of Bonaventure's mystical works, without the least exception: the union of the human soul in God through Jesus Christ. Though its tidy triads inevitably evolve a mystical "system," Bonaventure's final interest is not in methodology but love. He assumes, quite without discussion, the basic Augustinian notion that man is made for love, that he must and will have love, that he thirsts for perfect love and too often settles for its perverse or cruel parody. The "triple" way is, therefore, a love song, and its structure is epithalamic. Its subtitle is *alias Incendium Amoris*—"otherwise known as *The Fire of Love*"—and what the "union" of the unitive way is is the marital enjoyment of Christ the *sponsus*.

The purgative way prepares men for the knowledge, and hence the love of God, by separating them from sin—the necessary prolegomenon to spiritual growth at any stage. The illuminative way consists of a formation of morals in a redirection of love based on the imitation of Christ. The operations of purgation, illumination, and, eventually, of union, address three fundamental aspects of Christian "human nature" as described in the theological anthropology which Bonaventure shares with many other medieval writers in the Augustinian tradition. They are conscience, reason, and wisdom, all of which, in however blurred or muted shape or hue, are innate human faculties. The journey toward God begins in man's fumbling and confused recognition of the "spark" of wisdom which excites him to a principled response.[14] The "spark" (*igniculus*) pertains to the highest mode of the triple way, and to nourish it involves necessary preparation: purgation through the prick of conscience, illumination through the light of reason. Thus it is that Bonaventure's argument in the *De triplici via* constantly turns back upon itself, stitching and restitching a whole and apparently seamless cloth of spiritual demonstration. Bonaventure's intellectual method is to ideas as Dante's *terza rima* is to poetry. What a critic has said of Dante's verse applies as profoundly to Bonaventure's habit of thought: "It binds and looses."

It remains to be suggested how the works of a university professor and religious administrator, however profound his ideas or lucid his style, could have exerted so great an influence over the emerging popular cultures of vernacular Europe. Bonaventure is almost always linked with his great Dominican contemporary at Paris, Thomas Aquinas, just as are the two founders of the great mendicant orders themselves. Thomas is the Angelic, Bonaventure the Seraphic Doctor, twin beacons of the Church Militant in the heady days of the thirteenth century. Yet the impact of technical Thomistic thought on popular religion and its literary expression is insignificant. Indeed the influence of Thomism even in learned theological circles in the late Middle Ages, outside the immediate family of the Dominican Order, has been greatly exaggerated. Dante, it is true, is something of a pseudo-Thomist—to use the naughty but accurate phrase of M. de Gandillac—and a few Thomistic hymns established themselves in the familiar repertory of medieval hymnody; but even by a generous appraisal, Thomistic influence on popular literature before 1400 is insignificant.

[14] *De triplici via,* I, 15; *Opera,* VIII, p. 7; de Vinck, p. 71.

Bonaventure's works on the other hand, especially the mystical *opuscula,* had begun to circulate widely in vernacular translations and adaptations even before his death, and multiplied rapidly in the fourteenth century.[15] There are early versions of the *Itinerarium,* for example, in German and Catalan, and an early imitation in English. The major structural patterns of the *De triplici via* virtually monopolize fourteenth-century popular mysticism, and are fundamental to the most successful works of the *Devotio moderna.* And the Bonaventurean attitude to certain genre subjects—the Crucifixion, for example—is clearly visible in the Passion lyrics of a dozen different lands. The truth is that Thomas and the Dominicans generally despised poetry, or at least tried to, believing that the discursive theology of the *Summa* was a sufficient gloss to the revelation of Scripture. Bonaventure, on the other hand, was always a poet with a poet's intuition. For him the entire created order was a book in which the poetic images led the mind, captivated by truth and beauty, to look beyond the visible image to the divine exemplar.

Great writers have many lives. They are reborn in every generation of readers, always new, always different. Certainly the living importance of Bonaventure's literary achievement for the generations which followed his death, for late medieval religious literature of all kinds, would be difficult to exaggerate. In the polarized spiritual climate of the century of the Great Schism in the Church and of the Hundred Years' War, when the legal fictions which had imposed a workable unity on Christian Europe for many centuries seemed at last to be vitiated, at a time when religious thought seemed to

[15] See Kurt Ruh, *Bonaventura deutsch: ein Beitrag zur deutschen Franziskaner-Mystik und -Scholastik* (Bern, 1956).

stagnate in arid, pedantic scholasticism on the one hand or fly to hermetic and often anti-intellectual mystical systems on the other, Bonaventure's extraordinary spiritual imagination answered the articulated need of those who sought the path of continuity which could lead them surely through a forest of uncertainty and change. Even as he had been an arbiter of judicious compromise in the spiritual self-definition of the Franciscan Order in his own lifetime, he reached out through his writings to touch and to direct Christian thinkers of widely divergent sympathies. His music was the new song of charity, set in thrilling variations on themes by Saint Augustine; but he shared much in common as well with two of the greatest spiritual writers of the previous century, St. Bernard and Hugh of St.-Victor. From both of them he had learned a great deal, and he had their gift for speaking with a spiritual and poetic clarity that challenged all sorts and conditions of men.

His own circle of literary admirers, certainly, was very large, and extended from the academic halls of Garlandia to the *béguinages* of Flanders. The most basic university textbook of the Middle Ages after the Bible itself, the "set text" which was the shared challenge and perhaps adversity of thousands of university students, was of course the *Sentences* of Peter Lombard. Bonaventure's *Sentences* commentary is by any reckoning one of the most intellectually elegant of the scholastic period, and it immediately and permanently established for him an academic reputation of the highest order. At the same time the rigorous honesty of his prose, which avoided contrived complexities and faced real ones openly, made a deep impression on those Christian thinkers who were developing the schools of the *docta ignorantia*. Jean Gerson, the fascinatingly complex chancellor of the University of Paris at the end of the fourteenth century, once said that a single little book, *The Mind's Road to God,* was more valuable than all the literature which had ever been written. Most importantly perhaps, in the present context, Bonaventure was one of that limited number of medieval religious writers who created a verbal iconography of spiritual and mystical experience which proved to have the flexibility and the popularity to become a dominant spiritual mode.

In a literary climate in which what we would call plagiarism was a respectful convention by which aspiration paid its debt to achievement, Bonaventure's popularity is to some extent suggested by the wide body of literature which he never wrote but which circulated under his name. The most remarkable achievements of "pseudo-Bonaventure" are the *Sacrum Commercium,* the *Meditationes vitae Christi,* and such works as Rudolph of Biberach's *De Septem Itineribus Aeternitatis.* The flattering list of *spuria* is very long, comparable to the phantom works of Augustine or Bernard.

The *Septem Itineribus Aeternitatis* has, like several other works of its genre, enjoyed something of a shadow-life among the apocrypha of Bonaventure.[16] Its contemporary popularity must have been very great indeed, to judge from manuscript evidence alone, and it was not without its influence on the great spiritual giants of later centuries. In modern times, however, the work has fallen into obscurity. Peltier did publish a serviceable, though uncritical, edition of it in his ambitious *Opera Bonaventurae* in the late nineteenth century, and there has recently appeared an excellent and scholarly edition of the

[16] *De septem itineribus* is published in Peltier's edition of the *Opera* of Bonaventure (Paris, 1864-71), VIII, 393-482.

German redaction of the work found in a manuscript at Eisiedeln, the *Siben Strassen zu Got.*[17]

The *Septem Itineribus Aeternitatis* is in many respects typical of what might be called "popular" or "evangelical" mysticism of the fourteenth century. Built around several of the recurrent metaphors of twelfth-century spiritual literature, decorated with a schematic and harmonious organizational facade rich with the mystical significance of its numbers, the *Septem Itineribus* presents an incremental program for growth in the science of God. The German title captures rather better than the Latin does the real force of the book. Though it begins with a distinction between the two eternal "ways"—that which leads to eternal life and that which leads to death—the true structural focus of the book is not on the exploration of this tropological Pythagorean Y, but on the seven "steps" or trips of eternal life which can lead to an eventual and consuming union with God. These stages, which begin in a disciplined direction of the will, continue through the trained and graced exercise of the intellect to the spiritual union with God which is beyond the analysis of the rational faculties. Rudolph calls the seven "trips" *recta intentio, studiosa meditatio, limpida contemplatio, affectio caritativa, revelatio secreta, experimentalis praegustatio,* and *Deiformis operatio.* As is typical of the vocabularies of mystical writers, these terms are to some extent part of a privileged but easily recognizable lexicon of contemplative prose, the common coin of Bernardine and Bonaventurean psychology, and to some extent the verbal tokens of a private and quite hermetic interior language. In terms of its major move-

[17] Rudolf von Biberach, *Die Siben Strassen zu Got,* ed. Margot Schmidt (Quaracchi, 1969).

ments, however, there are three rather than seven steps. These are *imaginatio* or (what the German text calls *bildung*), *intellectio,* and *meditatio.* The psychological and affective faculties are lifted from "carnal" perception, to the operation of the rational intellect, to a stage of knowing God directly. These three stages are, easily enough, comparable with the three ways of Bonaventure or, for that matter, the movement from letter to sense to sentence in the analysis of a scriptural text. They are one of the staple triads of medieval thought, and in following them so precisely Rudolph of Biberach is submitting to a literary tradition of apparently inexhaustible fascination to medieval thinkers, though in his eventual downgrading of the imagination he is true to only half of the Franciscan tradition. I shall have something more to say of this matter in the next chapter.

One of the most elegant of formal handbooks of contemplation is the *Stimulus Amoris,* or *Sting of Love,* of Friar James of Milan.[18] Concerning this author we know very little, except that he is a keen Latin stylist, an alert student of Bonaventure, and a profoundly spiritual reader of the Bible. The obscurity which surrounds him derives in part from the fact that there are several medieval works which bear the title *Stimulus Amoris,* and that that of James of Milan appears in two rather different redactions.

The controlling images of the *Stimulus Amoris* are the Bonaventurean themes of illumination and ascent; and James follows his master in practice as well as precept by combining passages of speculative instruction with medleys of affective prayer. The thematic texts of the prologue come from the psalms. "To Thee, O Lord, have I lifted up my soul" (24:1) and "To thee have I lifted

[18] Ed. Quaracchi, 1905 (Bibliotheca franciscana ascetica medii aevi, 4).

up my eyes; who dwellest in heaven" (122:1). Unlike the *Itinerarium* or the *Triplici via*, however, the *Stimulus Amoris* does not develop a mathematics of spiritual progress. Its structure is in fact rather casual, combining chapters of moral instruction, practical advice, exemplary meditation, and spiritual speculation.

The spiritual doctrine of the *Stimulus Amoris* is marked by an optimism which grows from no naive discounting of ascetic necessities, but from a powerful belief in the efficacy of spiritual discipline. The last chapter of the work is entitled "That a man can become perfect in a short period of time"; in it he draws a sharp distinction between spiritual and physical alpinism. The physical mountaineer must take periodic rests in order to moderate his fatigue and reach his goal, but for the one who would climb the mountain of the Lord any relaxation, however brief, could be fatal. For the spiritual ascent grows ever swifter and keener with experience. "If the contemplative runs fast, then it is easy for him; when he walks along the flat ground, he begins to tire; if he rests, he loses his force."[19] Meditation on the Passion of Christ, recommended and described in one of the longest chapters in the little book, is a never-failing medicinal spring, and James of Milan leaves his readers with an injunction to return to it in time of need. "If you should become fearful on the mountain, run to the cave in Christ's side." If the climber finds that, after all, he simply cannot forsake the valley, "because he was born and raised there," he can at least live lovingly with his neighbor, sadly joining with him in lamenting his sins.[20] There is in this suggestion some of the plangency of the end of *Paradise Lost,* when "They hand in hand with

[19] *Stimulus amoris,* p. 127.
[20] *Stimulus amoris,* p. 129.

wand'ring steps and slow,/Through Eden took their solitary way."

The flourishing Franciscan literature of that extensive area of Europe in which various forms of the German language were spoken in the late thirteenth century perhaps owes its greatest debt to the saintly Friar David of Augsburg, one of the notable luminaries of the Franciscan provinces north of the Alps.[21] We have already found occasion to mention him as the teacher, colleague, and lifelong friend of Berthold of Regensburg. Like so many of the giants of the Golden Age of the Order, David's rich legacy to history is not reflected in a richness of biographical detail. He was probably born at Augsburg early in the thirteenth century, and he may have been educated at the Franciscan *studium* in Magdeburg. Though he performed a varied ministry, which included participation in some of the spectacular preaching tours through the Teutonic countryside, the great work of his life was the schooling of novices, first at Regensburg, then at Augsburg, and his literary career was almost entirely an adjunct to his vocation as a *doctor spiritualis.* He died in 1272. According to tradition, Berthold was in the middle of a sermon when he had the spiritual perception of his great friend's death. He immediately stopped preaching, and begged his auditors to pray for the soul departed. Then he led them in the recitation of the liturgical hymn *Iste confessor,* a simple hymn which "succinctly and aptly characterizes his friend."[22]

The qualities praised in *Iste confessor*—piety, prudence, humility, modesty, chastity, spiritual peace—were

[21] Kurt Ruh, "David von Augsburg und die Entstehung eines franziskanischen Schrifttums in deutscher Sprache," in *Augusta 955-1955* (Munich, 1955), pp. 71-82.

[22] Frances Mary Schwab, *David of Augsburg's "Paternoster" and the Authenticity of His German Works* (Munich, 1971), p. 180.

the qualities and special virtues of the religious life which defined the spiritual formation of David of Augsburg himself and which he tried to teach others in his enduring masterpiece, *De exterioris et interioris hominis compositione.*[23] It is possibly more accurate to describe this work as a trilogy than as a single book. Its first part, the *Formula novitiorum de exterioris hominis reformatione* is, as its name implies, a textbook for religious novices; the second two parts, written at a later date, are usually entitled the *Formula interioris hominis* and the *De septem processibus religiosi.* The textual history of the *De compositione* is complex and to some degree uncertain, but it is clear enough that the tripartite work in its final form—the form in which it enjoyed a wide popularity and came down to us in over three hundred manuscripts—is a thematically coherent and carefully unified work. It is radically trinitarian in its nature—both in its Augustinian anthropology and in its theory of the spiritual life.

Its major structural divisions derive from a beautiful passage in the *Golden Epistle* of William St.-Thierry, a work which was frequently attributed to Saint Bernard in the later Middle Ages: "Blessed Bernard, in his letter to the brethren of the monastery *de Monte Dei* (Bk. 1, Ch. V, n. 12) describes three stages in the religious life, that of beginners, that of proficients and that of the perfect. The first he speaks of as *animal,* i.e., earthly-minded who do not yet perceive the *things that are of the spirit of God* (I Cor. ii, 14), and must perforce busy themselves largely with outward endeavours, controlling and chastening the body lest it rebel against the spirit over which, in the days of sin, it once ruled. The second he calls

[23] Ed. Quaracchi, 1899; a new edition is pending. I cite the translation by Dominic Devas, *Spiritual Life and Progress* (London, 1937).

rational, for herein it is reason, belonging to man's higher nature and distinguishing him from irrational creatures as nobler than them all, and their master, which leads the soul to strive after self-knowledge and—the body being now subdued and brought into the soul's service—to purify herself and refashion herself towards that pristine dignity and beauty sullied of old and lost by sin. The third he calls *spiritual,* for in this stage the soul, created to God's image and supported by the grace of the Holy Spirit, rises above herself and tends towards Him to whose image she has been made, striving to make the likeness more perfect and to achieve the joy of union by way of knowledge and of love. The first stage is as the step to the second, the second to the third: *And there was a broad passage round about, going up by winding stairs, and it led into the upper loft of the Temple all round. Therefore was the Temple broader in the higher parts: and so from the lower parts they went to the higher by the midst* (Ezech. xi, 7)."[24]

The structure and intellectual orchestration of the *De compositione* should supply the answer to the question, not particularly useful but frequently asked, of whether David is an "ascetic" or a "mystical" writer; for of course he is both. The purpose of ascetic discipline is the subjugation of carnal, animal man whose sensibilities, disordered since the Fall, are a chaos of imperfect, incomplete, and at times positively and malignly misleading sensory data. The taming of Brother Ass, as Francis had called his own body, was in fact an elementary step in the ascent to God; but this first mile of the journey was also in some ways the hardest, and David of Augsburg makes it clear that religious discipline, though it be of itself carnal and exterior, is the absolute prerequi-

[24] *Spiritual Life and Progress,* I, pp. 79-80.

site for the spiritual possibilities of mystical knowing. The first part of the trilogy, called *The External Man,* therefore deals unashamedly but always sensibly with the external observances of the religious life.

Yet David always has an unerring aim for the spiritual truth which lies behind and consumes external practice, and his treatise on the outward man begins with this stirring appeal to inward truth: "You should always bear in mind, as of the very first importance, the reason why you came to religion, and what your purpose was. For what did you come? Was it not simply for God—to work for Him and to enjoy Him as your reward for all eternity?" The *De compositione* shares with other great ascetic works of the Middle Ages the power to animate outward forms, customs, rules, and regulations with a spirit of inward vitality. One thinks immediately of the *Rule of St. Benedict,* or of the simple *Rule of Saint Augustine,* which begins, "Ante omnia, fratres carissimi, diligatur deus, deinde et proximus, quia ista sunt praecepta principaliter nobis data. Qualiter autem nos oportet orare vel psallere describimus . . ."

The specific subjects which David of Augsburg finds it convenient to write about are such matters as obedience to superiors; deportment at the office, in chapter meeting, in the refectory, in the dormitory, at labor; on travel outside the monastery; on personal discipline within the community. He deals, in short, with the major topics of monastic discipline. Indeed the first book of the *De Compositione* is perhaps the most remarkable of the many thirteenth-century handbooks of conventual wisdom, and an impressive memorial to those within the Order who found no conflict between the "new" order of poverty and established and cherished medieval religious tradition. David of Augsburg clearly writes as one in that tradition. He speaks of the custom of kneeling at once before one's superior to recite a *culpa* when caught out. "This is an old religious custom handed down from the times of the most blessed father Benedict, and by St. Francis and other holy fathers."[25] For him, the religious life is both a pilgrimage with a hope of individual perfection and a cultural and spiritual quest with real obligations both to the past and to the future. "As far as in you lies, by word and example, you must try to hand on the Order to posterity such as, by your superiors, it has been handed to you. . . . Whether I am to be a sharer in the rewards or in the punishments of those who are to come after me must depend upon the kind of example, good or bad, that I leave behind me."

Among David's admonitions to his novices, none is more forceful than his commendation to them of appropriate reading, especially from the Scriptures. In this, as in other aspects of his life, his practice is as good as his preaching. Throughout the course of the *De compositione*, David cites a fairly wide range of medieval and classical authorities—including such authors as Ovid. He always does so according to his own canons of decorum, always appropriately, always without ostentation. A true Franciscan, David never strays far from the Bible in his search for literary authority. To the study of the sacred page David brought a thoroughness and a delicate intellectual inventiveness that cannot but make us wish that he had left behind some formal and sustained works of scriptural exegesis.

The outer shell of the religious life, if it be true religion, must coat and protect a radiant core of spiritual truth. Religion is an institution; David calls it a school. A school has its grounds, buildings, regulations, and tra-

[25] *Spiritual Life and Progress,* I, p. 9.

ditions—but what it teaches is not of the flesh but of the mind. The technical term which David uses is *reformatio mentis.* The word *mentis* has here the force of Pauline Vulgate tradition (esp. Romans 7:25), though it lacks the precision of definition which it was to take on in the special vocabulary of Bonaventure. The religious who undertakes and masters the exterior form of his religious vocation is a double fool if he gains no knowledge of the spiritual matters for which those externals are merely the necessary preparation. "University men who squander their time come home with nothing to show for it all but unpaid bills. We religious are like that, if after reckoning up the time we have spent in religion, we find we have nothing to show on the credit side but an exiguous measure of progress or—sadder acknowledgement still—that we were actually better and more fervent as novices than now after many years."[26]

The second part of David's trilogy is concerned with the sciences appropriate to the growth of the interior man. Its organization is schematic, and in many ways traditional. Its psychology derives from the rich tradition of Augustinian anthropology which finds the essential congruence between God and man in the soul's trinitarian structure of memory, will, and understanding. Its moral theology is disposed according to the familiar categories, already commonplace in the thirteenth century, of the seven capital vices and their "remedies."

Like the introductory book for novices, the sequel presents in schematic form a great deal of conventional medieval wisdom and science, such as, for example, the operation of the "appetites." What distinguishes it from "the former" book is its steady focus on interior life. That is, it is not merely a restatement or recapitulation

[26] *Spiritual Life and Progress,* I, p. 62.

of the moral counsels appropriate for the governing of the exterior man. Rather, David is concerned to demonstrate that moral action is grounded in inward and spiritual reality, that it can be analyzed according to a spiritual wisdom, and that it can be made to conform to the invisible law of charity written on the hearts of men, once the excrescences of sin have been scorched off by determined ascetic practice.

It is the third of the books which make up the *De compositione* which most clearly establishes David of Augsburg's mystical credentials. It is entitled the *Formula de septem processibus religiosi statu* (Seven Stages of Progress in Religion). The book on the exterior man provides a program of corporal discipline which can of itself create no more than the possibility of spiritual growth, and the book on the internal man describes the structure of spiritual human nature and a formula for beginning life in the spirit. The third book grows upon, and out of, the earlier two; it is a handbook for friars who are becoming the "proficients" of the spiritual life and seek to climb the ladder of religious growth. The seven stages of religious increment, like the seven liberal arts, are composed of a *trivium* and a *quadrivium.* David's *trivium* is fervor, travail (*labor*), and consolation; the *quadrivium,* temptation, the remedies, the virtues, and wisdom. This scheme, which is in part traditional and in part original with David, is clearly somewhat arbitrary, and the author himself says at the beginning of the work that not all religious will go through all stages. It is a characteristic of David of Augsburg that while he reverences the conventional formulae of medieval moral theology and even shows something of a penchant for what we would call scholastic categories, he always does so with tact, mental inventiveness and, above all, good common sense. One rarely feels constrained by arid formulations, in spite of the fact that one is confronted with "Six Outward Coverings to Adorn and Shield Holiness," "Seven Signs of Carnal Love," or "Three Degrees of Poverty."

David of Augsburg's own thought processes are tellingly pictorial, and he likewise has a pictorial analysis of human thought. The mind of a man is an undecorated edifice; his thoughts are the pictures which hang on the mind's walls. The mind of the religious must be a temple, adorned with a sacred imaginative iconography which is appropriate to a dedicated building. Theaters and taverns are adorned with vacuous and worldly scenes; temples, however, are decorated with scenes from sacred history and with mystical paintings (*mysticis picturis*). David describes the capital vices in terms of pictures painted by them in the mind: gluttony paints a groaning board, wrath paints contention, and so forth. These "pictures" are, of course, very much like actual representations of the deadly sins in pictorial art and their literary representations in such works as *Piers Plowman*—a work which David's *De compositione* indirectly illuminates in a number of ways.

His style is never portentous, but never drab either. His is capable of citing secular classics—such as the *Ars amatoria* of Ovid, whose authority he musters to discuss the virtue of patience—when it is to his purpose; and he reveals a felicitous metaphoric inventiveness. The religious should train his body to be obedient in the same way a juggler trains his dog. As the trained dog jumps to perform immediately upon command, so does the friar "jump from his bed for the Night Office, and obeying, throughout, the dictates of reason, shows himself alert at every exercise to which obedience may call him or which charity may demand from him or which devotion or any virtue may suggest to him."[27]

In those parts of the third treatise which deal explicitly with contemplative and ecstatic experience, David of Augsburg is reluctant to describe the indescribable ecstacy: " 'Ecstacy,' says St. Gregory, 'implies a joy ineffable which, whilst it cannot be expressed in words, betrays its presence by certain outward movements, its real, inward character remaining concealed.' Blessed is the people, says the Psalmist (88:16) that knoweth jubilation. He speaks of knowing it, not of describing it, since it baffles explanation."

The *De compositione* was destined, through its impact on the Brethren of the Common Life, the *devotio moderna,* and the popular spiritual life of the twilight Middle Ages, to exercise a very considerable influence beyond the friary close; yet it was not a work written for the lay world but for those "who would be perfect." We have already noted that it represents a closed conventualism much more obviously connected with early medieval monastic traditions than with the new apostolicism of the Franciscan Order. It is the sort of book appropriate for its audience, religious novices, and both in style and content it presents a limited conception of Franciscan life. We know that David's own religious career was a multifaceted one, and we are fortunate enough to have a number of his works in the vernacular versions which made them accessible to a wider audience than ever could have made a direct approach to the *De compositione.*[28]

We know from external evidence that David, like his friend Berthold, was a remarkable preacher, but we do

[27] *Spiritual Life and Progress,* II, p. 45.
[28] See Schwab, *David of Augsburg's "Paternoster,"* for a survey of his works.

not have any texts of vernacular sermons actually preached by him. We have instead a number of short spiritual tracts, the most interesting of which are the *Sieben Staffeln des Gebetes* (Seven Stages of Prayer), *Der Spiegel der Tugend* (The Mirror of Virtue), *Kristi Leben unser Vorbild,* (Our Model, the Life of Christ), and a commentary on the *Pater Noster.* The long-standing controversy concerning the authenticity of these and other works, as well as their complex relationships with other Latin and vernacular texts, has been very largely resolved by the careful work of Kurt Ruh and Sister Mary Schwab. We now know with virtual certainty that David of Augsburg wrote in German, and that his works enjoyed a wide diffusion. Kurt Ruh considers his contribution to the development of German prose a particularly important one.

The *Kristi Leben,* a brief pamphlet, offers the merest suggestion of the profound possibilities which Franciscan writers found in the gospel narratives, but it can in any event serve to introduce a genre of major importance in late medieval spiritual letters. One of the major tendencies of Christian spirituality in the Gothic period is its studied and varied concentration, both in matters of doctrinal theology and devotional practice, on the gospel life of Christ. The true *vita apostolica* begins in an intimate, familiar discipleship with the living Christ. Roggen and others have discussed this Christocentricity of spiritual vision as a defining feature of the Franciscan movement, and we have several times in this book, most notably in our brief survey of the themes of the Franciscan lyric, had occasion to remark upon its implications for the development of Franciscan literature. Those implications were profound both in terms of the content of Franciscan literature and in terms of its style. The thirteenth century abounds with diverse manifestations of Christian biography; it is the subject of lyric poetry, of the vernacular drama, of doctrinal handbooks, of meditative verse. It is so pervasive, indeed, that we may be in danger of overlooking its newness within its historical context; yet the fact is that the human person of Christ becomes an important subject of imaginative Christian literature only in the thirteenth century. The "life of Christ" is not entirely unknown as a literary genre in the earlier Middle Ages, to be sure, but the examples we have—gospel harmonies or diatesserons, or severely limited vernacular poetic redactions like the German *Heliand* and the Anglo-Saxon Christ poems—provide no genuine models for the extraordinary burgeoning of "biographical" genres in the thirteenth century.

For students of medieval Franciscan literature there is probably no single work which will command more study or offer more various suggestion than the *Meditationes vitae Christi,* and I shall find occasion to return to it in a final chapter which considers some of the broader aspects of Franciscan style and thought. It is also necessary, however, to say something of the fourteenth-century poems which reflect the immediate model of the *Meditationes,* for among them are several which are themselves important and even remarkable productions.

One of the first of these is an early fourteenth-century English poem in rhyming couplets; its incipit, which describes it as a translation from Bonaventure, describes the contents as "medytacyuns of þe soper of our lorde Ihesu and also of hys passyn and eke of þe peynes of hys swete modyr, Mayden Marye." These *Meditations on the Lord's Supper* have been ascribed to Robert Manning of Brunne, the author of *Handling Sin,* a work which also appears in the only known copy of the *Meditations.*[29] This ascription, though conjectural, is not improbable. Manning was a regular canon, not a Franciscan, but as we can tell from *Handling Sin* (a versified confession manual adapted into English from the *Manuel des Pechiez* of the Anglo-Norman William of Waddington), he shared with the Franciscans the desire to find popular literary expression for his pastoral theology. The poem, something over a thousand lines long, is an obedient but intelligent rendering of several of the best of the Thursday and Friday meditations, including the Last Supper, the betrayal, and the words from the cross. The translator has few original inspirations, but the verse is competent and at times quite moving.

The English-verse *Meditations* testify to the alacrity with which vernacular artists could respond to the originality of their Latin model, but it would be wrong to claim too much for them in their own right. Two Italian poets who wrote at a slightly later date, however, created poems out of the materials of the *Meditationes vitae Christi* poems which would be remarkable by any standard. They are Felice Tancredi da Massa and Niccolo Cicerchia.[30] Fra Felice was a *romitano* friar who wrote a long but exquisitely wrought poem in *ottava rima* stanzas on the childhood of Christ, *La fanciullezza di Gesu.* It is a work without clear generic models, though it has a distant relative in Ailred of Rievalux' *When Jesus Was Twelve Years Old.* The *Fanciullezza* has marked literary pretensions. Its elegant form, its self-conscious use of literary conventions of the high style, and its careful

[29] *Meditations on the Supper of Our Lord,* ed. J. Meadows Cowper (London, 1875).

[30] L. Cellucci, "Le 'Meditationes vitae Christi' e i poemetti che ne furono ispirati," *Archivum Romanicum,* XXII (1938), 30-98. The poems are edited by Giorgio Varanini, *Cantari religiosi senesi del trecento* (Bari, 1965).

attention to the details of poetic techniques all point to Fra Felice's serious artistic ambitions. An Augustinian, he brings to his poem not merely a coherent Augustinian theology but the authority of the saint himself, whom he formally invokes as his muse, after the Godhead and the Blessed Virgin, and who is repeatedly cited by name during the course of his poem. The ghost of Augustine is not the only spirit which inhabits Fra Felice's poem. Bonaventure is also there, and so is Dante Alighieri. He presents the *Fanciullezza* not as the honeyed dogmatic theology which at heart it is, but rather as the fruit of illumination, and, so far as the reader is concerned, an opportunity for ecstatic contemplation:

> Onde, lettor, i' ti prego, per Dio,
> che quel che nullo libro ha manifesto
> tutto l'attribuisca al pensier mio,
> e non dannar però el mie contesto.
> La voluntà mi tira con disio,
> la qual con devozion mi mosse a questo:
> quando l'anima sopra ciò si stende,
> molte cose mirando li comprende.[31]

Fra Felice uses the actual materials of the *Meditationes vitae Christi* only intermittently, but he is everywhere true to the affective strategies of the work even as he reshapes the materials to his own more ceremonial vision. The bottle of the *ottava rima* is new, but the wine is old, mellow, and rich. The stanzas move slowly, forming verse paragraphs of a felicitous wholeness, moving from poignant pictorial vignette to an explicitly structured meditation to a formal theological statement theoretical in its implications. Even as it is a work without clear precedent, the *Fanciullezza di Gesu* has little in the way of a specific literary posterity, at least outside of England.

[31] "Fanciullezza di Gesù," xxv; Varanini, *Cantari religiosi,* p. 199.

Its relationship to such a work as the English stanzaic *Life of Christ* is superficial and unimportant, though it does have a real spiritual rapport with the lyric tradition as one sees it developing in the northern countries.

The other poet who concerns us here, Niccolo Cicerchia, was also a Sienese, but we know practically nothing about him except, according to a manuscript notation, that he wrote one of his poems in 1364. In poetic inspiration as well as in poetic technique Cicerchia shares much in common with Fra Felice, and nowhere more obviously than in the debt he too owes to the *Meditationes vitae Christi.* Cicerchia wrote two poems. The first, on the Passion, enjoyed an extraordinary success. It is made up of 282 *ottava rima* stanzas which closely follow the Passion meditations in "John of Caulibus." Cicerchia's intuitive understanding of the liturgical aspects of the *Meditationes*—an understanding which is clearly underscored by the Latin liturgical phrases which lace the Passion—suggests that he was probably a religious, and manuscript provenence likewise suggests that the *Passione* was a common book in *trecento* Italian religious houses.

He was certainly a learned man, for "John of Caulibus," though his chief source and poetic inspiration, is by no means the only author to whom he turns. His other poem, *La Risurrezione,* though less well known in the Middle Ages, is in several respects both poetically more inventive and structurally challenging than the *Passione.* Though "popular" in the simplicity of their doctrinal statements, Cicerchia's poems, like the *Fanciullezza* of Fra Felice, grow out of a profound Augustinian intellectuality. All three of the poems I have mentioned display learned numerological conventions which have gone unremarked by the few modern critics who have dealt with these materials. Cicerchia's *Risurrezione,* for example, is composed of two books. The first has 85 stanzas, the second, 171 (i.e., $2 \times 85 + 1$). The proportion is that of the octave—for which, of course the *ottava rima* is itself brilliantly suited—and reflects the harmony of the Resurrection as described in a celebrated passage in the *De Trinitate* of St. Augustine.[32]

What is perhaps conceptually the most brilliant of the Franciscan "lives of Christ," one which adapted the mystical image of the tree to the affective biographical strategies of the *Meditationes vitae Christi,* is the strangely beautiful book called the *Arbor vitae crucifixae* of Ubertino da Casale.[33] As we have already seen, Ubertino was deeply enmeshed in the poverty controversy during the pontificates of Boniface VIII and John XXII. I find him the most tragic figure among the rigorist triumvirate who have come to be known as the "Spirituals." He was a close contemporary of Dante, who in fact mentions him in an ambiguous but apparently unflattering light in the twelfth canto of *Paradiso.* The poet paid homage to the friar in deed if not in word, however, for he borrowed from him details of his own Franciscan poetic myth.

Though Ubertino takes his central metaphor of the tree directly from Bonaventure's *Lignum vitae,* along with most of the specific topics for contemplation, he has quite consciously structured his own book in a different fashion. Bonaventure's little treatise, less than a tenth the size of Ubertino's, was divided into three main sections or ramifications dealing with Christ's "origins," with His Passion, and with His glorification. Ubertino has instead five books distributed among exactly one hundred and one chapters; both numbers have symbolic

[32] Augustine, *De Trinitate,* IV, vi, 10.
[33] *Arbor vitae crucifixae Jesu* (Venice, 1485); reprinted with an introduction by C. T. Davis (Turin, 1961).

importance. The first book deals with the pre-existence of Christ, Christ as creator, the prophecies of His coming, and His birth; it contains some of the most difficult theological concepts in the *Arbor vitae* and shows Ubertino in the light of speculative theologian perhaps in spite of himself. The following three books divide the major materials of the gospels into books on Christ's childhood, His ministry, and His Passion. The very lengthy fifth and final book, nearly as long as the previous four considered together, contains the materials for which the *Arbor vitae* has become famous, or rather notorious. In it Ubertino gives free reign to all his Joachimist historiography, his bittersweet vision of Franciscan history, his Dantesque denunciations of certain members of the Church hierarchy, and a series of eschatological reveries which are among the most remarkable poetic inventions of the Franciscan Middle Ages.

It is this final book of the *Arbor vitae* which has received the most thorough scholarly analysis. In it one can find brilliantly anthologized the major institutional and theological premises that fatally linked the poverty fanatics of the Franciscan Order with the wild and finally uncontrollable apocalypticism of the "true believers" of Joachimism. The prophetic repertory included a fervent and uncompromising commitment to spiritual *renovatio* and the destruction of the "carnal church," an adulation at times blasphemous of the person and function of Francis of Assisi, sixth angel of the Apocalypse and *alter Christus,* whose life and ministry was different from the Incarnation only by an analysis too fine always to be made, and a submission to a "definitive" religious rule no less authoritative and ineradicable than the very words of Scripture from which it was made. Such ideas are essential to the *Arbor vitae,* but that is not the same thing as saying that they are the work's essence. The concentrated examination of the ideas of the fifth section has had, I think, the unintended result of misrepresenting the whole book.

Were the *Arbor vitae* merely a brilliant if prolix monument to a doomed Franciscan Joachimism, its literary legacy, like that of the *Introductorius* of Gerardus of Borgo San Donnino, would probably only be found bottled in the formaldehyde of anti-mendicant satire and invective. But just as its inspiration and expression owed as much to Angela of Foligno and Bonaventure as to Joachim, it exercised an important and beneficial influence on such great spiritual masters of the fourteenth-century Observance as St. Bernardino and, later, on writers outside the Franciscan Order for whom the polemical topics of the fifth book of the *Arbor vitae* could have had only an archeological interest. It is clear from its use by García Jiménez de Cisneros, the profound ascetic theorist of Montserrat, for example, that Ubertino took his place among the scant dozen of spiritual authorities who compose the classical repertory of the "Franciscan springtime," men such as the author of the *Meditationes*, Bonaventure, and David of Augsburg.

The intellectual and spiritual influences on Ubertino were diverse, even eclectic, and they by no means harmonized easily into a monochrome consistency of thought and action. Ubertino *was* a serious intellectual figure. He studied at Paris; he was a lifelong disciple of Olivi, without doubt the most brilliant speculative mind of the "Spirituals" whose works have come down to us; he held lectorships under Ministers General both in Florence and in Provence. He showed a marked ability in academic debate, and in the conventional professional hair-splitting to which his opponents' charges of heresy drove him. Yet in the autobiographical prologue to the *Arbor vitae* Ubertino speaks with that brutal and studied anti-intellectualism which was also a major strain in thirteenth-century Franciscan thought and which viewed humane letters as vanities, at best inconsequential and at worst damnable. Frédégand Callaey has said of Ubertino that for him there was but a single science, the mystical science of the direct knowing of God, and his best teachers here were not the gowned and garrulous *magistri* of the Latin Quarter.[34] They were, instead, the simple and the illiterate: the saintly Sienese street vendor Pier Pettinaio and Angelo da Foligno, the housewife turned mystic.

The profound ambiguity of Ubertino's attitude toward organized learning in the Franciscan life is reflected in his attitude toward St. Bonaventure. His silent but massive debt to the Seraphic Doctor is everywhere apparent in the work. The *Arbor vitae* takes not merely its central structuring metaphor but also a number of its specific chapter headings from Bonaventure's *Lignum vitae.* Yet Ubertino is also explicitly dissatisfied with the moderating and conciliating tendencies of the *Legenda major.* According to Ubertino, Bonaventure suppressed evidence of Francis' hostility to lukewarm friars in order not to wash dirty linen in public; but he is far from certain that the attempt to avoid the scandals of the past has not helped to create the far more grievous scandals of the present.

It is the fate of Francesc Eiximinis, dictated by chronological accident, that he is forever appearing in this book as an afterthought. One must finally mention his beautiful *Life of Christ,* Franciscan to the core, one of a dwindling list of books that can still legitimately be

[34] F. Callaey, *Etude sur Ubertin de Casale* (Louvain, 1911), p. 123.

called neglected masterpieces.[35] It is a book which in its scholarly inaccessibility reminds us, no less than the *Meditationes vitae Christi* and the *Arbor vitae crucifixae*, that in many ways the study of Franciscan literature is an infant industry.

[35] See M. de Riquer, *Història de la literatura catalana,* II, p. 191.

6

Franciscan Style and the Literature of Late Medieval Europe

The earlier chapters of this book have been concerned with the internal history of medieval Franciscan literature, with its themes, its genres, with the spiritual agenda which masterfully controls elegant Latin works like the *Sacrum Commercium* and the *Stimulus Amoris,* and the evangelical mission which needed the *Summa confessorum* of John of Freiburg and the moralized tales of Nicholas Bozon. The body of literature which these concerns have led us to examine or at least to notice has been considerable both in its size and in its variety, and if there were no further significance to the concept of "Franciscan literature" than a few major monuments like the *Laude* of Jacopone da Todi or the mystical writings of St. Bonaventure, the topic would remain one of interest to students of medieval life and art.

But Franciscan literature has also an external history, a complex series of relationships with other late medieval literary traditions; and it is this history which can provide important if at times baffling evidence concerning certain broad aspects of the stylistic change observable in late medieval verbal and pictorial art. This external history gives an increased dignity to the phrase "Franciscan literature."

Stylistic change is a cultural mystery, among the most alluring mysteries, indeed, which are the object of humanistic study. To the historical critic of Western art in the Gothic period major stylistic shifts have been puzzling conundrums, easy enough to notice, but difficult to describe with precision, and almost impossible to account for in finally convincing ways. So far as literature is concerned, the thirteenth and fourteenth centuries, the first two centuries of the "Franciscan era," constitute a divide—though not, to be sure, the great divide—between major medieval styles. The newness of Jean de Meun, Dante, Boccaccio, and Chaucer lies not so much in their ambitious exploration of vernacular possibilities as it does in a conception of how fiction best achieves its ends.

The theological allegories of Alain de Lille, who died in the year that Francis returned from his captivity in Perugia, exerted an enormous influence in thirteenth-century literary circles and provided an academic model for serious Christian poetry throughout the literary centers of Europe. In their stylistic (as opposed to their intellectual) conception the *Anticlaudianus* and the *De planctu Naturae* have not come a very great distance from Martianus Capella or Prudentius. Alanian allegory is highly abstract and intellectual, characterized by an absence of serious dramatic intention or complex exemplification. When, a century later, Jean de Meun mined the rich quarry of the *De planctu* for his continuation of the *Roman de la Rose* he brought to his work an artistic intention which vivified Alain's abstract theological categories by channeling them through highly articulate literary "characters." Thus a concept of *Natura* does exist in the *Roman de la Rose* as a personified abstraction, but one who has distinct, engaging and individual literary characteristics as a fictional woman: she is a great talker, somewhat repetitious, at times amusingly ponderous. But Jean de Meun has also had the stylistic inspiration to consider other possible implications of "nature" understood in the full ambiguity of Pauline and Augustinian analysis through the manipulation of other highly engaging and individualized characters: an old whore who comically exults in that "human nature" which is ruled by the law of the members, or a vicious friar who is one of those by nature a "child of wrath." Geoffrey Chaucer, a century later still, would take a number of Jean's walking ideas and reanimate them in even more extraordinary ways in the Wife of Bath, the Pardoner, the Summoner, and other characters of such vivacity and sharpness that many critics have insisted that they must be the literary realizations of flesh-and-blood people Chaucer had seen on the dusty roads of fourteenth-century England.

A general stylistic movement from abstract and lapidary forms to ones which are highly exemplified and kinetic is of course characteristic of artistic development not merely in literature, but in the plastic and visual arts as well. In the cliché of cultural historians, Giotto is the painterly Dante—or Dante the literary Giotto, depending upon one's perspective; but unlike many clichés, this one is largely redeemed by its truth. The stylistic continuum shared by Giotto and Dante extends beyond the representational arts to include all major aspects of Gothic culture; it is usually, though rather inappropriately, described as emergent "realism," and it has connections with broad social and economic developments which seem clear enough at a distance and opaque up close.

Many historians of art and literature have been disposed to connect this "realism" with the tastes and interests of the rising middle class—a group which, as one historian has wittily put it, "has been rising so long in the pages of our history text books that they should now be visible only to the most powerful optical instruments." Thus the *fabliau*—the short comic tale, often earthy or positively obscene in its details, brilliantly exploited by such writers as Boccaccio and Chaucer—has often been called a "bourgeois" literary form; and Jean de Meun, the major author of the *Roman de la Rose,* has been described as a "bourgeois realist." Though patient and detailed study of the audience of the *fabliaux* or of Jean de Meun's literary context shows how untenable such characterizations actually are, the term "bourgeois" is not entirely useless in describing at least much of the subject matter of the works involved.

Other scholars have sought to explain the stylistic changes under consideration by reference to the spread of Aristotelian and Averroist ideas, at the University of Paris and at other centers of learning, to the concomitant rise of an experimental attitude toward the natural sciences, and even to the liturgical practice, new in the thirteenth century, of elevating the consecrated Host in the Mass. I do not propose a "Franciscan thesis" to vie for its temporary place among the voguish explanations of late medieval stylistic change, but I would claim that the Franciscan movement in its broadest sense was consistently and at many levels its agent and its conduit.

Since Franciscanism was itself merely a major part of a larger whole—a new vision of "apostolic" religion developed by the mendicant orders and others in response to the kinds of concerns represented by the Fourth Lateran Council—exclusively "Franciscan" claims must be avoided in what follows. Yet so far as the development of vernacular literature is concerned, the Franciscan influences were so various, and Franciscan mental habits so distinctive even among the mendicant orders, that it is useful to speak of a Franciscan literary style which was itself a part of the broader literary developments of the thirteenth and fourteenth centuries and an instrumental conduit through which stylistic change flowed into the vernacular continuum. Thus conceived, "Franciscan style" is a far broader concept even than that which has been posited by, for example, F. J. E. Raby in his fine discussion of thirteenth-century Latin poetry.[1] It goes well beyond Franciscan writers and makes claims not merely on religious literature but also on secular works like the *Roman de la Rose* and the *Canterbury Tales* which adopt a formally anti-fraternal attitude. The Franciscan movement legitimized for the late Middle Ages new literary subjects and new literary fashions; and it helped to create a popular taste for the "classical," the exotic, the pathetic, and for an increasingly emotional and vicarious literary participation in complex and tactile fictions which spoke among other things of observed life. The remarks which follow do not pretend an ambitious treatment of the larger meaning of Franciscan style. Like the book as a whole, they are explicitly introductory in intention, seeking rather to ask than to answer.

At the very heart of the new conception of Franciscan religious life there is an impulse which, turned to reading and writing, could not fail to suggest marked changes

[1] F. J. E. Raby, *A History of Christian-Latin Poetry from the Beginnings to the Close of the Middle Ages* (Oxford, 1927), pp. 415 ff.

in literary style and taste. That these changes have been insufficiently noted and inadequately studied so far, as I would claim, argues merely that other revolutionary aspects of medieval Franciscanism, particularly in the realms of social history and the history of Christian doctrine, have made more prominent claims on the scholar. "Franciscan religion," as I have repeatedly argued, combined what might be called the traditional aspirations of Western monasticism with an ambition for a powerful evangelical mission in the world. From such a geminated asceticism, often implicit in the spiritual life of the early Christian centuries but articulated as a broad social ideal only in the century of the Lateran reforms, the disparate genres of Franciscan letters almost naturally evolved.

Yet there is at least one other major issue involved in "Franciscan literature" which has so far largely been ignored. That is the history of the imagination itself. The fictions of literature are products of the human imagination, and literary criticism, at least since the second half of the eighteenth century, has been much concerned with attempting to define or at least describe the operations of the artistic imagination in the formulation of fictions and the invention of poetic images. There is virtually no such discussion in what we usually think of as the literary criticism of the Middle Ages. The literary historian interested in the medieval theory of the imagination will find a rich but in many ways frustrating body of material in a perhaps unexpected place, in formal ascetic documents. Such documents are rich because they frequently discuss the very topics of interest to the modern investigator: the nature of the imagination, its psychology and physiology, the nature and function of poetic imagery, and so forth. They are frustrating because of the consistently hostile, or at best the highly ambiguous attitude which monastic tradition takes toward the imagination and its operations.

An excellent example of this ambiguity is provided by a famous work of popular Benedictine spirituality contemporary with Franciscan origins, the *Speculum Ecclesiae* of St. Edmund of Abingdon. This work of popular instruction, which grew out of a more specifically monastic *Speculum Religiosorum,* enjoyed a very broad popularity in Latin, English, French and other vernacular versions. The basis of its popularity is not difficult to find. It presents, in an accessible and effective way, the basic elements of the science of God and of moral theology. Though it takes as its text "See your vocation" (I Cor. 1:26), a text most appropriate for "us religious men," the *Speculum* in fact has at times a distinctly pastoral drift not inappropriate for a work from the pen of England's chief shepherd. At first blush, the *Speculum Ecclesiae* has a number of "Franciscan" characteristics: affective Marian piety, schematic contemplation of the physical Passion of Christ, an insistence on penance. It explains the familiar three levels of contemplating God—in His creation, in His Scriptures, and in Himself—and insists on the utility of even the first two, imperfect modes, and particularly, of course, on contemplating through the Scriptures. But it likewise reveals a hostile unease with "carnal images," that is, with the mental conception of things created. Such carnal—or, as we might say, imaginative—contemplation is both imperfect and dangerous, and it should be left behind by anyone with a sophisticated approach to the knowledge of God.[2] St. Edmund Rich draws upon diverse sources: his dogmatic scheme comes largely from Hugh of St.-Victor, his affective piety from

[2] Edmund of Abingdon, *Speculum Religiosorum and Speculum Ecclesie,* ed. Helen P. Forshaw (London, 1973), pp. 44-45.

St. Bernard, and with both he shares an essentially closed ascetic attitude toward the possibilities of the literary imagination.

If, after reading the *Speculum Ecclesiae,* we turn to the *Meditationes vitae Christi,* a work that might almost be described as a Franciscan "answer" to it, we shall immediately be struck by a marked increment of stylistic vision. The two works have much in common, and the differences between them are largely those of practice rather than precept.[3] Though I have discussed the *Meditationes* as an example of a virtually "pure" Franciscan work, its affective qualities and techniques are by no means unprecedented in medieval spiritual writing. Indeed, it reveals close and explicit connections with a rich tradition of Cistercian meditative literature of the twelfth century, and in particular with certain works of St. Bernard, which have long been recognized as its direct and principal literary sources.

Yet the qualities which bind it to the monastic spiritual tradition are for our purposes less important than those which boldly strike out in new literary directions. The author of the *Meditationes* shares with Bernard, from whom he borrows freely, a powerfully visual literary imagination which presents the reader vividly realized scenes from the domestic life of Christ and His Mother. Where the Franciscan writer departs from Bernard is in the complexity of his literary vision. For him it is a unifying vision which combines the dialectic of the interior life with a clear evangelical intent made explicit in a

[3] There is no critical text of the entire Latin version; uncritical texts can be found in the older editions of Bonaventure, including that of Peltier. The *Meditations on the Life of Christ,* trans. Rosalie B. Green and Isa Ragusa (Princeton, 1961), is an excellent rendition of the medieval Italian version. I shall cite the French edition of Paul Bayart: *Jean de Caulibus* [pseudo-Bonaventure], *Méditations sur la vie du Christ* (Paris, 1958). A new and critical Latin edition is badly needed.

programmatic meditative agenda. The literature of Cistercian meditation as we find it in Bernard's *Sermons on the Canticles* and elsewhere, on the other hand, is beyond question highly inventive, lushly imaginative, powerfully affective. But it is also carefully circumscribed by a specifically "religious" cast of mind which self-consciously distinguishes its intentions from the affective energies of secular art.

The same Bernard whose pen has given us some of the most dramatic and imaginative renditions of sacred history in all of medieval literature can also reveal, when he speaks as a theorist, a closed monastic contempt for the imagination's artefacts. We may recall his well-known strictures against Romanesque architectural ornament in his *Apology to the Abbot William.* "What excuse can there be for these ridiculous monstrosities in the cloisters where the monks do their reading, extraordinary things at once beautiful and ugly? Here we find filthy monkeys and fierce lions, fearful centaurs, harpies, and striped tigers, soldiers at war, and hunters blowing their horns. . . . All round there is such an amazing variety of shapes that one could easily prefer to take one's reading from the walls instead of from a book. One could spend the whole day gazing fascinated at these things, one by one, instead of meditating on the law of God."[4] Bernard speaks of visual and plastic art, but in terms which reveal a typically medieval identification of the strategies of the verbal and the visual.

The importance of his attitude for the literary historian lies as much in what he does not say as in what he does. He does not, as has sometimes been thought, attack all imaginative art designed to control and move

[4] *Apologia,* XII, 29; *The Works of Bernard of Clairvaux: Treatises I* (Spenser, 1970), p. 66.

an audience. He does not even attack a special category of "vain" or "profane" art, as other medieval moralists frequently do. Rather, he says that the affective, glittering pomps of art, appropriate by condescension to the primitive spirituality of the carnal world of laymen, are inappropriate distractions in the houses of those who would be perfect. He clearly, if somewhat grudgingly, acknowledges the power of imaginative representations, and he approves the initiatives of bishops seeking to instruct their flocks through their use. However, "it is not the same for monks and bishops. Bishops have a duty toward both wise and foolish. They have to make use of material ornamentation to rouse devotion in a carnal people, incapable of spiritual things. But we no longer belong to such people."[5] William of Saint-Thierry, in his beautiful *Golden Epistle*, puts the matter in the starkly military terms of scriptural language when he discusses the question of the architectural elegance of monastic churches. "I beg you therefore, while we are pilgrims in this world and soldiers on earth, let us not build for ourselves houses to settle down in but make tents we can leave at a moment's notice, we who are liable to be called away from them in the near future to our fatherland and our own city, to the home where we shall spend our eternity. We are in camp, we are campaigning in a foreign country."[6]

The consequences of this Cistercian attitude to the artistic products of human imagination, an attitude coherently developed at length in a number of twelfth-century spiritual masterpieces, have an importance which I think has not yet been fully explored. The stark con-

[5] *Apologia*, XII, 28; *Treatises I*, p. 64.

[6] "Epistola ad Fratres de Monte Dei," I, xxxvii, 151; *The Golden Epistle*, trans. Theodore Berkeley (Spencer, 1971), pp. 60-61.

trast of Cistercian failure and Dominican success in the campaign against heresy in the Midi in the first half of the thirteenth century, for example, surely has less to do with the superior "spirituality" of the friars than it has to do with markedly differing conceptions of the religious life. The monastic aspiration excluded popular religion designed for "a carnal people, incapable of spiritual things." The mendicant conception of religious life, on the other hand, was much broader, for it combined the "apostolic" mission of preaching and teaching to such people with the radical alienation of a pilgrim Church. That this union, firm in theory, was fragile in practice, is attested to by both the internal and external histories of the mendicant orders; and within the Franciscan Order in particular the poverty controversy was cruelly to test the validity of the formulation.

In a work like the *Meditationes vitae Christi,* however, the literary unity of this religious conception remains perfectly and effectively intact. The book is a major monument of ascetic *meditatio* in a clearly defined tradition. It is organized according to a highly intellectual and "mystical" scheme, based both upon the symbolic numerology of perfection and upon conventional religious practices and liturgical devotions. Its fifty-sixth meditation, a consideration of the four obstacles to contemplation, even contains a traditional attack on the *imaginatio* in the very language of Bernard and William of Saint-Thierry. In contemplation "one must be deaf, dumb, and blind: see nothing at all, hear nothing at all, take no pleasure of any sort in speaking."[7] Yet this is only part of the spiritual regimen of the work, the most theoretical and doctrinaire. In the introduction the author counsels a quite different course. Here the reader

[7] Bayart, *Méditations,* p. 180.

is firmly enjoined to *imagine* with the full sensory vivacity of vicarious participation the details of Christ's life. Indeed, the reader's response to the verbal pictures painted so richly by the author should be precisely that of immediate "carnal" sensation: "Make yourself present at the conversations and deeds reported of the Lord Jesus. Hear Him as with your own ears; see Him as with your own eyes. . . ."[8] The reader is permitted, indeed encouraged, to *imagine* details of Christ's life which may be without specific scriptural warrant; he is advised to consider alternative visualizations or mental dramatizations of the same scriptural "scenes."

To be sure, there is in the mind of "John of Caulibus" no conflict or dichotomy of the kind which I have suggested, for there is no danger in "fleshly imaginings" when the imagination's object is the Word made flesh. Yet the fact of the matter is that his Franciscan vocation, at once an ascetic and an evangelical vocation, makes the author comfortable with affective literary techniques and open about experimenting with them.

The peculiar and "double" impulse of the *Meditationes* can be gauged to some degree by the history of its varied and powerful influences on later writers. As Fischer has shown, the text spread widely and rapidly, and its early popularity, though probably always greatest in its native Italy, has left a rich depository of manuscripts throughout Europe.[9] Its influence on popular lyric poetry, on the development of the vernacular drama, and on iconographic conceptions in the visual and plastic arts was both immediate and profound. One scholar who has worked closely with the late medieval Irish text of

[8] Bayart, *Méditations*, p. 22.

[9] Columban Fischer, "Die 'Meditationes vitae Christi': Ihre handschriftliche Überlieferung und die Verfasserfrage," *AFH, XXV* (1932), 3-35, 175-209, 305-348, 449-483.

the work has this to say: "The *Meditationes* has been variously referred to as a life of Christ, a biography of the Blessed Virgin, the fifth gospel, the last of the apocrypha, one of the masterpieces of Franciscan literature, a summary of medieval spirituality, a religious handbook of contemplation, a manual of Christian iconography, one of the chief sources of the mystery plays." All this and more is true, yet I think the same scholar fails to consider the work's full complexity when he attributes its success almost entirely to its affective techniques of pathetic narrative: "Its appeal was to the heart rather than to the head."[10]

In fact, it is arguable that the most remarkable achievement of the *Meditationes* was not its popular success among (to use once more Bernard's words) "a carnal people incapable of spiritual things," but rather the deep impress it made upon the very cadre of professed contemplatives. The late medieval successors to Bernard, who we might think at first would be most uncomfortable with the work's affective and imaginative techniques, found in it an appeal to both heart and head. It was a book much revered by a variety of fourteenth-century mystical writers, and it is easy enough to identify its stylistic influences on the thought and prose of major works of the *devotio moderna.* Most surprisingly of all, perhaps, is its demonstrable influence on the most radical and isolated ascetics such as Carthusians. "Pseudo-Bonaventure" exerted upon Ludolph of Saxony an influence crucial both in conceptual and stylistic terms, and Ludolph's *Vita Christi,* one of the enduring masterpieces of late medieval contemplative piety, can be said to be a foster daughter of St. Francis. And the English rendition of the *Meditationes, The Blessed Mirror of the Life*

[10] *Smaointe Beatha Chríost,* ed. C. Ó Maonaigh (Dublin, 1944), pp. 325-326.

of Our Lord Jesus Christ, was undertaken by Nicholas Love, an early fifteenth-century prior of the charterhouse at York.

For the Gothic audience of the late medieval period, an audience which the *Meditationes* both addressed and helped to create, the Franciscan conjunction of an imaginative fiction operating within the world of sensible objects with a profound inner spirituality which sought to transcend the corporeal world proved altogether particularly satisfying. If the stylistic impulse to some degree domesticated the mysterious, it also opened new and exciting contemplative possibilities. The contemplative claim on the *Meditationes* is by no means a shallow one. Indeed, it *is* a formal meditative work both in its imposed structure and in its internal strategies. Its specific audience is a religious community or at least a certain Poor Clare of the author's acquaintance. Indeed, there are enough explicitly Franciscan hints in the work to demonstrate beyond question the religious context of its creation. It may even be the case, as has been argued by some scholars facing the book's structural peculiarities, that the "contemplative" sequence which runs from the forty-fifth to the fifty-eighth chapter is really a handbook on meditation which existed independently of the larger work. All this is to say that in its sources, its subject matter, and its spiritual attitudes the *Meditationes* clearly belongs in a cloistered tradition.

At the same time, the truly popular character of the work, suggested not by a lack of learning or of theological sophistication but rather by the familiar, domestic foundation of its imaginative appeal, is marked throughout. There is a consistent appeal to felt experience, to the authority of ocular demonstration, and to what might be called eyewitness reporting. These qualities are immediately apparent even in the opening pages of the book, which deal in a highly imaginative way with speculative theological questions concerning the motivations for divine initiative in the plan of human salvation. The first meditation describes the powerfully emotive intercession of the angels on behalf of fallen man—one of the many parts of the book for which the only apparent source is the happy and vivid imagination of "John of Caulibus."

By comparison with this meditation, analogous attempts by Milton in *Paradise Lost* seem not so much baroque as wooden. The second meditation is devoted to the Bernardine debate between the "four daughters of God"—Mercy, Justice, Truth, and Peace. This literary topic, based on the text and exegetical elaborations of a psalm verse ("Mercy and truth have met each other; justice and peace have kissed" [Ps. 84:11]), had been developed at some length by Bernard in his first sermon on the Annunciation, and it appears widely in a number of different forms in medieval European literature. John's use of the material, however, altogether lacks the quality of a schooled demonstration of a literary convention. For him the debate is not a dramatic homiletic adornment but an actual event; Bernard is for him not its inventor or popularizer but its most elegant reporter. "Thus a great debate arose among them, which the blessed Bernard retells with great eloquence. As for me, I shall only report the essentials. I shall frequently use his very words, which flow like honey, but I shall leave out many details in order not to be too long."[11] The author thus masks his own very considerable literary inventiveness with the modest claim of an editor or anthologist of a reliable chronicle. This is not, of course, so much a self-

[11] Bayart, *Méditations,* p. 26.

conscious literary guise as it is a pervasive stylistic attitude toward his materials. The elements of Christian biography from whatever source—the Scriptures, apochryphal tradition, the rich repository of twelfth-century spiritual literature, his own imagination—are seen not as frozen, iconic stone tableaux, captured forever within the chiselled confines of a quatrefoil border, but rather as kinetic, lively, and malleable scenes in the mimetic theater.

The *Meditationes*, though the unique work of a distinctive literary genius, can be said to be stylistically typical of a much wider range of Franciscan letters, particularly lyric poetry, homiletic literature, and the drama. Beyond that, the work is a very useful stylistic index of certain general tendencies in late Gothic narrative quite outside the arena of what we usually think of as religious literature, for the Franciscan literary style, like the Franciscan conception of the religious life itself, was radically incarnational, seeking to reestablish in a flesh-and-blood world a vibrant realization of the transcendent. The *Canterbury Tales* of Geoffrey Chaucer, one of the most stunning achievements of medieval "secular" literature, includes among its wide repertory of tales a scurrilous attack on friars which makes witty use of a specialized mendicant vocabulary and a penitential sermon closely based on a Franciscan manual. Both are brought without wrenching into a rich secular context without for a moment compromising their serious religious intentions.

The willingness of Franciscan literature to visualize concrete, verbal images is naturally and inevitably connected with a special perception of the human nature of Jesus Christ. It is not surprising that the Passion meditations of the *Meditationes vitae Christi* enjoyed a wide popularity as a separate book, or that the Franciscans are so intimately involved with the development of the literary and visual iconography of the Passion and its liturgical cult.[12] Yet the attempt to keep always before their eyes an image of the crucified Christ in vivid verisimilitude is merely a conspicuous instance of a wider stylistic tendency in Franciscan thought, and especially in the writings of the mystics, to find a language of literal objectification for all kinds of spiritual experience.

In the minds of the friars, as we can see in the documents of the poverty debate, the continuity between the apostolic life described in the New Testament and the apostolic life of the fraternal rule was literal and unbroken. Medieval Carmelites maintained and believed that their Order had been founded on Mount Carmel by Elijah and Elisha. Francis' own biography is full of episodes which recreate in their literal details spiritual vignettes from the Scriptures. At the time of his conversion he became not merely like the rich young man of Matthew 19; he became that man. The *poverello*'s total aspiration to the religious life was a crucifixion, and the "new" miracle of the stigmata underscored a new stylistic vision which sought to incarnate spiritual metaphors. There was of course little new about the idea of the religious life as spiritual crucifixion in the thirteenth century. The metaphoric monastic "crucifixion," like the metaphoric monastic "warfare," has clear linguistic warrant in the Bible, and it was a commonplace of eremetic and Benedictine literature alike. Refracted through the stylistic prism of Franciscanism, however, such a concept would have a totally new appearance. One need only compare the way in which Franciscan writers speak of spiritual crucifixion with the way in which the theme is typically

[12] *Meditaciones de Passione Christi olim S. Bonaventurae attribuitae,* ed. M. J. Stallings (Washington, 1965).

treated in twelfth-century monastic tradition to become aware of the significant difference.

Consider, for example, a letter of Adam of Perseigne to his spiritual friend Margaret. Its subject is virginity, which Adam writes of in the traditional imagery of wedding with Christ. In paragraphs interwoven with the mystical language of the Cistercian liturgy, Adam encourages the nun to grow from the infantile and innocent suckling of the paps (*ubera*) of Mother Church to the mature and virile consummation of divine love. "I reckon that, by the grace of God, you have arrived at that age when you will no longer play with Christ in the cradle, as a breast-sister (*collactanea*), but, now ready to be crucified with Christ, you can eat more solid food. In fact, 'for the sake of the words of his lips, you wish to walk hard paths'; and you feel the strength, you who, in imitation of the Crucified One, put your glory in the merits of the Cross. For indeed if you do not refuse to copulate with your husband on such a bed, you shall achieve one day the glory of a nuptial bed which knows nothing of cross or pain."[13]

Such imagery is arresting, perhaps even shocking, in its superficial sexuality; but it immediately calls for a kind of purely intellectual analysis through which any apparent claims of the letter of the metaphor are subsumed in a spiritual "understanding." This is generally true of the Cistercian spiritual writers, including Bernard, who, for all his affective daring, spends little energy in creating a sustained and coherent literal texture. For such writers, the scriptural metaphors which they appropriate and in some instances build upon operate in precisely the way in which St. Augustine, in *On Christian Doctrine,* shows the "carnal" language of the Scriptures

[13] Adam de Perseigne, *Lettres I,* ed. Jean Bouvet (Paris, 1960), p. 108.

to work. In Franciscan imagery, on the other hand, there is a marked tendency to press metaphoric language as far as it can go, and to advance significant claims for the letter of metaphor.

We can perhaps demonstrate the difference by considering a passage from Hendrik Herp's *Spieghel der Volcomenheit.*[14] In spite of its title, this fifteenth-century work has more in common with the *Meditationes* than with the *Speculum Perfectionis.* That is, it is a schematic, detailed guidebook to Christian perfection, organized around a systematic presentation of moral theology and a specific program of practical spiritual exercises. Though it shows, as one would expect, a number of strong local influences—particularly of the Rhineland mystics and other Low German spiritual writers—it is a profoundly Franciscan work by a profoundly Franciscan writer. Its very lack of originality and its wide diffusion in both Latin and vernacular versions lend it acceptable credentials as a representative text. In the fifth chapter of the first book Herp addresses the mortification of the imagination, which he says is capable of entertaining three kinds of mental images. The first of these are the random images which invade the mind "like the ebbing of the sea and the flight of birds." Though not in themselves sinful, such vacuous occupation of mental energy is an impediment to perfection and must be controlled. The second kind of images—those associated with the "pleasurable thought" of concupiscent desire—are of course actively sinful and, unless extirpated, deadly.

Yet there is a third category of images which are in themselves explicitly good, and those are images which reduce daily experience to the Christ-life of the gospels.

[14] Hendrik Herp, *Spieghel der Volcomenheit,* ed. Lucidius Verschueren, 2 vols (Antwerp, 1931).

Herp has this to say: "I would not want you to be without thoughts and mental images at all, but I would propose for you the image of Jesus Christ. . . . If you eat, dip each of your morsels into His wounds. If you drink, think of the draft He drank on the Cross. If you wash your hands or body, think of the blood which washes your soul. When you go to bed think of the bed of the Cross and rest your head against the pillow of the Crown of Thorns."[15]

For Herp, "spiritual crucifixion" is no less *spiritual* than it is for Adam of Perseigne. But it is at once considerably more physical. In what I am loosely calling Franciscan style the spirit not merely conquers but in a sense also redeems the letter of metaphoric word and act. Probably the purest example which one can adduce is the miracle of the stigmata, the sign which early Franciscan writers universally took to be the seal of the true "newness" of Francis and his movement, but Franciscan biography abounds with telling examples. All Christians in all times and places have mourned the death of Christ. In the ninety-second chapter of the *Speculum Perfectionis* Francis walks alone near the Portiuncula, weeping and lamenting in a loud voice. "And a spiritually-minded man who met him, fearing that he was suffering from some painful ailment, said to him, 'What is your trouble, brother?' But he replied, 'I am not ashamed to travel through the whole world in this way, bewailing the Passion of my Lord.' At this, the man joined him in his grief, and began to weep aloud."[16] Such a vignette neatly summarizes one of the major movements of Franciscan literature; for the Franciscan poets taught medieval

[15] *Spieghel der Volcomenheit,* II, pp. 42-48.
[16] *Speculum Perfectionis,* 92; *Omnibus,* p. 1226.

Europe to weep—and to praise, rejoice, lament, adore—out loud, in public, wih exuberant physical participation.

The problem of the confusion of the "real" and the "metaphorical" in religious experience, and particularly in mystical experience, became very acute in the world of the *gothique flamboyant.* Indeed, in the mystical writings of the Rhineland mystics and others coherent patterns of experience seem to break down altogether. In a justly famous passage in the prologue to the *Incendium amoris* Richard Rolle records his surprise at the carnal operations of the Spirit. "I cannot tell you how surprised I was the first time I felt my heart begin to warm. It was real warmth too, not imaginary, and it felt as if it were actually on fire. . . . I had to keep feeling my breast to make sure there was no physical reason for it."[17] By the time Rolle wrote, such bizarre language was commonplace; but it is very far from the traditional world of monastic spirituality. The medium which introduced it and popularized it was the unitive vision of the Franciscan spirit which created the Christmas crib at Greccio and smarted with the fiery tears of Angela of Foligno.

Medieval Franciscan literature is, furthermore, not prudish in its language. One of the peculiar qualities which thickens the *Cronica* of Salimbene is the author's linguistic honesty in mentioning unmentionable subjects. Ascetic rigor and high seriousness were often the inspirations behind a freedom of satirical expression which we would be wrong to call libertinism but which will not fall easily into preconceived notions of cloistered piety. What Giotto was not ashamed to paint in the Last Judgment of the Scrovegni Chapel, the friars openly preached. We shall find a particularly exuberant and

[17] *The Incendium Amoris of Richard Rolle of Hampole,* ed. Margaret Deanesly (Manchester, 1915), p. 145.

imaginative collation of themes of sexual and monetary cupidity. It is not surprising to me that Luke Wadding, in some ways a spiritual throwback to pre-Tridentine innocence, gives François Rabelais a proud page in his bibliography of Franciscan writers.[18]

That the fraternal movement coincided with a number of major social changes in Western Europe, changes to which it responded and which to some extent it helped to shape, is one of the clichés of thirteenth-century history. Though the word "urban" has been somewhat compromised for us by special modern circumstances unknown in the Middle Ages or in any period of our history before industrialization, we may with caution speak of the friars as "urban apostles." Caution is necessary because they were likewise "rural apostles" for whom the agricultural countryside was often an important missionary field. In general, Franciscan houses were established where people were or where they frequently came or passed by—that is, in the towns, at crossroads and on pilgrimage routes, near markets and fairs. So marked is this phenomenon that a group of French historians, studying the growth of towns in the French countryside, has taken the establishment of a mendicant house as an important sign of such growth. The social structures of the new towns of the thirteenth century are themselves complex, but it is clear that the new centers typically included a fairly broad spectrum of commercial life: merchandising, professional and artisan services, staple manufacturing.

We have already seen that the penitential manuals of the friars addressed in new ways the moral problems of a commercial society and a money economy. Such con-

[18] See Etienne Gilson, "Rabelais Franciscain," in *Les idées et les lettres* (Paris, 1955), pp. 197-241.

cerns as usury, the "just price," and so on were of course not absent from the moral theology of the older tradition, as the example of the circle of Peter the Chanter at Paris makes abundantly clear. But the friars did popularize what might be called mercantile morality, created a popular language in which to debate it, and made it a respectable subject of learned and literary discussion.[19] Social and economic historians have been alert to these developments, and have begun to use evidence from literature and the visual arts to make exciting reformulations about the nature and meaning of thirteenth-century social change. It has been argued, for example, that iconographic evidence demonstrates the increasing importance which the sin of avarice came to have in popular conceptions of the seven capital vices.[20]

Likewise, it has been speculated that just as the "Benedictine" spirituality of the high Middle Ages found its metaphoric ascetic strength in the symbolic renunciation of feudal power, fraternal spirituality of the late medieval period found its self-image in poverty, the symbolic rejection of *wealth*.[21]

To despise wealth and to renounce money was not the same thing as to ignore the commercial world. In fact the truth of the matter, only superficially paradoxical, is that the friars, in their labored distinctions between *pecunia* and *denarium* and in their profound concern with developing a casuistry of the marketplace, introduced economic man into Western literature as a respectable

[19] Barbara Rosenwein and L. K. Little, "Social Meaning in the Monastic and Mendicant Spiritualities," *Past and Present*, LXIII (1974), pp. 4-32.

[20] Lester K. Little, "Pride Goes before Avarice: Social Change and the Vices in Latin Christendom," *American Historical Review*, LXXVI (1971), pp. 16-49.

[21] Barbara Rosenwein, "Feudal War and Monastic Peace: Cluniac Liturgy as Ritual Aggression," *Viator*, II (1971), 129-157.

"literary topic." The misers, spendthrifts, dicers, and wastrels of the *fabliaux*, the *novelle*, the *artes moriendi*, and the morality plays of the Renaissance can trace a direct ancestry to the *piazza* theology of mendicant apostles. Neither *The Merchant of Venice* nor *Romeo and Juliet* would have been the same plays without the remote and palimpsest presence of Raymond of Pennyfort and Master Alexander of Alexandria.

The friars' special interest in the sin of usury is frequently and often comically alluded to in prose fiction of the thirteenth and fourteenth centuries, and particularly in the Italian *novella*. Two of the most charming short stories in Sacchetti's *Trecentonovelle* can give some suggestion of the comic possibilities inherent in the subject. One of the stories, already mentioned in an earlier chapter, describes the Lenten preaching of an Austin friar who was conducting a mission at the church of Santa Reparata among a congregation made up almost entirely of poor and indebted wool workers. The friar preached each night after the working day in the darkened church, and his theme was always the same: usury, and the moral dangers of money lending. After several nights of this, a crusty old worker shouted out from the darkened nave: "It seems to me that you can preach of nothing but usury. I want to make it clear that you are wasting your words, for we are borrowers, not lenders! Give us some comfort as debtors, or we can do without your preaching!" The friar, no doubt startled but still alert, immediately began preaching on the text "Blessed are the poor"![22]

Another of the *novelle* deals with a Dominican engaged in a similar Lenten mission in a Tuscan town. Noting that few people attended his preaching while they flocked

[22] *Trecentonovelle,* no. 100, in Franco Sacchetti, *Opera,* ed. Borlenghi, pp. 320-322; se p. 125 above.

to hear other friars, he devised a startling plan to attract an audience. During a sermon, he announced to his sparse audience that he had discovered a major blunder in the received teachings about usury. Money lending, far from being a sin, is meritorious, he claimed, and publicly announced that he would devote a major Sunday sermon to demonstrating the truth of this new position with subtle theological reasoning. When word of this new revelation spread, the entire countryside flocked to hear him on a Sunday. Always promising his fiscal sermon, but always putting if off for one reason or another, he drew large crowds to his mission all through Lent. Finally, on Palm Sunday, he delivered the promised defense of money lending. His sermon began magnificently, as he demonstrated beyond cavil that money lending was charitable. "It is charity and nothing else to succor one's neighbor, and a loan is succor; therefore I say that loans may be made, and that they are licit; what is more, he who makes the loan gains merit." It is only at this point that the friar's true "subtlety" becomes apparent. "But where is the sin?" he asks, rhetorically. "The sin is in the collecting! But to loan money and not to collect it back, that is no sin but extraordinary charity!"[23]

The satiric intention in the two stories is of course different. In the one, the friars are being gently mocked for a tendency to fall into an unexamined academicism; in the other, the people's appetite for novelty and their venal desire to find religious approbation for carnality (what the Wife of Bath calls a "gentle text") are exposed. What both share in common is a demonstration of mendicant spiritual opportunism, and of the friars' willingness to speak of the marketplace and their expertise in doing so.

[23] *Trecentonovelle,* no. 32; *Opera,* pp. 128-132.

But nowhere in late medieval literature will we find more vivid pictorial recreation of mercantile life in the towns than in the sermon literature, and among the marketplace preachers none is more remarkable than St. Bernardino of Siena (1380-1444). By all contemporary accounts the most moving preacher of his day (Pius II said of him that men listened to him as they might have listened to St. Paul), Bernardino returns time and again to the special moral problems associated with buying and selling, particularly in an extended series of sermons in the *Quadragesimale de Evangelio Aeterno.*

Although the recorded Latin versions of most medieval sermons probably give us but a general idea of an actual sermon as delivered—when they were in fact delivered at all—we are fortunate in the case of Bernardino in having texts of unusual authority. In the first place, they are real sermons, not closet compositions. Furthermore, we have from Bernardino, in addition to important autographs, some essentially verbatim transcriptions of vernacular sermons. According to the scribe of the Sienese sermons of 1427 the transcribed Italian text represents with total accuracy sermons as actually delivered by Bernardino, who would, says the scribe, first write them on a wax tablet and then, after delivery, transcribe them into a book, all on the same day—a feat he regards as something of a minor miracle.[24] These sermons abound with what are in effect dramatic dialogues, but dialogues in a realistic and domestic style which has become current once again in serious literature only in our age of kitchen-sink drama.

We may consider, for example, a passage in which Bernardino sets out to show that what we would now

[24] S. Bernardino da Siena, *La Fonte della vita,* ed. G. V. Sabatelli (Florence, 1964), p. 40.

call price haggling involves "numerous lies, perjured promises, falsity, and terrible sales techniques (*scilosismi mercantanteschi e terribili*)." He posits a conversation between a customer and a merchant about a pair of slippers.

' "What do you want for these slippers?"

"I want twenty soldi for them."

"I swear on the Bible I won't pay that."

"You should take them. I promise you—they're the the real thing."

(He lies through his teeth.)

"What lower price will you take for them?"

"I won't take less—I swear on the Bible; I couldn't sell these shoes for eighteen soldi." (There's another lie!)

"Will you take fifteen?"

"No! I promise you, you won't find a better pair of slippers in this town than these."

"I won't give you more than fifteen soldi." (Now you are lying, too.)

"OK. Give me eighteen soldi. I've gotten that price many times before."

"I swear on the Bible, I won't give you more [than fifteen]."

"And I swear on the Bible, you won't have them then."

'And finally they are sold for seventeen soldi, after each of them has made many false oaths and told many lies!'[25]

When Boccaccio, Chaucer, and Langland satirized the friars as venal money grubbers, they would address an audience which the friars themselves had largely created and in a significantly new literary language that the friars themselves had made possible. Franciscan style could make so large and so various an impression on the face

[25] *La Fonte della vita,* pp. 385-386.

of late medieval literature because it reflected that unitive vision of Franciscan religion which found no corner of God's world unworthy of redemption. Literary history has long regarded with studied admiration the vessels of gold and silver which are among the showiest ornaments in the museum of the medieval spirit; but there are other vessels, too, humbler vessels of terra cotta and of wood, and they too are worthy of our admiration. In the *Cantico di frate sole,* which must remain after any analysis our purest model of what Franciscan literature can mean, God is praised not merely through the great celestial bodies which were His work on the third day but through the earth, air, fire, and water which were the indivisible elements of His material world.

Index

The following index includes references to works of medieval literature, to the names of medieval and modern writers, and (on a highly selective basis), to the major intellectual topics of the book. In listing the names of medieval writers, and in some cases of modern ones, euphony or common practice, rather than a severe canon of consistency, has been the guide. Thus one finds *Jakob van Maerlant* but *James of Milan*; or *John of Parma, Jean de Meun*, and *Pecham, John*. For indexed items with two or more listings, **figures in bold print** indicate the more important entries.